The Bible Speaks

The Bible Speaks

ROBERT DAVIDSON

THE SAINT ANDREW PRESS
EDINBURGH

© 1959 by Robert Davidson

First published in 1959 by
Skeffington, London and
Thomas Y. Crowell Company, New York

Re-issued in 1974 by
The Saint Andrew Press
121 George Street
Edinburgh

ISBN 0 7152 0241 3

Printed in Great Britain by
T. & A. Constable Ltd., Edinburgh

ACKNOWLEDGEMENTS

Thomas Nelson and Sons Limited for permission to use throughout the Revised Standard Version of the Bible, copyrighted 1946 and 1952. Faber and Faber Limited for the quotation from D. M. Baillie's God was in Christ *used in Chapter* 1.

TO

Elizabeth

Contents

Preface to Re-Issue

It may seem strange to re-issue unchanged a book on the Bible which first appeared in 1959 and which has been out of print for many years. The justification for doing so is that people continue to ask for it on the grounds that it attempts to do something that is all too seldom done: to present a picture of the thought of the Bible as a whole. The study of the Bible never stands still. There are many parts of this book, particularly in the Old Testament section, that I would wish to recast or to slant differently if I were re-writing it today; yet I am as convinced as ever that the central thesis of the book is sound: that the Bible in spite of the rich variety of material to be found within it, is in a deep sense one book, Old and New Testament, part of one continuous story. If the re-issue of this book, in spite of its imperfections, can help some people to a new glimpse of the oneness of this story I shall be satisfied. I am grateful to the Saint Andrew Press, and in particular to its Publisher Mr Tim Honeyman, for taking the risk of re-publication.

Robert Davidson

University of Glasgow   Professor of Old Testament
Language and Literature

Preface to First Edition

'Certain authors,' wrote a great Frenchman, 'speaking of their works, say "My book", "My commentary", "My history", etc. . . . They would do better to say "Our book", "Our commentary", "Our history", etc., because there is in them more of other people's than their own.'[1]

There is indeed more of other people's than of mine own in this book. Shamelessly, yet gratefully, I have drawn on the labours of others; how shamelessly and how gratefully only those conversant with the subject will fully realize.

I am more personally and immediately indebted to Dr. Wm. Lillie, Head of the Department of Biblical Study in the University of Aberdeen, and to my father-in-law, Rev. R. A. Robertson, M.A., of Nicolson Street Church, Edinburgh, both of whom read the manuscript and rid it of many infelicities of expression and errors of judgement. The dedication is a totally inadequate acknowledgement of the debt I owe to my wife, whose encouragement and advice have been invaluable, and who, amid the constant demands of a young family, found the time and the energy to turn into legible type increasingly illegible handwriting. This is our book.

[1] Pascal, *Pensées*, section 43 (Everyman's edition).

King's College   R. D.
  University of Aberdeen

Introduction

The family gather in the farm cottage on Saturday evening; a simple meal is shared; the father, priest in his own home, takes the family Bible, reads a passage, then leads the others in prayer—such is Robert Burns' picture of the family in Scotland some hundred and fifty years ago.[1]

It is a picture which was still familiar to many fifty years ago; family life with the Bible in the place of honour at its centre, and that for a very good reason. Was not this the book which laid bare the inmost heart and purpose of the Almighty? Was not this the book which had an uncannily appropriate word to say to men in their varied needs; the word of consolation in sorrow, the word of rebuke to pride, the word of forgiveness for sin, the word of challenge for daily life? This was no ordinary book. God Himself was its author. Whether it spoke of the creation of the world in six days (Gen. i) or told of the love of God (John iii. 16); whether it described a serpent with a remarkable gift of speech (Gen. iii) or warned of the universal sinfulness of men (Rom. v. 12 ff.) it spoke with a unique authority.

Today the picture is very different. For one thing, the whole pattern of family life has changed. With the Women's Institute and the Men's Club, the Boy Scouts and the Girl Guides, the Country Dancing and the cinema, with shift-work and homework, there is seldom an evening when the whole family gathers as a family. If, perchance, such an evening does come, the family circle will form not round the Bible but round the television set. Furthermore, seeds of suspicion about the Bible are deeply implanted in our minds. We have all heard echoes of a conflict between the Bible and modern science, and we are reasonably sure that the scientists won.

[1] Cf. *The Cotter's Saturday Night.*

If the Bible is going to ask us to believe that the world was created by a word from God in six days, then so much the worse for the Bible. Are not Christians themselves in a bit of a muddle over the Bible? Some claim that the Bible, 'as originally given'—whatever that may mean—is the infallible word of God, free from all errors of fact or judgement. Others, equally sincere, protest that to claim this is to misunderstand the Bible, that in many ways it is a very human book, subject to human error and frailty, and that when we describe it as 'the Word of God' we must clearly indicate what we do and what we do not mean by that phrase.

Perhaps our bewilderment is even deeper and more personal than that. If once the Bible spoke clearly to men about God and about themselves, does it still? We all know that children, being self-willed, like the rest of us, sometimes flout the wishes of their parents. We would all be shocked, however, if parents dealt with such a 'stubborn and rebellious' child by hauling him before the city magistrates so that the magistrates might inflict the death penalty. Yet this is what parents are enjoined to do in Deuteronomy xxi. 18-21; only one instance among many where ordinary people, who make no claim either to be very good, or to be deeply religious, follow a line of conduct higher than that laid down in certain parts of the Bible.

Nor are we less puzzled when we try to come to terms with what the Bible has to say about God. Many of us would agree with the words of two school-teachers, who, on the basis of the frustrating attempt to teach Scripture to unwilling schoolboys, wrote:

'In the Bible, the works of God are plain for all to see; the simpler the intelligence, the plainer they seem. But now "God moves in a mysterious way" and for the plain man, that is usually equivalent to saying He does not move at all. The problem of miracles reveals our difficulty in an acute form. . . . In face of this, no amount of teaching to the contrary will convince the ordinary boy that in the Bible we have a picture of how God works in the world today. To him the whole thing is irrelevant, and a religion based on the Bible alone is a religion out of touch with the modern world.'[1]

[1] Cf. V. Gollancz, *More for Timothy*, p. 277.

In the Bible God apparently speaks directly to men, but does He speak at all to men today, and, if so, how? God spoke to Moses, according to Exod. iii, through a burning bush, but our 'burning bushes' are atomic piles, and who or what speaks there? According to Luke ii. 8 ff. shepherds gazing up into the night sky saw a host of angels and heard them singing, 'Glory to God in the highest and on earth peace among men with whom he is pleased.' Their modern counterparts, gazing into the night sky, see 'Sputniks', and what is the message they proclaim?

The Bible spoke, but does it still speak? Of course there are parts of the Bible which are immortal on any reckoning, e.g. the 'Shepherd Psalm' (Ps. xxiii), the Inescapable God (Ps. cxxxix), the Sermon on the Mount (Matt. v-vii), the three parables in Luke xv. Such passages have an indisputable right to be included in an anthology of the best in the scriptures of the great world religions.[1] So to treat the Bible, however, is to be guilty of a serious misunderstanding.

Much of the Bible is history, a record of certain events that happened. They were hardly 'world-shaking' events in our usual sense of these words. They concern the life of a particular nation, a small, politically insignificant nation; they concern a particular man born within this nation, a man who lived his entire life in Roman-occupied Judea. Here is a record of events and, stranger still, the claim that these events are charged with a unique significance.

The Bible tells the story of the escape of some Hebrews from slave labour in Egypt, probably somewhere about the beginning of the thirteenth century B.C. (cf. Exod. i-xiv). But to the Bible this is no mere 'escape' story; it is a mighty act of deliverance wherein God chooses for himself a people to be the instrument of His purposes in the world. The Bible tells the story of the birth at Bethlehem of Jesus (Luke i). But to the Bible this is no mere birth story, not even the birth story of one destined to be an infant prodigy; it is the story of God come as man among men, to share our human life. A record of events, charged, it is claimed, with unique significance, and the story of human response to these events, such is the Bible.

We are invited to see in the Bible, not the history of man's

[1] Cf. *The Pocket World Bible,* ed. by R. O. Ballou.

search to explore the ultimate mysteries of life, but God conde-
scending to make Himself known to man. If this be true, then
obviously the Bible is of supreme importance and must still have
something to say to us; for the God who thus once made Himself
known is 'the same yesterday and today and for ever' (Heb. xiii. 8).

If it be true—but is it? That question each one of us must answer
for himself, but we have no right to attempt to answer it unless we
are honestly concerned to know what the Bible does say. It is astonishing how sadly misinformed many otherwise highly intelligent
people can be. Fred Hoyle wrote a fascinating book called *The
Nature of the Universe*. In it he gives us the modern astronomer's
picture of our expanding universe, a picture which staggers the
imagination. In conclusion, he gives certain personal views about
the place of man in what he calls this 'wholly fantastic universe'.
Inevitably he finds himself asking and endeavouring to answer the
kind of questions about human destiny with which the Bible is concerned. Christians, he believes, on the basis of the Biblical tradition,
hold to one of two things: either our life goes on beyond death in
some kind of unending time sequence (a horrible alternative to
extinction, since three hundred years is the most he could possibly
endure of himself with his obvious limitations), or our present
limitations are so removed that nothing recognizably 'me' remains.
'It strikes me as very curious,' he says, 'that Christians have so little
to say about how they propose eternity should be spent.'[1] All of
which is indeed very curious. A closer look at what the Bible is
concerned to say on this issue might have removed some of the
difficulties.

The Book of Acts[2] tells the story of how Philip, one of the
early evangelists, met a high-ranking Ethiopean court official
reading a passage from the Old Testament. Philip asked him, 'Do
you understand what you are reading?' 'How can I,' comes the
reply, 'unless someone guides me?'

This book is written in the hope that some people will find in
it just such a guide to the thought of the Bible. It is in no sense
an anthology of carefully selected 'highlights' from the Biblical

[1] *The Nature of the Universe*, p. 117.
[2] Cf. viii. 26 ff.

writings. Many familiar passages are omitted. It is an attempt to place before the reader the main themes of the Bible, and, with a word of explanation, to allow the Bible to speak for itself. It is not a substitute for the Bible. At best it is hoped that it may be useful as a series of stepping-stones upon which some may safely cross the river of difficulty and misunderstanding to the challenging world on the other side.

I

God and Man

The story of the Bible can only be understood in the light of certain assumptions it makes about God and Man.

The Creation Hymn (Gen. i) invites us to view the world as the handiwork of a Creator God, Who rejoices in the goodness of what He has created, a Creator whose continuing activity is seen in the continuing life of nature.

From this belief in God as Creator, Biblical writers draw certain conclusions.

1. In a world where gods were ten a penny, a Hebrew prophet of the sixth century B.C. can claim 'there is no other god'.

2. In a world where images of the gods abounded, there was no image of the God of Israel. He remained 'unseen', nothing in His creation being adequate to represent Him.

In the purposes of this Creator, man holds a unique place. He shares the frailty of all created things; but not only is he lord over the rest of creation, he is made 'in the image of God', i.e. he stands in a responsible personal relationship with God. This is his true greatness and his tragedy, for, as the myths in Gen. ii–xi show, man has become God's problem child, saying 'No' to God, and placing self at the centre of life. The result is man strangely ill at ease, on the run from God and at loggerheads with his fellow man.

Against this background, the Bible unfolds its story of the encounter of God and Man in history.

I

MANY people find a visit to the opera a puzzling experience, especially when the opera is sung in a language other than their own. To enjoy an opera to the full, a programme is a wise investment. The 'programme notes', before giving a synopsis of the story, introduce us to the leading characters and tell us something about the background to the events in which they participate. Thus, even before the curtain rises, we may feel at home with what is to come. This first chapter is by way of 'programme notes'. In it we shall take a glance at the leading characters and the strangely tangled relationship between them, before we turn to listen to the great themes of the Biblical score.

If we begin with God the Creator, you must not assume that the faith of the Bible began with speculation about the creation of the world. What the Bible has to say about God is rooted in a series of events *within* human history, events in which, claims the Bible, God was confronting man.

'I am the LORD your God, who brought you out of the land of Egypt, out of the house of bondage' (Exod. xx. 2).

This is far more central to the witness of the Old Testament than belief in God the Creator. But our present concern is with 'programme notes', and if we are to understand the story of God's activity in human history, perhaps it is as well to begin with certain statements about God and Man, in the light of which alone the story of God's action becomes meaningful.

The Bible speaks of *God the Creator*.

'By faith we understand that the world was created by the word of God . . .' (Heb. xi. 3).

This is the way in which the Bible invites us to look at our vast mysterious universe, becoming vaster and more mysterious every day as the scientist probes more deeply into its secrets. It did not just happen; it is not the fruit of an accident. It owes its very existence to the creative power of God. The Bible uses many different pictures in its attempt to describe God's relationship to the universe.

God is the architect or master-builder, planning and supervising the most ambitious of all building projects—the world. Here is the way in which the Book of Job depicts God as replying to a man who has been led by bitter anguish to query the workings of providence.

> 'Where were you when I laid the foundations of the
>   earth?
> Tell me if you have understanding,

Who determined its measurements,
  —surely you know!
Or who stretched the line upon it?
On what were its bases sunk
  or who laid its corner stone . . . ?'
                    (Job xxxviii. 4-6, cf. Ps. civ. 5)

Or God is a potter who shapes and forms the world as the potter shapes and forms the vessels on his wheel.

'For lo, he forms the mountains', claims the Book of Amos iv. 13; while in Gen. ii. 7 we are told that 'the LORD God formed man of dust from the ground'.

The master-builder, the potter—these are pictures drawn from the activity of men in an attempt to describe, however inadequately, what God does. We call such language about God 'anthropomorphic', and the Bible is full of it from beginning to end. But there is another word the Bible uses when it refers to God's making of the world, a word which it never uses when it is talking about what men do.

'In the beginning God *created* the heavens and the earth' (Gen. i. 1). Thus begins the magnificent Creation Hymn in Genesis i. It is a hymn, not a scientific theory. In its intention it neither contradicts nor needs to be reconciled with the scientific picture of how the world and life came to its present form. It seeks to ask and to answer questions which go *behind* all our scientific questions. *Why* does the world exist? It came into being, claims this hymn, as an expression of the will of an all powerful God. 'In the beginning God created . . .' Day and night, the heavens, the earth and the seas, plants and trees, stars, sun and moon, birds, fish, mammals, and last, but by no means least, man—all dependent for very existence upon God the Creator (Gen. i. 1-26)—such is the theme of the hymn.

But let us look at its opening verses more closely. 'In the beginning God created the heavens and the earth. The earth was without form and void, and darkness was upon the face of the deep; and the Spirit of God was moving over the face of the waters. And God said let there be light; and there was light. And God saw that the light was good' (Gen. i. 1-4).

The writer of these words lived in a world where there were many stories about how the world had come into existence—cosmologies we call them. Often they are stories describing a bitter conflict between the gods of chaos associated with the unruly primeval waters, and the gods of order. Thus in the Akkadian Creation Myth we hear of how Marduk, the champion of the gods, slew Tiamat, 'split her like a shell fish into two parts';[1] with one part he makes the heavens, with the other part the earth. Although there are faint echoes of such stories in these opening verses of Genesis (echoes of the primeval waters of chaos; an echo perhaps of Tiamat in the Hebrew word 'tehom' translated 'the deep') how utterly different is the Creator God of whom the Bible speaks. Here there is no conflict among the gods; there is but one unchallenged Creator who has but to speak and His word is charged with creative power.

'And God said let there light and there was light' (Gen. i. 3).

A Psalmist is but dotting the 'i's' and crossing the 't's' of this statement when he writes:

> 'By the word of the LORD the heavens were made,
> and all their host by the breath of his mouth.
> He gathered the waters of the sea as in a bottle,
> he put the deeps in storehouses.
> Let all the earth fear the LORD,
> let all the inhabitants of the world stand in awe
> of him!
> For he spoke and it came to be
> he commanded and it stood forth.'
>
>   (Ps. xxxiii. 6–9)

Not only so, but God passes a verdict on what He has done.

'And God saw that the light was *good*' (Gen. i. 4).

Five times more in the course of the hymn, as the climax to a new creative act of God we hear the same refrain—'and God saw that it was good'.

[1] Cf. J. B. Pritchard, *Ancient Near Eastern Texts relating to the Old Testament*, pp. 60 ff. Tablet IV line 137.

Throughout the Bible there runs a rich vein of rejoicing in the world of God's creation . . . *for it is good.* There is no thought here, such as we find in many religions and philosophies, that God is to be found only by withdrawing from the evil grasp of this 'material' world to some purely 'spiritual' existence. It is God's world, God's good world, and we are summoned with all creation to rejoice in it.

'Praise the LORD. Praise the LORD from the heavens,
　　praise him in the heights.
Praise him all his angels
　　praise him all his host!
Praise him sun and moon,
　　praise him all you shining stars!
Praise him you highest heavens
　　and you waters above the heavens
Let them praise the name of the LORD!
　　For he commanded and they were created
And he established them for ever and ever;
　　he fixed their bounds which cannot be passed.
Praise the LORD from the earth,
　　you sea monsters and all deeps,
fire and hail, snow and frost,
　　stormy wind fulfilling his command!
Mountains and all hills,
　　fruit trees and all cedars!
Beasts and all cattle,
　　creeping things and flying birds!
Kings of the earth and all peoples,
　　princes and all rulers of the earth!
Young men and maidens together,
　　old men and children!'

(Ps. cxlviii. 1–12)

This triumphant anthem by the whole choir of creation is caught up in the Book of Revelation which puts this song of praise upon the lips of the heavenly host gathered round the throne of God.

'Worthy art thou, our LORD and God,
to receive glory and honor and power,
for Thou didst create all things
and by thy will they existed and were created.'

(Rev. iv. 11)

A modern writer truly describes the Biblical view of creation as 'a picture of such divine exhilaration in creation as forces us, if we are asked to say summarily why God made the world, to affirm that he made it for fun. There is no purpose in it save the purpose of joy; the joy of the Maker in the joy of His making, and the derived and reciprocal joy of the world in itself and in Him who made it.'[1]

In speaking of God the Creator the Bible, however, does not intend to draw our attention to a God who *once* 'in the beginning' demonstrated His creative power. The God of the Bible is no celestial engineer who invents the complicated mechanism of the world, sets it in motion, then leaves it to run according to its own momentum. Creation is not some past event, but a continuing work of God. Everything existing now depends upon and witnesses to the ever present creator God. In Psalm 104 there is a strangely interwoven pattern of past and present. After celebrating in verses 5–9 God's past creative activity, how He set the earth on its foundations and created mountains and valleys by imprisoning the unruly waters of chaos within strict bounds, the Psalm suddenly switches to the present:

'Thou *makest* springs gush forth in the valleys
they flow between the hills,
they give drink to every beast of the field;
the wild asses quench their thirst.
By these the birds of the air have their habitation,
they sing among the branches.
From thy lofty abode thou waterest the mountains;
the earth is satisfied with the fruit of thy work.

[1] A. Millar, *The Renewal of Man*, p. 54.

Thou dost cause the grass to grow for the cattle,
and plants for man to cultivate
that he may bring forth food from the earth
and wine to gladden the heart of man,
oil to make his face shine
and bread to strengthen man's heart.'

(Ps. civ. 10–15)

An enumeration of the rich and varied wonders of the world calls forth a cry of adoration:

'O LORD how manifold are thy works
In wisdom thou hast made them all
the earth is full of thy creatures.'

(Ps. civ. 24)

And these same creatures

'. . . all look to thee
to give them their food in due season.
When thou givest to them, they gather it up;
when thou openest thy hand
they are filled with good things,
When thou hidest thy face they are dismayed
when thou takest away their breath they die
and return to their dust.
When thou sendest forth thy Spirit they are created;
and thou renewest the face of the ground.'

(Ps. civ. 27–30)

'When thou sendest forth thy Spirit they are created'; the Hebrew word "Spirit" means primarily "wind", not the soft caressing breeze, but the wind which whips across the desert driving the sand hither and thither, a symbol of terrifying and irresistible power. So the "Spirit of God" is God powerfully in action in the world. This same Spirit which in the beginning was "moving over the face of the deep" (Gen. i. 1) to bring order out of chaos, is continually creatively at work renewing the gift of life to all living things. The thought of a continuously creating God is not so strange to us today as it once might have been. A modern astronomer claims that 'of all the various possibilities that have been suggested, continuous creation is easily the most satisfactory'.[1] Of course he does not bring in God, but this is his explanation of the mechanism of the universe as we know it.

To look at the world in this way, in the light of God its Creator, enables us to avoid two errors. We are saved from worshipping the world, or regarding God as nothing more than the sum of everything that is, Nature with a capital 'N'. This is pantheism which, by blurring the distinction between ourselves and God, renders impossible any real personal relationship between us and God. Nor may we regard God as some 'absentee landlord' or, as a recent writer has put it, 'an important outsider who is brought in to inaugurate a society but couldn't be expected to attend its ordinary meetings'.[2]

The Bible speaks of a God who, standing outside the world as its Creator, is yet ever present creatively in this world which in the beginning He created.

II

From this belief in God the Creator the Bible draws certain conclusions.

There was a serious overcrowding problem in the celestial mansions in Biblical times. The writers of the Bible lived in a world of numerous gods, many of them personifications of nature in her differing aspects, sun gods, moon gods, gods of life-giving rain, gods of death dealing drought; others among them national deities of one particular people. Here is an inscription which describes the religious scene in Babylon:

'There were altogether in Babylon fifty-three temples of the great gods, fifty-five shrines dedicated to Marduk, three hundred shrines belonging to earth divinities, six hundred shrines for celestial divinities, one hundred and eighty altars to the goddess Ishtar, one

[1] F. Hoyle, *The Nature of the Universe*, p. 104, cf. pp. 102–7.
[2] J. R. Macphail, *The Way, the Truth and the Life*, p. 1.

hundred and eighty to the gods Nergal and Adad and twelve other altars to various deities.'[1]

There were Jews in Babylon in the sixth century B.C., Jews deported there by a Babylonian conqueror who had ravaged their countryside and razed to the ground the temple of their god in Jerusalem. If the God of these Jews had simply been their national deity, then this national catastrophe would have been seen as proof that Marduk, the god of Babylon, had conquered the god of Israel. Among these Jewish deportees was the anonymous author of Isaiah xl–lv. Far from feeling that the God of his fathers has been discredited, he firmly insists that the God of Israel is the one true God, the Creator of everything.

'For thus saith the LORD
who created the heavens (he is God!)
who formed the earth and made it (he established it;
he did not create it a chaos,
he formed it to be inhabited!)
"I am the LORD *and there is no other*".'

(Isa. xlv. 18)

Because this God is the Creator of everything there can be no other effective gods. The many other gods whose shrines and images abound are merely powerless idols upon whom the writer of these chapters pours forth biting scorn. He can talk of such gods as being no more than 'burdens on weary beasts' when their panic-stricken worshippers seek to salvage what they can in their desperate flight from the doomed city.

'Bel bows down, Nebo stoops,
their idols are on beasts and cattle;
these things you carry are loaded as burdens on weary
    beasts.
They stoop, they bow down together
they cannot save the burden
but themselves go into captivity.'

(Isa. xlvi. 1–2, cf. Isa. xliii. 9 ff)

[1] Quoted by G. Contineau, *Everyday life in Babylon and Assyria*, p. 279.

On the contrary, the God of Israel, far from being a man-made idol carried unceremoniously by his worshippers out of the city, is the God who declares:

> 'I have made and I will bear
> I will carry and I will save.'
>   (Isa. xlvi. 4)

It is a startling claim. The ancient world was generally tolerant in matters religious. Which god or gods a man worshipped depended upon the community in which he lived, and upon what he expected his religion to do for him. The farmer naturally rendered homage to the gods who were responsible for the fertility of the land; a warrior king would be the devotee of the warrior god of his people. No great qualms were felt in transferring allegiance or in adding one more god to the list of desirable objects of worship. The Old Testament bears eloquent witness to the ease with which the people of Israel added the worship of the gods of the people among whom they settled to that of the God who had brought them up out of captivity in Egypt.

The modern mind and more than one contemporary religion, e.g. Hinduism, are equally tolerant, claiming that men may journey to the one truth along many different paths. But in the Bible there is a hard core of intolerance, a developing conviction that the God to whom the Bible witnesses is the only God, the Creator of everything beside whom all other gods are as nothing. Thus a Psalmist invites the worshippers in the temple at Jerusalem to

> 'sing to the LORD a new song . . .
> For great is the LORD and greatly to be praised;
> he is to be feared above all gods.
> For all the gods of the peoples are idols;
> but the LORD made the heavens.'
>   (Ps. xcvi. 4–5)

A startling claim, but no more startling than another fact which springs from the same source. In a world of innumerable images of the gods, there was no image of the God of the Bible.

'You shall not make yourself a graven image, or any likeness of anything that is in the heaven above, or that is in the earth beneath, or that is in the water under the earth; you shall not bow down to them or serve them; for I the LORD your God am a jealous God . . .' (Exod. xx. 4–5).

The spade of the archeologist has corroborated this, the second commandment of the Decalogue. While hundreds of figurines of Canaanite gods and goddesses, particularly a nude female goddess of fertility, have been unearthed in Palestine, and pictorial representation of deities in tree or animal form abound in the ancient Near East, no image of the God of Israel has come to light.[1] At a later date the Jews in the Graeco-Roman world were to be accused of being *atheists* not simply because they refused to worship the gods whom other peoples worshipped, but because in a world where every god and goddess was known from statues and images of one kind and another, there was no statue, no image of the God whom the Jews claimed to worship. Did they really worship a god, or were they dangerous atheists in disguise?

But to the Bible God is

> 'the LORD who made all things
> who stretched out the heavens above
> who spread out the earth . . .'
>
> (Isa. xliv. 24)

Between the Creator and what He has created there is an absolute difference which may not be blurred. Nothing in the world can adequately represent Him who stands for ever beyond and behind the world, the source of its very existence.

The Bible speaks of God, the sole and continuing Creator of all that is.

III

The Bible speaks of *Man*. What is man? There is no question more 'alive' than this in our world today; no question to which a

[1] Cf. W. F. Albright, *From Stone Age to Christianity* (2nd ed. 1957), p. 266.

more perplexing variety of differing answers is being given—a reference in a card index system or a dreamer of dreams, a useful, or expendable, drone in a totalitarian hive or an immortal soul, the victim of hidden impulses and half conscious desires or a scientific animal? What is man?

The Bible asks this question and suggests its answers.

> 'O LORD what is man that thou dost regard him
> or the son of man that thou dost think of him?
> Man is like a breath,
> his days are like a passing shadow.'
>
> (Ps. cxliv. 3–4)

Another Psalmist traces God's pity for man to the fact that

> 'he knows our frame,
>   he remembers that we are dust.
> As for man his days are like grass;
>   he flourishes like the flower of the field,
> for the wind blows over it and it is gone,
>   and its place knows it no more.'
>
> (Ps. ciii. 14–16; cf. Isa. xl. 6–9)

A breath, a passing shadow, dust, grass, the flower of the field—all symbols of the frailty, the transitoriness of human life. Man is not immortal, not a little god. He is part of the created world. He remains for ever a creature. According to the earlier of the two creation stories in Genesis, 'the LORD God formed man of dust from the ground and breathed into his nostrils the breath of life; and man became a living being' (Gen. ii. 7). Life and all our vital powers are thus seen to be God's gift; but they are not our permanent possession. There is a limit set against every human life. In this respect man is no better than any other living creature:

'For the fate of the sons of man and the fate of the beasts is the same; as one dies, so dies the other. They all have the same breath and man has no advantage over the beasts for all his vanity. All go to one place; all are from the dust and all turn to dust again' (Eccles. iii. 19–20).

It is a healthy douche of cold water flung in the face of our pre-
sumptuousness. The Bible does not think of man as an uneasy
alliance of immortal soul and perishable body, the body acting as an
unfortunate drag on the soul in its quest for what is eternal. Man is a
unity of vital forces, a 'living being' whose life breath comes from
God. He is utterly and always in all parts of his being dependent
upon the God who will one day withdraw from him the life that He
has given, as He withdraws it from every other living creature.

> 'When thou takest away their breath, they die
> and return to their dust.'
>
> (Ps. civ. 29)

Yet if in this respect, man is like every other living creature,
from the tiniest insect to the largest mammal, the Bible attributes to
man a dignity that belongs to no other creature.

> 'When I look at thy heavens, the work of thy fingers,
> the moon and the stars which thou hast established;
> what is man that thou art mindful of him,
> and the son of man that thou dost care for him?
> Yet thou hast made him little less than God,
> and dost crown him with glory and honor.
> Thou hast given him dominion over the works of thy
>   hands;
> thou hast put all things under his feet,
> all sheep and oxen,
> and also the beasts of the field,
> the birds of the air and the fish of the sea,
> whatever passes along the paths of the sea.'
>
> (Ps. viii. 3–8)

What is man? . . . 'made little less than God, crowned with glory
and honor, given dominion over all things'. What does this mean?

'Thou hast given him dominion over the works of thy hands.'
Man's lordship over the rest of creation is stressed in the Creation
Hymn in Genesis i. We are told that after the creation of man and

woman 'God blessed them and God said unto them, "Be fruitful and multiply, and fill the earth and subdue it; and have dominion over the fish of the sea and over the birds of the air and over every living thing that moves upon the earth" ' (Gen. i. 28 cf. v26). We take this lordship for granted. Every new scientific discovery underlines it. We harness the power in water for our use; we probe the inmost secrets of the atom; we either domesticate (i.e. make part of *our* life) other living creatures or regard them as fit objects for a 'Zoo Quest' or a journey into outer space. We are, within limits, the lords of creation, even if we do not always recognize that this lordship is at best a delegated authority given us by God.

But there is more in man's dignity than this. In the Hymn of Creation, God's creative activity reaches its climax on the sixth day with the creation of man. 'Then God said, "Let us make man *in our image, after our likeness*, and let him have dominion over the fish of the sea . . ." ' (Gen. i. 26). 'Image', 'likeness'—two words of similar meaning brought together to stress a certain kinship between God and man, and it is perhaps this, not simply man's lordship over other creatures, which Psalm viii has in mind in referring to man as 'made little less than God, crowned with glory and honour'.

What does the Bible mean when it speaks of man as made 'in the image of God'? The phrase 'the image of God' occurs only three times in the Old Testament (Gen. i. 26–27; Gen. v. 1–3; Gen. ix. 5–6), but it may be claimed that the thought which lurks, perhaps originally but dimly felt, in these words, is basic to the whole Biblical understanding of man. 'Made in the image of God'—these words have been interpreted in many different ways. Do they refer to man's upright physical structure or to his possession of reason or to his creative ability? It is doubtful whether any of these explanations is adequate. The words apply to man and *to man alone* in the Bible. What, we may ask, is the distinctive mark of human life according to the Bible? Is it not simply this, that between God and man there can take place a conversation?

'But the LORD called to the man and said to him, "Where are you?" And he (i.e. man) said . . .' (Gen. iii. 9–10).

'God called to him out of the bush, "Moses, Moses", and he said "Here am I" ' (Exod. iii. 4).

'Now the word of the LORD came to me saying. . . . Then I said . . .' (Jer. i. 4 and 6).

This is the recurring pattern of the Bible. God speaks, man hears and man replies. Here is the crowning glory of man; not his artistic ability, not his scientific genius, not his technological skill, but the fact that he is made for encounter with God. There is no true understanding of man, claims the Bible, unless we see him in the context of this relationship with God.

Nor can man ever wholly shake himself free from this encounter.

'Whither shall I go from thy Spirit?
Or whither shall I flee from thy presence?
If I ascend to heaven, thou art there!
If I make my bed in Sheol (i.e. the vague shadowy abode
    of the departed) thou art there.
If I take the wings of the morning and dwell in the ut-
    termost parts of the sea,
even there thy hand shall lead me
and thy right hand shall hold me.
If I say "Let only darkness cover me
and the light about me be night"
even the darkness is not dark to thee,
the night is bright as the day;
for darkness is as light to thee.'

(Ps. cxxxix 7–12)

Created by God to live in God's world, created to stand in intimate personal relationship with God, such is the glory of man, made 'in the image of God'.

Such is the glory of man, but such is also the stuff out of which his tragedy is woven.

A drowsy parent, jumping out of bed in the middle of the night to answer a baby's cry may be tempted to think there would be something to be said for exchanging the baby for a doll! But even the most expensive, blue-eyed, golden-haired, walkie-talkie doll has one incurable failing in our eyes. It is a thing. It may say 'Mama', but it can never express the love which is there when a young child,

C

lisping the same syllables, throws tiny arms round a mother's neck. A doll can never love or truly be loved; a baby can. Yet there would be certain advantages in having a doll rather than a baby. At least a doll does not grow up to sulk or say, 'No, I won't.' But it is in the very nature of a 'person' that he or she can do and say such things. A child may be a problem child—every child is, more or less!

It needs no great imagination to understand why God preferred to put into his world babies rather than dolls, men rather than puppets. Because He loves and wishes love in return, He took a risk and made us free responsible persons. And His children become His problem children. Something goes wrong in the relationship between God and man.

This is an essential part of the background to the story of the Bible. It is the theme of some of the stories in the early chapters of Genesis, stories which we call 'myths'. Like many another good word, the word 'myth' has fallen on evil days. 'It is pure myth', we say, meaning, 'There is not a grain of truth in it.' But this is not what we mean when we call the Garden of Eden story in Gen. ii. 15 ff. 'myth'. To use the word 'myth' in this connection is to assert two things—on the one hand we are saying, this is not a historian's account of something that once happened;[1] and on the other hand we imply that this is a story told to convey some lasting truth about the world and ourselves.

Jesus left no treatise on 'The Moral Imperative—our obligations to other people'; he told a story, the parable of the Good Samaritan, which brings us face to face with other people and their claims upon us. The Old Testament contains no learned discussion on the sinfulness of human nature, but it does tell certain stories which help us to see man as God's problem child.

Man, so the story goes—and woman, created from man to be a 'helper fit for him' (Gen. ii. 18)—once enjoyed an idyllic life in a wonderful garden. When dinner time came they had but to stretch out a hand. The fruit of every tree in the garden was theirs to eat, with one exception—'of the tree of the knowledge of good and evil

---

[1] A genuine historical event, however, may provide material for the myth, e.g. Floods in Mesopotania lie behind the Biblical myth of the Flood in Gen. 6 ff.

you shall not eat, for in the day that you eat of it you shall surely
die' (Gen. ii. 17).

'Now the serpent was more subtle than any other wild creature
that the LORD God had made. He said to the woman, "Did God say,
'You shall not eat of any tree of the garden'? And the woman said
to the serpent, 'We may eat of the fruit of the trees of the garden;
but God said, 'You shall not eat of the fruit of the tree which is
in the midst of the garden neither shall you touch it lest you die'."
But the serpent said to the woman, "You shall not die. For God
knows that when you eat of it your eyes will be opened, and you
will be like God knowing good and evil." So when the woman saw
that the tree was good for food and that it was a delight to the eyes,
and that the tree was to be desired to make one wise, she took of its
fruit and ate; and she also gave to her husband and he ate. Then
the eyes of both were opened, and they knew that they were
naked . . .' (Gen. iii. 1–7).

There are many questions we might ask about the story. Indeed
such 'myths' were probably told to suggest answers to many different questions. We shall focus our attention on only one aspect of
the story. Something has gone wrong in this idyllic existence. We
may find it difficult to swallow the tale of a talkative serpent, but it is
at least obvious that there is 'a fly in the ointment'. The root of the
trouble is plain. Man and woman deliberately disobey God. This is
the story of 'man's first disobedience' or rather of everyman's daily
disobedience to God. If we ask why man chose to disobey we may
see the answer in the words with which the serpent cunningly baits
the temptation, 'You shall not die . . . *you will be like God.*' Man
wants to put himself at the centre of the universe where only God
can rightly be. He thinks he knows best. 'Self',' self-centredness',
this is at the root of what the Bible calls 'sin'.

We may see the same emphasis in another myth in Gen. xi, a
myth told mainly to give primitive man's answer to the question,
'Why are there so many different languages in the world?' The
story tells of how men decided to build the original skyscraper, of
how God objected and turned their skyscraper into a heap of rubble.
It is a strange story. In the background there is the memory of
the great multi-storied temple towers or 'ziggurats' which were a

characteristic feature of the Mesopotamian landscape. These lofty temples were an expression of man's deep piety. On the topmost storey was a shrine. Hither came the god whose permanent abode was in the heavens to make contact with the faithful on earth. To the writer of the Biblical myth, however, such a building was a sign, not of piety, but of man's presumption and self-assertion. Notice the motive which, he alleges, prompted the builders: 'Come, let us build ourselves a city and a tower with its top on the heavens, and let us make a name for ourselves, lest we be scattered abroad on the face of the earth' (Gen. xi. 4). A tower to penetrate into the heavens, the urge to make a name for themselves—this, to the Bible, is sin, a way of indicating man's preoccupation with self, with setting himself at the centre of things.

There is no easy-going optimism about man in the Bible. Time and again it draws our attention to something radically amiss with man, that is to say, with us. A Psalmist in a moment of deep contrition was vividly aware of this wrong within.

> 'Have mercy on me, O God, according to thy stead-
> fast love:
> according to thy abundant mercy blot out my trans-
> gression.
> Wash me throughly from my iniquity and cleanse me
> from my sin
> For I know my transgression and my sin is ever be-
> fore me.
> Against thee, thee only have I sinned
> and done that which is evil in thy sight,
> so that thou art justified in thy sentence
> and blameless in thy judgement.
>
> (Ps. li. 1–4)

Hundreds of years later a man of great moral earnestness and disarming honesty was to note a strange twist in his daily living. 'I do not understand my actions. For I do not do what I want, but I do the very thing I hate. . . . I do not do the good I want, but the evil I do not want is what I do' (Rom. vii. 15 and 19).

And who among us has not known this experience?

Man wishes to be the master of his own fate, to take his own way rather than God's way. Inevitably there follows estrangement. The story of the Garden tells how, after man and woman had disobeyed 'they heard the voice of the LORD God walking in the garden in the cool of the day, and the man and his wife hid themselves from the presence of the LORD God among the trees of the garden. But the LORD God called to man and said to him, "Where are you?" And he said, "I heard the sound of thee in the garden, and I was afraid because I was naked and I hid myself" ' (Gen. iii. 8–10). Into the world of innocence has come a guilty conscience. Man is on the run from God.

Not only do things go wrong between man and God. There is in consequence friction between man and man. How can it be otherwise if the world is populated with little units of self-centredness, each bent on placing 'self' in the centre of the stage? The story of the Garden is followed by a story of jealousy and murder. Cain, jealous because God had looked with greater favour on an offering brought by his brother Abel than on his, 'said to Abel his brother, "Let us go into the field." And when they went into the field Cain rose up against his brother Abel and killed him. Then the LORD said to Cain, "Where is Abel your brother?" He said, "I do not know; am I my brother's keeper?" And the LORD said, "What have you done? The voice of your brother's blood is crying to me from the ground . . ." ' (Gen. iv. 8–10).

'Am I my brother's keeper?' There speaks the authentic voice of self-centred man. The world has reaped, and is still reaping, a bitter harvest from this strange human perversion.

These ancient myths speak to us of present truths. They help us to look into our own hearts. Perhaps we may best gather up what they have to say to us about man by listening to a modern theologian as he tells us another 'myth'.

'I would tell a tale of God calling His human children to form a great circle for the playing of His game. In that circle we ought all to be standing, linked together with lovingly joined hands, facing towards the Light in the centre, which is God ("the Love that moves the sun and the other stars"); seeing our fellow creatures all round the circle in the light of that central Love, which shines on them and beautifies their faces; and joining with them in the dance of God's great game, the rhythm of love universal. But instead of that, we have, each one, turned our backs upon God and the circle of our fellows, and faced the other way, so that we can see neither the Light at the centre nor the faces on the circumference. And indeed in that position it is difficult even to join hands with our fellows! Therefore instead of playing God's game we play, each one, our own selfish little game, like the perverse children Jesus saw in the market-place, who would not join in the dance with their companions. Each one of us wishes to be the centre, and there is blind confusion and not even any true *knowledge* of God or of our neighbours. That is what is wrong with mankind.'[1]

But it is time to lay aside the programme notes. We are ready now to listen to what the Bible has to say to us as it unfolds the great drama of God and Man on the stage of human history.

[1] D. M. Baillie, *God was in Christ*, p. 205.

PART ONE

The Old Testament

2

God in Action

The faith of the Old Testament turns upon certain events in history in which it is claimed God is to be seen in action.

1. The Hebrews speak of their pilgrim forefather Abraham coming from Mesopotamia in response to a call from God. Here is an emphasis characteristic of the Biblical witness—the initiative lies with God.

2. Central to the Old Testament understanding of God is the Exodus, the deliverance of enslaved Hebrews from Egypt towards the beginning of the thirteenth century B.C. This is declared to be a mighty act of God, delivering and choosing for Himself a people. The Hebrew name for God, YHWH, stresses the dynamic, active nature of God.

The importance of the Exodus is illustrated in worship and daily conduct.

(a) Worship in the Ancient Near East as a whole, centred upon 'nature' gods. In Israel, accepting certain of the great occasions of the religious year from her neighbours, it centres upon the God of history.

(b) The daily conduct of the Israelite is to be a grateful response of obedience to the God who has done great things for His people. Thus the 'Ten Words' begin with a reference to the Exodus.

3. Throughout the nation's history, the Old Testament traces the hand of God. To the Israelites, struggling for a foothold in Canaan in the twelfth century B.C., God is the warrior God of his people, leading them to victory.

To the prophet Jeremiah, in the seventh and sixth centuries B.C., he is the God who orders events, even the destruction of His own people, to fulfil His purposes.

*To the anonymous prophet of the exile in Babylon, He is the God
alive to accomplish a new deliverance for His people.*
This is the 'living God', the God who acts.

WHAT is God? Many a Scottish boy and girl used to know the
answer to this, the fourth question in the Shorter Catechism.
'God is a Spirit, infinite, eternal, and unchangeable in His being,
wisdom, power, holiness, justice, goodness and truth.' If we ask,
whence comes this succinct definition of the nature of God agreed
upon by the worthy Assembly of Divines which met at West-
minster in 1647, the answer is plain. The authors wish us to be in
no doubt. In the course of the definition they use that essential aid
to erudition, the footnote, no fewer than nine times to direct our
attention to the Bible, five of the references being to Old Testament
passages, four to New Testament passages and, interestingly
enough, of the four New Testament passages two contain direct
quotations from the Old Testament. It is as if we are being presented
with a skilfully selected mosaic of Old Testament ideas. Yet if we
turn over the passages of the Old Testament expecting to find some
such neat definition of God, we are in for a disappointment. The
Old Testament is far less interested in describing what God is, than
in pointing to what God does; far less concerned that we should
think correctly about some Being who is infinite and eternal than that
we should face a dynamic, living, active God Who makes Himself
known to men in and through events. Here is the God of newspaper
headlines rather than the God of our quiet reflective moments.

The Book of Joshua ends with the account of a memorable
gathering of the tribes at Shechem. The tribes are struggling to
make good their foothold in Canaan. In the tradition of some of
them there lay the nightmare of Egyptian oppression and the
wonder of deliverance; others may never have heard of Egyptian
enslavement. The sole hope for them all lay in unity. Joshua knew
that the one bond which could effectively unite such a motley
group of tribes in a country whose broken terrain encouraged the
'parish pump' mentality was common allegiance to one God. What
takes place at Shechem, however, is not a representative gathering of
theologians issuing, after weary hours of argument and discussion,

an agreed statement of belief. Instead 'Joshua said to all the people, "Thus says the LORD, the God of Israel, 'Your fathers lived of old beyond the Euphrates, Terah, the father of Abraham and of Nahor; and they served other gods. Then I took your father Abraham from beyond the River and led him through all the land of Canaan, and made his offspring many. I gave him Isaac; and to Isaac I gave Jacob and Esau. And I gave Esau the hill country of Seir to possess, but Jacob and his children went down to Egypt. And I sent Moses and Aaron and I plagued Egypt with what I did in the midst of it; and afterwards I brought you out. Then I brought your fathers out of Egypt, and you came to the sea; and the Egyptians pursued your fathers with chariots and horsemen to the Red Sea. And when they cried to the LORD, he put darkness between you and the Egyptians, and made the sea come upon them and cover them; and your eyes saw what I did to Egypt; and you lived in the wilderness a long time. Then I brought you to the land of the Amorites who lived on the other side of the Jordan; they fought with you and I gave them into your hand, and you took possession of their land and I destroyed them before you. Then Balak the son of Zippor, king of Moab, arose and fought against Israel, and he sent and invited Balaam the son of Beor to curse you, but I would not listen to Balaam; therefore he blessed you; so I delivered you out of his hand. And you went over the Jordan and came to Jericho, and the men of Jericho fought against you, and also the Amorites, the Perizzites, the Canaanites, the Hittites, the Girgashites, the Hivites and the Jebusites; and I gave them into your hand. And I sent the hornet before you, which drove them out before you, the two kings of the Amorites; it was not by your sword or by your bow. I gave you a land on which you had not labored, and cities which you had not built, and you dwell therein; you eat the fruit of vineyards and oliveyards which you did not plant!' " ' (Joshua xxiv. 2–13).

The form of this passage may date itself long after the time of Joshua but the content is traditional. It reads like a history lesson full of strange names and strange places. It *is* a history lesson, for the God of the Old Testament is the God who comes in and through the strange pattern of events which is a nation's history.

When we celebrate harvest thanksgiving, our thoughts dwell on

God the Creator, the goodness of His daily providing, the constancy of seedtime and harvest. We sing the praise of God who

> 'sends the snow in winter,
> The warmth to swell the grain,
> The breezes and the sunshine
> And soft refreshing rain.'

But when an Israelite came to the sanctuary to present to God the first fruits of harvest, this was the song of praise on his lips:

'A wandering Aramean was my father; and he went down into Egypt and sojourned there, few in number; and there he became a nation, great, mighty and populous. And the Egyptians treated us harshly, and afflicted us and laid upon us hard bondage. Then we cried to the LORD the God of our fathers, and the LORD heard our voice and saw our affliction, our toil and our oppression; and the LORD brought us out of Egypt with a mighty hand, and an out-stretched arm, with great terror, with signs and wonders; and he brought us into this place and gave us this land, a land flowing with milk and honey. And behold now I bring the first of the fruit of the ground which thou, O LORD, has given me' (Deut. xxvi. 5–10).

Here again we find a history lesson, the *same* history lesson, pin-pointing certain significant events—the wanderings of the Hebrew pilgrim fathers, the unforgettable deliverance from cruel oppression in Egypt leading eventually to the settlement in a promised land. These were vital events in the life of the Hebrew tribes; vital and hence remembered in the historical sagas of the people however much these sagas in the form in which we now have them may be the product of later reflection; vital because in them men of faith saw not merely the passing panorama of events but the activity of the living God. Let us look more closely at certain of these events to see what they have to tell us about this God.

A

'I took your father Abraham from beyond the River (i.e. the Euphrates) and led him . . .' (Joshua xxiv. 3).

Early in the second millenium B.C. the northern region of the Mesopotamian valley was overrun and settled by Semitic tribes whom the Babylonians were to call 'Amorites', i.e. Westerners.[1]

From one of these settlements, Haran, the Hebrews traced the coming of their great ancestor Abraham. There is nothing unusual in the movement westwards towards the Mediterranean of a semi-nomadic family group under the leadership of father Abraham. What is strange is the reason which, according to the Bible, prompted the migration. Neither wander-lust nor the urgent necessity of fresh pasturage for the flocks nor dreams of conquest beckoned their wandering 'Aramaean'.

'Now the LORD said to Abram, "Go from your country and your kindred and your father's house to the land that I will show you. And I will make of you a great nation, and I will bless you and make your name great, so that you will be a blessing. I will bless those who bless you and him who curses you I will curse; and by you all the families of the earth will bless themselves! So Abram went as the LORD had told him" ' (Gen. xii. 1–4).

These opening verses of Genesis xii mark the point at which the narrative of Genesis becomes firmly anchored to history. Chapters i–xi contain in the main 'myths', told to reveal to us certain truths about God and Man. Now we are summoned to take the caravan route westward from Haran, sometime perhaps in the eighteenth century B.C., as a family group takes to the road in response to a call from God. *God takes the initiative.* He speaks to a particular man at a particular time. He bids him, not as we might expect, to search diligently for truth, goodness or beauty, but to pack his bags and venture forth into the unknown with nothing to sustain him but a promise of greatness for his descendants. Puzzling, disturbing though this incident may be, it sets the pattern for what the Bible has to say to us about God. We would be well advised to shelve our questions until we have looked a little more closely at the total pattern. Of course if this is the kind of God with whom we have to deal, there is only one thing a man can do. A New Testament writer puts it in a nutshell in words which are a fit summary of the life and character of Abraham. 'By faith Abraham obeyed when

[1] Cf. G. Ernst Wright, *Biblical Archeology*, chapter II.

he was called to go out to a place which he was to receive as an inheritance; and he went out not knowing where he was to go' (Heb. xi, 8). He obeyed. There was only one other possibility. He might have disobeyed this God who had taken the initiative.

B

'I sent Moses and Aaron . . . then I brought your fathers out of Egypt' (Joshua xxiv. 5 and 6).

The Book of Genesis traces the fortunes of Abraham and his descendants Isaac, Jacob and Joseph until some five hundred years after Abraham moved from Haran the stage is set for that never-to-be-forgotten event which became central for the faith of the Old Testament. Some of Abraham's descendants who had gone to settle in Egypt in more auspicious days now found themselves treated as slaves. The hand of the oppressor lay heavily upon them. Once again God takes the initiative. The call comes to Moses as he tends his father-in-law's flocks in the wilderness. Arrested by a strange sight, a burning thorn bush, burning yet apparently never burned, Moses hears a voice saying to him: 'I have seen the affliction of my people who are in Egypt, and have heard their cry because of their taskmasters; I know their sufferings and I have come down to deliver them out of the hand of the Egyptians and to bring them up out of that land to a good and broad land, a land flowing with milk and honey' (Exod. iii. 7–8).

Comforting words, but Moses is in for a shock; *he* has been chosen as a human instrument through which this mighty act of deliverance is to be accomplished. The excuses come tumbling out. He is not a fit man for the job; the people won't recognize his credentials.

'If I come to the people of Israel and say to them, "The God of your fathers has sent me to you," and they ask me, "What is his name?" what shall I say to them?' God said to Moses, 'I Am Who I Am', and he said, 'Say this to the people of Israel, "I am has sent me to you." ' God also said to Moses, 'Say this to the people of Israel, "The Lord, the God of your fathers, the God of Abraham, the God of Isaac and the God of Jacob has sent me to you"; this is my name for ever and thus I am to be remembered throughout all generations' (Exod. iii. 13–15).

'What is his name?' This is not the opening question in some 'Guess Who' party game. There is an Egyptian story[1] of how the supreme God 'Re' had many names, one of them a carefully guarded secret. The goddess Isis plots to discover the secret name so that the supreme power may be hers. This secret name was the key to Re's character and power. 'What is his name?' that is to say, 'What is he really like, what can he do?'

The reply Moses received hardly seems illuminating at first sight —'I am who I am.' Perhaps it conjures up in our minds a picture of a rather pompous official drawing himself up to the full height of his self-assured dignity and saying, 'Don't ask silly questions.' 'I am who (or what) I am' or 'I will be who (or what) I will be'—all these translations are possible. This is the explanation given in this passage of the meaning of the peculiar personal name YHWH by which God was known to the Hebrews, the name translated LORD in this passage and elsewhere in the text.[2] YHWH—the original meaning of this four consonant Hebrew word has been much disputed.[3]

Exodus iii. 13–16, however, links it with the verb 'hayah' to be, i.e. YHWH represents the third person singular of the verb 'to be'; the meaning is therefore 'He is' or 'He will be'. That this is the correct etymology of the word YHWH may well be doubted, but it does serve to underline much of what the Old Testament has to say about God. Moses wanted a thumbnail sketch of the character of God to take to the people; he was given instead a promise, a promise of One actively present with his people. When Moses first tried to wriggle out of the responsibilities laid upon him in the vision of the burning bush, 'Who am I that I should go to Pharaoh and bring the sons of Israel out of Egypt?' (Exod. iii. 11), God met his protests with a promise, 'But I will be with you' (Exod. iii. 12). Moses was being sent into the front line, but he had this assurance that God would be there in action by his side. This same assurance Moses is now commanded to bring to his oppressed fellow countrymen. The God who

[1] J. B. Pritchard (ed), *Ancient Near Eastern Texts*, p. 126.
[2] The A.V. translation *Jehovah* is an impossible hybrid form first used in the sixteenth century A.D. The name is usually rendered as *Yahweh* in modern discussion.
[3] Cf. E. Jacob, *Theology of the Old Testament*, pp. 48 ff.

had been with Abraham, with Isaac and with Jacob, the God whose activity could be traced in the past, this same God is to be present and active now and will be present in whatever lies ahead. We cannot tie a neat label to the God of the Old Testament and catalogue Him as one among many exhibits in a Universal Religious Museum. He is, if we may say so, a disconcerting character, disturbingly alive, ever going into action—YHVH, He assuredly is, He assuredly will be with us. Certainly the Old Testament believes that at this moment when an oppressed people bowed beneath the taskmaster's lash, God went into action. The story of what happened according to the Biblical narrative is found in Exodus, chapters v–xv. It is a strange story—a series of inconclusive interviews between Moses and the Pharaoh of Egypt; the terrifying plagues which smite the Egyptians; Pharaoh temporizing until the eleventh hour, unwilling, no doubt, to lose a convenient pool of cheap labour; the wonder of the Sea which parted to allow the Israelites to pass and surged back to engulf the pursuing Egyptians. It is all rather breathless, perhaps bewildering. What happened at certain points we may never know, but one fact stands indisputably —a group of people once cowed by slavery found themselves, much to their surprise, free. They could give no adequate explanation of what had happened except to say, 'Here was the hand of God'. This was the decisive event in the religious experience of the nation. Just as for the Christian there can be no understanding of God which is not rooted in the life, death and resurrection of Jesus of Nazareth, so the man of faith in Old Testament times could never omit this from his confession of faith, 'I am the LORD your God who brought you out of the land of Egypt, out of the house of bondage' (Exod. xx. 2). Like some inevitable refrain, these or similar words haunt the pages of the Old Testament.

The Book of Deuteronomy depicts the people of Israel standing, their hearts very much in their mouths, on the borders of the promised land. The promised land was already occupied by a people numerically and materially much stronger. Occupation means war. The people are afraid. Listen to the morale-restoring words of Deuteronomy vii. 17–19 'If you say in your heart, "These nations are greater than I; how can I dispossess them?" you shall not be afraid of them, but you shall remember what the LORD your God did to Pharaoh and to all Egypt, the great trials which your eyes saw, the signs, the wonders, the mighty hand and the outstretched arm by which the LORD your God brought you out; so will the LORD your God do to all the peoples of whom you are afraid' (cf. Deut. iv. 34).

A prophet of the eighth century B.C., bitterly conscious of his people's waywardness and infidelity to God, recalls God's dealings with the people in the following words:

> 'When Israel was a child I loved him,
> And out of Egypt I called my son.'
>
> (Hos. xi. 1)

Another prophet depicts God as exclaiming in similar vein:

> 'O my people what have I done to you?
> In what have I wearied you? Answer me!
> For I brought you up from the land of Egypt,
> and redeemed you from the house of bondage;
> and I sent before you Moses, Aaron and Miriam . . .'
>
> (Mic. vi. 3–4)

How deeply this belief in the God who delivered His people out of captivity in Egypt penetrated into the very marrow of the religious consciousness of the Hebrew people may be seen if we look briefly at two facets of their religious life and thought where we might well expect it not to occur.

I

Every faith which seeks to wield a lasting influence upon men clothes itself in action. Together in a sanctuary or at a recognized holy place, the worshippers *do* certain things which give expression to their faith or indeed play a vital part in that faith. The world of the ancient Near East was well acquainted with such cultic acts; they had an essential function in religion. In a way in which it is difficult for us in our artificial Western communities to realize, a

D

man knew himself to be a child of Nature, terrifyingly dependent on Nature's annual bounty. His gods were gods of fertility who had to be assisted in their yearly struggle with the gods of aridity and death; the powers of order had to be fortified against the primeval powers of chaos which ever threatened to break in and engulf human life.[1] This was the theme which was re-enacted dramatically, sometimes with the king of the community in the leading rôle, at the great New Year Festival held in the autumn. The life-giving god died, smitten by the god of death; died only to be raised in triumph to scatter his enemies, to re-establish life out of death, order out of chaos. Thus was the welfare of the community ensured for the coming year. This cultic pattern, with infinite variation, is found throughout the ancient Near East with the solitary exception of Israel. Certainly Israel has her great religious occasions and her autumnal New Year Festival, the Feast of Tabernacles; certainly she assimilated from the Canaanite peoples among whom she came to dwell, certain features of this 'nature' cult; certainly she took over, sometimes with little alteration, cult hymns associated with that religion—Psalm xxix is an example; *but* what was celebrated, perhaps dramatically re-enacted, in the Temple at Jerusalem was subtly different. Whereas Canaanite religion centred dramatically on the myth of Creation, Israelite worship celebrated not only the power of YHWH as Creator, but more importantly the mighty acts of YHWH in history, and in particular that mighty act whereby He delivered His people out of captivity in Egypt.

From their Canaanite neighbours the Israelites took over a Feast of Unleavened Cakes celebrated annually at the beginning of the barley harvest; in their own semi-nomadic past there was Passover, originally perhaps a festival in which the herdsman offered the firstborn of his flock to the deity who gave fertility. Unleavened Cakes; Passover—originally two entirely distinct religious festivals connected with different aspects of the mystery of life in field and flock. But look what happens to them in the Book of Deuteronomy, which, although its present form dates from the seventh century B.C., may well be echoing an older tradition.

'Observe the month of Abib, and keep the passover to the LORD

[1] Cf. S. H. Hooke (ed.), *Myth and Ritual.*

your God; for in the month of Abib the LORD your God brought you out of Egypt by night. And you shall offer the passover sacrifice to the LORD your God, from the flock or the herd, at the place which the LORD will choose, to make his name dwell there. You shall eat no leavened bread with it; seven days you shall eat it with unleavened bread, the bread of affliction—for you came out of the land of Egypt in hurried flight—that all the days of your life you may remember the day when you came out of the land of Egypt. No leaven shall be seen with you in all your territory for seven days; nor shall any of the flesh which you sacrifice on the evening of the first day remain all night until morning. You may not offer the passover sacrifice within any of your towns which the LORD your God gives you; but at the place which the LORD your God will choose to make his name dwell in it, there you shall offer the passover sacrifice, in the evening at the going down of the sun, at the time you came out of Egypt. And you shall boil it and eat it at the place which the LORD your God will choose; and in the morning you shall turn and go to your tents. For six days you shall eat unleavened bread; and on the seventh day there shall be a solemn assembly to the LORD your God; you shall do no work on it' (Deut. xvi. 1–8). Here the two originally separate festivals have been dovetailed into one, and, even more significantly, the whole has been linked to the story of the Exodus from Egypt. The date of the festival recalls the date of the Exodus (verse 1); the unleavened bread is said to owe its origin to the haste in which the people quit Egypt (verse 3); the Passover victim is to be sacrificed 'in the evening at the going down of the sun, at the time you came out of Egypt' (verse 6). Just as surely as Good Friday and Easter remind the Christian of God's mighty act in the death and resurrection of Jesus, so Passover was the Israelites' constant reminder of that day when, thanks to God, he came out of the land of Egypt.

II

'But, Daddy, why can't I do that, why *must* I do this?' 'Just because I say so'—a familiar conversation? It was obviously not unknown in Old Testament times. There is a passage in the Book of Deuteronomy which speaks to this situation, and incidentally provides a harassed parent with a much better answer than 'Just because I say so.' 'When your son asks you in time to come, "What is the meaning of the testimonies and the statutes and the ordinances which the LORD our God has commanded you?" then you shall say to your son, "We were Pharaoh's slaves in Egypt; and the LORD brought us out of Egypt with a mighty hand; and the LORD showed signs and wonders, great and grievous, against Egypt and against Pharaoh and all his household, before our eyes; and he brought us out from there, that he might bring us in and give us the land which he swore to give to our fathers. And the LORD commanded us to do all these statutes, to fear the LORD our God, for our good always, that he might preserve us alive as at this day. And it will be righteousness for us, if we are careful to do all this commandment before the LORD our God, as he commanded us" ' (Deut. vi. 20–25). Thus the Exodus from Egypt becomes a vital factor even in the day to day conduct of the man of faith in the Old Testament. His life is to be a life of grateful obedience to the God who has done good things for him. Significantly, that great summary of basic morality the Decalogue (the 'Ten Words'), which in essence goes back to the time of Moses, begins not 'I am a moral God therefore you must be good,' but 'I am the LORD your God who brought you out of the land of Egypt out of the house of bondage' (Exod. xx. 2; Deut. v. 6).

Thus, whenever the faithful Israelite joined the joyful crowd which thronged the sanctuary on the great occasions of the religious year, whenever he sought to order his life in obedience to God, he found himself face to face with that living God who took the initiative in delivering His people out of bondage in Egypt.

> 'I will call to mind the deeds of the LORD;
> yea I will remember thy wonders of old.
> I will meditate on all thy work,
> and muse on thy mighty deeds.
> Thy way, O God, is holy.
> What god is great like our God?

Thou art the God who workest wonders,
who hast manifested thy might among the peoples.
Thou didst with thy arm redeem thy people,
the sons of Jacob and Joseph.
When the waters saw thee, O God,
when the waters saw thee they were afraid,
yea, the deep trembled.
The clouds poured out water;
the skies gave forth thunder;
thy arrows flashed on every side.
The crash of thy thunder was in the whirlwind;
thy lightnings lighted up the world;
the earth trembled and shook.
Thy way was through the sea,
thy path through the great waters;
yet thy footprints were unseen.
Thou didst lead thy people like a flock
by the hand of Moses and Aaron.'

                                        (Ps. lxxvii. 11–20)

C

An Israelite in the twelfth century B.C., however, engaged in the desperate struggle to secure and maintain a foothold in the land of Canaan was not dreaming nostalgically of the 'good old days' of the Exodus when God had acted so wonderfully. He was squaring his shoulders to face the grim tasks of the day in the firm conviction that this same God was still acting, the God of the embattled ranks of Israel going into action with His people. The Book of Judges contains, in chapter v, one of the oldest extant portions of Hebrew literature. It commemorates, as so many folk ballads do, a battle fought between the people of Israel and their Canaanite adversaries 'at Ta'anach, by the waters of Megiddo' (v. 19). A torrential deluge turned the battlefield into a quagmire, effectively immobilizing the feared Canaanite chariotry. The Israelite forces swept down to victory from the heights of Mount Tabor. Sisera, the Canaanite commander-in-chief, fled from the field to meet his death at the hands of a woman. This memorable victory was not celebrated by the publication in the official *Israelite Gazette* of a series of awards for gallantry, nor by the bestowal of a knighthood on the Israelite commander Barak. Instead the prophetess Deborah leads the people in what has been well described as 'a triumphal Te Deum to Yahweh, Israel's God'.[1] After an opening stanza which summons the people and their leaders to bless the LORD, the victory ode continues:

> 'Hear, O kings; give ear, O princes;
> to the LORD I will sing,
> I will make melody to the LORD,
> the God of Israel.'

> (v. 3)

Vividly the poem depicts the God of Israel coming from His abode in the south country to go into action.

> 'Lord, when thou didst go forth from Seir,
> when thou didst march from the region of Edom,
> the earth trembled and the heavens dropped,
> yea the clouds dropped water.
> The mountains quaked before the LORD,
> yon Sinai before the LORD,
> the God of Israel.

> (v. 4–5)

Wherever the people travel they are bidden 'repeat the triumphs of the LORD' (v. 11). Though some of the tribes making up the Israelite confederacy shamefully failed to rally to the standard in the hour of crisis, the very elements, controlled by the LORD, fought on behalf of the Israelites.

> 'The kings came, they fought;
> then fought the kings of Canaan,
> at Ta'anach, by the waters of Megiddo;
> they got no spoils of silver.

[1] Moore, *Judges*, International Critical Commentary, p. 134.

From heaven fought the stars,
from their courses they fought against Sisera.
The torrent Kishon swept them away,
the onrushing torrent, the torrent Kishon.'

(v. 19–21)

This was the LORD's doing and it was wonderful in the sight of His people.

Let us turn the pages of Old Testament history till we come to the seventh century B.C. The Kingdom of Judah, tiny and politically powerless, is all that remains of the once powerful kingdom that the Israelites had established under David and Solomon. It is a difficult, a perplexing age for men of faith. For the first half of the century King Manasseh kept Judah out of trouble by faithfully licking the boots of his Assyrian imperial overlord. The country was at peace, but it was the peace of death as far as true religion was concerned. There had been a revival of religious practices such as human sacrifice which had long been seen to be inconsistent with true faith; Assyrian deities were worshipped in the temple at Jerusalem, the inevitable religious expression of political bondage. This was a world where might seemed right, where cruelty and oppression abounded. The second half of the century witnessed a strong reaction to Manasseh's policy. His son Amon was liquidated in a palace intrigue. Josiah, a young lad of eight years of age, succeeded to the throne in 639 B.C. to inaugurate a period which was to be marked by an ill-starred religious revival and a resurgence of nationalism which spelt doom for the Kingdom of Judah. Into this situation steps one of the greatest figures of the Old Testament, Jeremiah. There came to him in his youth the staggering conviction that God had laid his hand upon him. He had been called to be a 'prophet', that is to be God's spokesman in declaring to his age God's purposes, and in summoning the people to face God's demands. Jeremiah did not exactly relish his commission. He had his hesitations and his doubts. Personal diffidence lay behind some of them, but beyond personal diffidence there lay a deeper problem. What kind of faith could be adequate for the perplexing age in which he lived?

'And the word of the LORD came to me saying, "Jeremiah, what do you see?" And I said, "I see a rod of almond!" Then the LORD said to me, "You have seen well for I am watching over my word to perform it"' (Jer. i. 11–12). An almond twig bursting into life is the first sign of spring in Palestine. The seeming spell of death which winter has cast upon the countryside is broken. The Hebrew word for an almond twig is, appropriately, 'shaqed'—the 'wakeful' tree. Gazing at such a 'shaqed' one day Jeremiah is gripped with the overmastering conviction that this God who has called him is 'shoqed', wakeful, alive, watching over His word to perform it. God is ever on the *qui vive*, in control, working out his purposes even when we cannot see them. This faith was the stay of Jeremiah throughout a lifetime of misunderstanding, persecution, increasing loneliness and intense inner turmoil, a lifetime played out against the sombre backcloth of the death throes of his country. Some forty years after the vision of the almond twig, as the Babylonian armies closed in to give Judah the *coup de grâce*, Jeremiah found himself the most dearly hated man in Jerusalem. He was a self-confessed traitor, advocating that the citizens should desert to the Babylonians. There was a temporary lifting of the siege of the city while the Babylonians withdrew to settle scores with an Egyptian Expeditionary Force which threatened to come to the rescue of Jerusalem. As the Babylonians withdrew King Zedekiah of Judah sent a message to Jeremiah asking him to pray for the city. The reply he received was hardly reassuring.

'Then the word of the LORD came to Jeremiah the prophet: "Thus says the LORD, God of Israel: Thus shall you say to the king of Judah who sent you to me to enquire of me, Behold, Pharaoh's army which came to help you is about to return to Egypt, to its own land. And the Chaldeans shall come back and fight against this city; they shall take it and burn it with fire. Thus says the LORD, Do not deceive yourselves saying, The Chaldeans will surely stay away from us, for they will not stay away. For even if you should defeat the whole army of Chaldeans who are fighting against you, and there remained of them only wounded men, every man in his tent, they would rise up and burn this city with fire"' (Jer. xxxvii. 6–10).

There is very little political or military realism in the picture of a handful of wounded men sacking a city. Jeremiah was convinced, however, that the real threat to Jerusalem came not from the Babylonians, but from God. In the stirring events of the day he saw, not merely the clash of armies, but God in action writing 'finis' to a sorry chapter in the nation's history. This was the LORD's doing, even if it seemed, to many people, catastrophic.

Jeremiah ended his life in exile somewhere in Egypt. Many of his fellow countrymen were exiled to Babylon. Nearly half a century of exile induced in some of these Babylonian exiles a mood of pessimism. God had forgotten them.

> 'My way is hid from the LORD,
> and my right is disregarded by God.'
>
> (Isa. xl. 27)

To such people the unknown poet-prophet who composed Isaiah xl ff. brought good news. In words which consciously echo the great events of the Exodus he reminds them of God:

> 'who makes a way in the sea,
> a path in the mighty waters,
> who brings forth chariot and horse,
> army and warrior;
> they lie down, they cannot rise,
> they are extinguished, quenched like a wick.'
>
> (Isa. xliii. 16–17)

But faith cannot be restored simply by the memory of what is past, however good that past may be.

> 'Remember not the former things,
> nor consider the things of old.
> Behold I am doing a new thing;
> now it springs forth, do you not perceive it?
> I will make a way in the wilderness
> and rivers in the desert.

> The wild beasts will honour me,
> the jackals and the ostriches;
> for I give water in the wilderness,
> rivers in the desert,
> to give drink to my chosen people,
> the people whom I formed for myself
> that they might declare my praise.'
>
> (Isa. xliii. 18–21)

As God had acted, so he was about to act again, to deliver his people, to prepare a way for them.

We have listened to the Hebrews recalling the stories of their distant forbears; we have heard the triumph song of the Exodus echoing throughout the Old Testament tradition. We have shared in the battle cry of Hebrew warriors in the twelfth century B.C.; we have pondered the words of prophets from the seventh and sixth centuries B.C. At every point we hear the same refrain. This is the story of God's activity, of God in action in the events which constituted a nation's history.

There is a vivid phrase which the Old Testament sometimes uses to describe God. It speaks of 'the living God'. What that meant may best be seen in a passage in the Book of Jeremiah which contrasts the LORD, the God of Israel, with the gods of other peoples.

> 'Thus says the LORD:
> "Learn not the way of nations,
> nor be dismayed at the signs of the heavens
> because the nations are dismayed at them,
> for the customs of the peoples are false.
> A tree from the forest is cut down,
> and worked with an axe by the hands of a craftsman.
> Men deck it with silver and gold;
> they fasten it with hammer and nails
> so that it cannot move.
> Their idols are like scarecrows in a cucumber field,
> and they cannot speak;

they have to be carried
for they cannot walk.
Be not afraid of them,
for they cannot do evil,
neither is it in them to do good".'

(Jer. x. 2-5)

Herein is the difference between the LORD and the idols of other nation's worship—they cannot do anything, either evil or good.

'There is none like thee, O LORD
thou art great and thy name is great in might.
Who would not fear thee, O King of the nations?
For this is thy due;
for among all the wise ones of the nations
and in all their kingdoms
there is none like thee.
They are both stupid and foolish;
the instruction of idols is but wood!
Beaten silver is brought from Tarshish,
and gold from Uphaz.
They are the work of the craftsman
and of the hands of the goldsmith;
their clothing is violet and purple;
they are all the work of skilled men.
But the LORD is the true God;
he is the living God and the everlasting King.
At his wrath the earth quakes,
and the nations cannot endure his indignation.'

(Jer. x. 6-10)

The LORD, 'the living God'—this is not an assertion that God exists, but that He is a God who does things, who acts, who is ever active fulfilling his purposes amid the affairs of men.

This one 'living God' was the 'odd man out' among the many pantheons of the ancient world. He is still the 'odd man out' in much of our thinking. At a popular level, there are many people who believe that there must be a 'someone, somewhere' to account for this mysterious universe. At a more philosophical level men have often convinced themselves that they can reason their way to a God who is the source of all goodness, beauty and truth. The 'someone, somewhere' and 'the source of all goodness, beauty and truth' have this in common—and it is part of their attractiveness—they are not liable to do anything. They are safely 'there', not disconcertingly in action 'here'. We may think about them, we may draw inspiration or comfort from them, but they are not liable to interfere with us, nor, unsought, to do anything for us. The atheist in the Bible is not the man who, taking a searching look at life, concludes, 'There is no God'; he is the man who, like many of us, confesses to a belief in God, but says, or at least lives on the assumption that 'He will do nothing' (Jer. v. 12). To believe in God and to banish Him as an idle spectator to the touchline of the universe—this is atheism. The God of whom the Bible speaks is the master player in this game of human life and destiny. He is the God whom we meet in action in the history of His people, Israel.

3
This Holy God

'*Holy*' *is the word characteristic of God. Psalm xcix helps us to see its varied meaning in the Old Testament.*

1. Ps. xcix. 1–3. That dread 'mysterious otherness' *which separates God from man. Stories from the early days of the settlement in Canaan (twelfth-tenth centuries* B.C.*) show how this 'holiness' is regarded as dangerous when not properly channelized. This apparently primitive idea serves to stress that spirit of reverence out of which all true worship springs.*

2. Ps. xcix. 4–5. The call to the prophet Isaiah (742 B.C.*) reveals this holiness as a* moral holiness *contrasting sharply with the sinfulness of man. God is holy in righteousness. 'Righteousness' and 'justice' in the Old Testament range far beyond the normal meanings we give to these words. Righteousness is not an abstract quality but a description of how God acts. Since the Old Testament sees God as the deliverer of His people, righteousness has a strongly gracious flavour, and is linked with 'steadfast love'.*

3. Ps. xcix. 6–9. The Holy One of Israel. *Along with the Exodus the Old Testament associates the Covenant between God and His people. The word describing the attitude to one another of parties bound together in covenant is 'chesed', 'steadfast love', faithfulness, loyalty, rather than kindness.*

The prophet Hosea (eighth century B.C.*), drawing upon his own experience of loving a faithless wife, stresses this 'steadfast love' of God, constant mid all His people's inconstancy. It is Israel's hope in the hour of national catastrophe (cf. Isa. xl–lv). God's relationship to Israel is seen in the way God is described as Father, Shepherd, and Redeemer.*

God's steadfast love for His people is the supreme demonstration of His righteousness.

THERE is an everyday saying that 'actions speak louder than words'. Unless there is some strange abnormality in a man, what he does is our surest guide to what he is. Estimating the value of a testimonial is always a difficult task, but at least we have something upon which to base a fair judgement if it contains not merely a general description of character, but also a record of what the person has done. We have just seen that the Old Testament is at heart a record of certain events in which God was believed to be in action. From sharing in the wonder of these events, or from pondering upon their meaning, the writers of the Old Testament were led to make certain assertions about what God is. 'The so-called "attributes" of God are inferences drawn from the way he has acted.'[1]

There was a period of frustration and despair in Florence Nightingale's life when she found herself frequently giving God instructions as to how He ought to order His universe to better purpose. Realizing one day what she was doing, she wrote down on a scrap of paper, 'I *must* remember that God is not my private secretary.' There is in the Old Testament a word which is the ultimate safeguard against adopting towards God the 'private secretary' attitude; the word 'holy' (Hebrew root *q-d-sh*), a word used only of God and hence of certain people, places and things in the world which are thought of as belonging to God. Holiness is of the very essence of God, so that when the prophet Amos declares, 'The Lord God has sworn by his holiness' (iv. 2) he means that God has taken the most solemn of oaths; he has sworn by His own very nature. Psalm xcix with its three stanzas each finding its climax in a reference to God as holy, will act as our guide as we seek to understand what the Old Testament means when it speaks of 'this holy God'.

[1] G. Ernst Wright, *God Who Acts*, p. 84.

I

Fundamental to the word 'holy' is the recognition of that 'Mysterious Otherness',[1] that awesome power of which the Hebrew was made vividly aware in his encounter with God.

> 'The Lord reigns; let the peoples tremble!
> He sits enthroned upon the cherubim; let the earth
>   quake!
> The Lord is great in Zion;
> he is exalted over all the peoples.
> Let them praise thy great and terrible name!
> Holy is he!'
>
> (Ps. xcix. 1–3)

—enthroned, exalted, His name great and terrible; holy is He, and before this holy God men and nations tremble.

This dread divine power can be either dangerous or beneficent to men, like electricity, which, when properly controlled and insulated, can give us heat, light and energy, but which in itself may be fatal. This finds vivid illustration in the stories about the 'ark' in the books of Samuel. In the time of their wandering in the desert, and in the days of the conquest of Canaan, the ark was to the people of Israel a very holy object. What precisely the ark was has been much disputed. Some have seen it as a Throne for the invisible God of Israel. Others claim it to be a box which originally contained either some long sacred object or the stone tablets on which were written 'the ten words' or commandments given to Israel at Mount Sinai. Whatever form it took, the ark was intimately associated with God, indeed to some it may have been God, present in the midst of His people to bless, travelling with them in their wanderings, carried with them into battle. One disastrous day the Israelites were decisively defeated by their enemies the Philistines. Worse than military humiliation was the fact that the ark was captured (cf. 1 Sam. iv). In triumph the Philistines carry the ark into the temple of their god Dagon. Strange things begin to happen. The statue of

[1] Cf. R. Otto, *The Idea of the Holy.*

Dagon crashes to the ground; disease and death ravage the Philistine cities. The source of the trouble is traced to the ark. It is the ark of the God of Israel; its holiness is dangerous to the Philistines. A hastily convened gathering of Philistine civic heads decides, 'Send away the ark of the God of Israel and let it return to its own place that it may not slay us and our people' (1 Sam. v. 11). Guided by their priests, the Philistines, after taking steps to placate the offended holiness, load the ark on to a cart and send it to the Israelite border where, much to their relief, the oxen bearing the sacred load shamble off in the direction of the Israelite village of Bethshemesh. At Bethshemesh the ark is returned to the care of the Levites. They can handle it safely since they have been duly consecrated for this task. That is to say, they have been chosen from among the people, and by certain rites have been 'made holy'—for that is what consecrated means. Curiosity, however, got the better of some of the ordinary village folk of Bethshemesh. God, we are told, 'slew some of the men of Bethshemesh because they looked into the ark of the LORD; He slew seventy of them and the people mourned because the LORD had made a great slaughter among the people. Then the men of Bethshemesh said, "Who is able to stand before the LORD, this holy God?" ' (1 Sam. vi. 19–20). The villagers did not sleep easily in their beds till the ark moved on.

There is a similar story in 2 Samuel, chapter vi. David with a stroke of genius had decided upon Jerusalem, recently captured from the Jebusites, as the religious and political capital for the new united kingdom he was trying to create out of tribes which had hitherto known no permanent political bond. As part of his policy he had the ark brought to Jerusalem. At one point on the way the oxen stumbled, the ark was in danger of falling. A certain Uzzah put out his hand to steady the ark. His motives may have been exemplary, but he was struck dead. An unconsecrated person had made contact with this dangerous holiness.

Now there is nothing unique in all this. Parallels to these ideas have been culled from many primitive peoples. Historians of religion normally use the Polynesian terms 'mana' and 'tabu' to describe this beneficent and dangerous holiness.[1] It is easy to give a superficial

[1] Cf. R. H. Codrington, *The Melanesians*, pp. 118 ff.

smile and dismiss the whole thing as non-moral if not indeed immoral. Yet there is something here of lasting importance for our
understanding of God, something which was to be richly developed
in the Old Testament. God may be described in startlingly human
language in the Bible. He sees (Gen. vi. 12); he listens (Exod. xvi. 12);
he laughs (Ps. ii. 4); he is angry (Ezek. vii. 8); he repents (Gen. vi.
6); he has feet (Ezek. xliii. 7), hands (Ps. cxxxix. 5), eyes (Amos ix.
4), ears (Ezek. xxii. 14), arms (Jer. xxvii. 5); *but* the Bible never
imagines that God is simply another member of the Human Club,
not even an Honorary Member. There is always an awareness of an
ultimate and unbridgeable difference between God and man. It is
this difference to which the word 'holy' points. 'I am God and not
man, the Holy One in your midst' (Hos. xi. 9). Out of the awareness of this mysterious, awesome otherness of God springs that
which gives birth to all true worship, namely reverence which has
been well described as 'the response of body and soul to lofty
mysteries deeply felt and only partially understood'.[1]

Remember how God's call came to Moses, destined to be the
great leader of His people in the hour of their emergence as a nation.
'. . . God called to him out of the bush, "Moses, Moses." And he
said "Here am I." Then He (i.e. God) said, "Do not come near: put
off your shoes from your feet for the place on which you are standing is holy ground" ' (Exod. iii. 4–5). The place was holy because
it was the place where this mysterious 'Other' chose to encounter
Moses; hence the sign of humble, if not fearful reverence, the re-
moval of the sandals from the feet; hence the command, 'Do not
come near,' for the first effect of such holiness is to keep man at a
distance, to make him vividly aware of the dread difference between
himself and God. Many centuries later, the thirties of the eighth
century B.C. found the people of Judah anxiously scanning their
northern borders. There was talk of a conspiracy among her
northern neighbours. People lived in daily dread of invasion.
Politicians hurriedly looked for a policy which would best meet the
immediate threat. In the urgency of imminent peril God was forgotten. Neither people nor politicians regarded Him as a relevant
factor in the issues of the day. One man and the little group of

[1] Interpreter's Bible, Vol. I, p. 873.

E

disciples who gathered round him saw more deeply. A more deadly peril confronted Judah than the threatened northern invasion.

'For the LORD spoke thus to me with his strong hand upon me, and warned me not to walk in the way of this people, saying: "Do not call conspiracy all that this people call conspiracy, and do not fear what they fear, nor be in dread. But the LORD of hosts, him shall you regard as holy; let him be your fear and let him be your dread" ' (Isa. viii. 11–13).

A fatal familiarity was taking God for granted. There was need of the reminder that God was holy, and because of His holiness ought, and alone ought, to evoke from the people a response of reverent fear and dread.

That the prophet Isaiah should summon His people to look at their lives in the light of this holy God was but the natural outcome of that majestic vision of the holiness of God which summoned him to his life's work. The year is 742 B.C. An aged, ailing king sits on the throne of Judah. Isaiah goes to the Temple perhaps to share in one of the great religious festivals which celebrated the Kingly power of Yahweh. Participating in the ritual and the ceremonial the prophet glimpses the divine reality which is being symbolized in the worship.

'In the year that King Uzziah died I saw the Lord sitting upon a throne, high and lifted up; and his train filled the temple. Above him stood the seraphim; each had six wings: with two he covered his face, and with two he covered his feet and with two he flew. And one called to another and said:

> "Holy, holy, holy is the LORD of hosts;
> the whole earth is full of his glory!"

And the foundations of the thresholds shook at the voice of him who called and the house was filled with smoke' (Isa. vi. 1–4).

The invisible King exalted on His throne, His royal robes filling the temple; the seraphim, 'the burning ones', mysterious, unearthly, partly human creatures attendant upon God; the vibrating door-posts, the swirling smoke, all provide fit setting for that awesome 'otherness' which finds expression in the chant of the seraphim with its thrice repeated 'Holy . . . Holy . . . Holy'.

Yet this holiness which serves to stress God's difference from man does not make Him a remote distant God. 'The whole earth is full of his glory,' and the word glory (Kabod) which means literally 'weight' always refers to the burning splendour of *God's presence* in the world. This mysterious God is present and disturbingly present.

'And I said, "Woe is me! For I am lost; for I am a man of unclean lips and I dwell in the midst of a people of unclean lips; for my eyes have seen the King, the LORD of hosts!" ' (Isa. vi. 5)

Here we are in touch with one of the distinctive turns which the Old Testament gives to the word 'holy'. An essential part of the 'otherness' of this holy God is a terrifying moral purity.

II

The opening stanza of Psalm xcix brought us face to face with the awesome mystery of God's nature; the second stanza continues:

> 'Mighty King, lover of justice,
> thou hast established equity;
> thou hast executed *justice*
> and *righteousness* in Jacob.
> Extol the LORD our God;
> worship at his footstool!
> Holy is he!'
>
> (verses 4–5)

In similar vein Psalm xcvii begins:

> 'The LORD reigns; let the earth rejoice;
> let the many coastlands be glad!
> Clouds and thick darkness are round about him;
> righteousness and justice are the foundation of his
>   throne.'
>
> (verses 1–2)

Here we find a characteristic linking of the holiness of God with 'justice' and 'righteousness'. The prophet Isaiah is but playing a variation on the same theme when he says:

'The LORD of hosts is exalted in justice,
and the Holy God shows himself holy in righteousness.'
(Isa. v. 16)

That this phrase 'holy in righteousness' indicates a God whose very nature involves a moral perfection which shows up with alarming clarity the sinfulness of man is evident from Isaiah's temple vision already cited. Isaiah feels lost; he is conscious that not only he personally but the society in which he lives stands condemned (cf. Isa. vi. 5). Such is the outcome of an encounter with this holy God. The Old Testament from first to last is profoundly conscious that, whatever be the case with other religions, the God of Israel is a God who makes inexorable moral demands. We shall see later what this involves for everyday living.[1] But when the Old Testament talks of God as 'holy in righteousness' it means rather more than this. The trouble with the words 'justice' and 'righteousness' is that we all think we know what they mean. The figure which looks impassively down upon the Central Criminal Court in London is that of Lady Justice, blindfolded, holding in her hands an equally balanced pair of scales. Utter impartiality, one law for rich and poor, wise and foolish, Prime Minister and tinker, that is the source from which much of our thinking about justice springs, and it is a source zealously to be guarded. Righteousness we tend to regard as a somewhat abstract moral quality, difficult perhaps to define, but highly to be commended, except when we come across the 'self' variety—in other people. Now all this may serve us very well as a rough and ready guide to the everyday meaning of these words, but it serves us ill when we turn to the Old Testament, not to mention the difficulties it raises in the interpretation of the New Testament. We must look more closely at the words as they are used in the Old Testament.

'*Righteousness*' (Hebrew root *ts-d-q*) perhaps means originally

[1] Cf. pp. 88 ff.

'conforming to a certain norm'. In Arabic, for example, you may talk of a 'righteous' date—edible variety—meaning a date which is up to standard, all that a desirable date ought to be. The Old Testament talks of 'right' sacrifices—'sacrifices of righteousness' in the A.V.—intending thereby sacrifices offered in accordance with correct ritual practice (Deut. xxxiii. 19; Ps. iv. 5); or again just balances, a just ephah, a just bath—literally 'balances of righteousness', etc.—to indicate scales, weights and measures which, as we would say, conform to the official standards laid down by H.M. Inspectors of Weights and Measures (Ezek. xlv. 10; Lev. xix. 36). The way in which 'righteous' was applied to people and their actions is well illustrated by the scarcely edifying story of Tamar and her father-in-law, Judah, in Genesis xxxviii. Neither Judah nor Tamar appears in the story as a paragon of virtue, but in the *dénouement* Judah is compelled to say of Tamar, 'She is more righteous than I inasmuch as I did not give her to my son Shelah' (Gen. xxxviii. 26). The whole story hinges on the ancient custom of 'levirate' marriage (cf. Deut. v. 5–10) by which, when a man died childless, it was the duty of his brother or nearest kinsman to marry his widow and thus seek to perpetuate the family name. There could be no greater tragedy for the Hebrew than the extinction of the family. Judah, as head of the family group, had failed to ensure that Tamar was given her rights according to this custom, hence he is led to acknowledge that in the light of accepted custom she is 'in the right', the innocent, he the guilty party. We are here moving in the realm of 'justice', with which righteousness is so closely connected in the Old Testament. Indeed, it is not going too far to say that in the message of the great prophets, justice and righteousness are like Siamese twins.

'*Justice*' (mishpat, from the root *sh-p-t*) refers to the activity of a judge, not simply to his passing sentence but to the whole process which begins with two parties pleading their case and ends with one party being declared 'in the right' and the other 'in the wrong'. In the earliest strands of the Old Testament the administering of justice is the responsibility of the sheikh or head of the family group, and it is as such that Judah is called upon to judge Tamar. Later in more settled village communities justice is in the hands of the 'elders', that is to say the heads of families who meet in the open space near the entrance-gate to hear cases of dispute involving members of the community and to give their decisions in the light of the immemorial customs of their people[1] (cf. Deut. xxi. 18–21; Ruth iv. 1 ff.). Because of this, 'misphat' may mean simply traditional practice or custom, witness 2 Kings xvii. 33 where we are told concerning the 'Displaced Persons' whom the Assyrians settled in Samaria after they had conquered and exiled the native Israelites, that 'they feared the LORD, but also served their own gods after the manner (mishpat) of the nations from among whom they had been carried away'. There was, however, always the possibility of cases arising which did not seem to be covered by the traditional practice of the people, or cases in which, because of conflicting evidence, decision was difficult. In such circumstances recourse was had to God; that is to say, to the local sanctuary where in the presence of God either by means of a solemn oath or by the consultation of some kind of sacred oracle, the case was decided. This is the procedure advocated in cases involving breach of trust as in Exod. xxii. 7–9.

'If a man delivers to his neighbor money or goods to keep, and it is stolen out of the man's house, then if the thief is found he shall pay double. If the thief is not found, the owner of the house shall come near to God, to show whether or not he has put his hand to his neighbor's goods. For every breach of trust, whether it be for ox, for ass, for sheep, for clothing, or for any kind of lost thing of which one says, "This is it", the case of both parties shall come before God; he whom God shall condemn shall pay double to his neighbor.'

Behind this procedure there lies the thought that God is the ultimate judge and can be relied upon to give right judgement.

The people of Old Testament times were to become only too familiar with corruption in the administration of the law. It was said of the sons of Samuel, unworthy sons of a noble father, that they 'did not walk in his ways, but turned aside after gain; they took bribes and perverted justice' (1 Sam. viii. 3). In the eighth and seventh centuries B.C., a period of rapid social change which witnessed the growth of a class of capitalists and the ruin of many a small peasant farmer, it is the repeated complaint of the prophets

[1] This system of administering justice was to be modified by the emergence of the monarchy and the increasing tendency to centralization of power in Jerusalem.

that the law courts provide no redress for crying wrong. Listen to
Amos describing the situation in Samaria, the wealthy capital of the
Northern Kingdom towards the middle of the eighth century B.C.

> 'For I know how many are your transgressions,
> and how great are your sins—
> you who afflict the righteous, who take a bribe,
> and turn aside the needy in the gate.'
>
> (Amos v. 12)

A few decades later Isaiah has this to say about justice in Jerusalem the capital of the Southern Kingdom:

> 'Your princes are rebels
> and companions of thieves.
> Every one loves a bribe
> and runs after gifts.
> They do not defend the fatherless
> and the widow's cause does not come to them.
>
> (Isa. i. 23)

Money talks. Those who most need the protection of the law are
least likely to receive it. In striking contrast the Old Testament
depicts God as one who judges, and in His judgements always gives
right decisions; He judges in righteousness. Hence the binding
together of 'justice' and 'righteousness' in an attempt to say something about the very nature of God. In this respect the God of
Israel differs not only from all fallible human judges, but also from
'other gods'. There is a famous courtroom scene in the Book of
Psalms. In the celestial Central Criminal Court, the God of Israel
sits in judgement upon other gods.

> 'God has taken his place in the divine council;
> in the midst of the gods he holds judgement:
> "How long will you judge unjustly
> and show partiality to the wicked?
> Give justice to the weak and the fatherless;
> maintain the right of the afflicted and the destitute.

> Rescue the weak and the needy;
> deliver them from the hand of the wicked".'
>
> (Ps. lxxxii. 1–4)

Because of this failure on the part of the other gods the very foundations of the universe are shaken, just as the whole fabric of society is undermined when true justice is perverted (cf. Amos iii. 9 ff.).

> 'They have neither knowledge nor understanding,
> they walk about in darkness;
> all the foundations of the earth are shaken.'
>
> (verse 5)

The court scene reaches its climax with the sentencing of these gods to a most ungodlike fate:

> 'I say, "You are gods,
> sons of the Most High, all of you;
> nevertheless you shall die like men,
> and fall like any prince".'
>
> (verses 6–7)

The Psalm fittingly concludes with a plea to God, the righteous judge of all the earth:

> 'Arise, O God, judge the earth;
> for to thee belong all the nations!'
>
> (verse 8)

We may learn a great deal about the Old Testament outlook from this Psalm. The writer accepts the common Near Eastern mythology of the heavenly council of the gods. The Old Testament is not interested in philosophical arguments in favour of monotheism, belief in the existence of one God, and one God alone. Yet the people of Israel, or at least the faithful within Israel, were practical monotheists long before they ever attempted to state their creed in so many words. They were far too busy facing the demands laid upon them by exclusive loyalty to a God who acted with power as Sovereign of both nature and history, to bother denying the existence of the gods of other nations. Nothing is more basic to their practical monotheism than the assertion that the LORD their God judged and ruled the world in righteousness.

It is this conviction which presents some of the greatest problems to faith in the Old Testament. The Book of Job, for example, wrestles not simply with the problem of suffering, but with the apparent injustice of undeserved suffering in a world ordered and ruled by God (cf. Job xxiii. 1–7; xl. 7 ff.). It is the impossibility of reconciling his present suffering with belief in *this* God that racks the soul of Job.

To say, however, that God as judge always gives 'right' or 'righteous' decisions still leaves us asking one vital question. What makes God's decisions 'right' decisions? What, in other words, is the norm of God's righteousness? This is the point at which our everyday use of the word 'righteousness' becomes totally inadequate for an understanding of the Bible. The Hebrew did not wrestle with the meaning of the 'good life', assert that 'righteousness' is of the very essence of such a life, and then conclude that such 'righteousness' must belong to the very nature of God. He pointed to the way in which he saw God acting in the world, and said, 'that is righteousness'. Righteousness is not some abstract moral quality; it is rather a description of a series of events in history, 'righteous acts' in which God was making Himself known. Thus the great victory which God granted to His people at the famous battle 'by the waters of Megiddo'[1] is described in Judges v. 11 as 'his righteousnesses'; and the R.S.V. correctly translates:

> 'there they repeat the *triumphs* of the LORD,
> the *triumphs* of his peasantry in Israel.'

Just because 'righteousness' is for the Old Testament a transcript of what God does in the furtherance of His purposes in the world, bare 'justice', in the sense of legal rights, cannot fathom the depths of its meaning.

[1] Cf. pp. 53–55.

'Thus says the LORD: "Let not the wise man glory in his wisdom, let not the mighty man glory in his might, let not the rich man glory in his riches; but let him who glories glory in this, that he understands and knows me, that I am the LORD who practise kindness, justice and righteousness in the earth; for in these things I delight, says the LORD" ' (Jer. ix. 23–24).

The Siamese twins 'justice' and 'righteousness' have a strange bedfellow, the Hebrew word 'chesed', inadequately translated 'kindness', a word vital for our understanding of the holiness of this holy God.

III

'Moses and Aaron were among his priests,
Samuel also was among those who called on his name.
They cried to the LORD and he answered them.
He spoke to them in the pillar of cloud;
they kept his testimonies
and the statutes that he gave them.
O LORD our God, thou didst answer them;
thou wast a forgiving God to them,
but an avenger of their wrongdoings.
Extol the LORD our God,
and worship at his holy mountain:
for the LORD our God is holy.'

(Ps. xcix. 6–9)

The LORD *our* God is holy. Again and again, at least thirty times in our present Book of Isaiah, both in that section of it (1–39) which comes in the main from Isaiah the prophet in Jerusalem, towards the end of the eighth century B.C., and in the later anonymous chapters (40 ff.) which date from the bitter days of exile in the sixth century B.C., we find God described as 'the Holy One of Israel'. Thus after holding out to the dejected exiles a promise that Israel is to be the instrument of divine judgement in the world, Isaiah (chapter xli) continues:

'And you shall rejoice in the LORD;
in the Holy One of Israel you shall glory.'
(xli. 16; cf. i. 4; v. 19; xii. 6; xlviii. 17)

It is part of the essential holiness of God for the Old Testament
that He has entered into a peculiar relationship with one out of all
the nations of the world, and that a nation neither politically nor
culturally in the first rank, the people of Israel. When the writers of
the Old Testament seek to describe this relationship which exists
between God and Israel, they use the word 'covenant' (berith). How
basic to the thought of the whole Bible this idea of the 'covenant' is,
may be seen by the fact that we still describe the two parts of our
Bible as the Old and New Testaments, and 'testament' is simply the
Latin form of the word 'covenant'. Covenant was a familiar word
to the nomadic peoples of the Ancient Near East. They used it to
describe those solemn agreements between two parties which made
peaceful co-existence possible. You will find such a covenant described in Genesis xxxi. 44 ff. Jacob and his father-in-law, Laban,
have one thing in common in this ancient story; they are both past
masters in treachery and deceit. Their relationship reaches a point
at which Jacob thinks it wiser to put as many miles as possible
between Laban and himself. When Laban catches up with his erring
son-in-law there follows a scene of angry recriminations, of charge
and counter-charge which might easily have ended in bloodshed
(xxxi. 25–43). Family solidarity, however, prevails and Laban says,
'Come now, let us make a covenant, you and I; and let it be a witness
between you and me' (xxxi. 44). A cairn of stones is erected as
witness to the covenant—the close connection between God and
such stone heaps and pillars is well attested in primitive thinking
(cf. Gen. xxviii. 22)—and the participating partners share in a
covenant meal, the pledge of their new brotherhood. Any violation
of the covenant will call down upon the violator the judgement of
the god—or gods—who guarantee the covenant (verse 53).

Likewise, in the moving story of the friendship of Jonathan and
David, we are told how, at the outset, their friendship was cemented
by a solemn pledge. 'Then Jonathan made a covenant with David
because he loved him as his own soul' (1 Sam. xviii. 3). This

covenant, renewed in an hour of crisis (1 Sam. xxiii. 18), bound them to one another in lifelong devotion (cf. 2 Sam. v. 1–5).

The Old Testament writers take this word 'covenant' and use it in a unique way to explain what is happening to the nation of Israel in the purposes of God. The wonder of deliverance from slavery in Egypt is, as we have seen,[1] indelibly stamped upon the Old Testament tradition; but equally clearly and in close connection with what happened at the Exodus, there is the story of the wonder of the meeting between God and the people at the sacred mountain, Mount Sinai. Deliverance from Egypt so vividly commemorated in the victory chant of Miriam:

> 'Sing to the LORD for he has triumphed gloriously,
> the horse and his rider he has thrown into the sea.'
>
> (Exod. xv. 21)

is followed in Exodus xv. 22—xviii. 27 by the story of the pilgrimage, albeit a not entirely joyful or willing pilgrimage to Mount Sinai, or Horeb, according to another tradition (cf. Deut. v. 2). There to the delivered people God comes shrouded in His terrifying, mysterious holiness:

'On the morning of the third day there were thunders and lightnings and a thick cloud upon the mountain, and a very loud trumpet blast, so that all the people who were in the camp trembled. Then Moses brought the people out of the camp to meet God; and they took their stand at the foot of the mountain. And Mount Sinai was wrapped in smoke, because the LORD descended upon it in fire; and the smoke of it went up like the smoke of a kiln, and the whole mountain quaked greatly' (Exod. xix. 16–18).

The mountain is so dangerously holy that the people dare not approach it; only Moses, the chosen servant of God, may ascend the mountain. God comes to remind the people in the first instance of what He has done for them. 'I am the LORD your God, who brought you out of the land of Egypt, out of the house of bondage' (Exod. xx. 2). Then He makes certain demands upon the people[2] (Exod. xx. 3 ff.).

[1] Cf. pp. 46 ff.
[2] Cf. chapter 4.

There follows in Exodus xxiv. 3–8 the account of the ratification of the covenant between God and the people. At the foot of the mountain there is erected an altar, symbol of the presence of God, and twelve pillars representing the twelve tribes of Israel. Blood is taken from sacrificial victims, half of it thrown upon the altar, half of it sprinkled upon the people when they renew their pledge of obedience to the known demands of God. 'Moses took the blood and threw it upon the people and said, "Behold the blood of the covenant which the LORD has made with you in accordance with all these words"' (Exod. xxiv. 8). The blood upon altar and people is the sign of the bond which now unites God and the people in the one sacred fellowship. Notice that throughout the *initiative comes from God*; He delivered, now He appears to make the covenant with the people. This is 'the covenant which the LORD has made with you' says Moses. It is His doing, not the people's; the people's part in the covenant is that of response to God's initiative. This covenant is more truly described as a 'gift' than as a legal contract. We find the same emphasis among the stories which the Hebrews told about their great pilgrim father, Abraham. At a dark moment in Abraham's life, when he seriously doubted whether the God who had called him to venture out into the unknown could fulfil His promises, we read that 'the LORD made a covenant with Abram' (Gen. xv. 18) reassuring him of future blessing.

Now the word which describes the proper attitude of those who have entered into solemn covenant is the word 'chesed', translated 'kindness' in Jeremiah ix. 24. Chesed is one of those untranslateable words, though 'faithfulness' is usually nearer the mark than 'kindness'. It stands for that attitude which guarantees the covenant and makes it strong and lasting; the exact opposite of the attitude which regards binding treaties as mere scraps of paper to be torn up at will. So we read in 2 Samuel x. 1–2, 'After this the king of the Ammonites died and Hanun his son reigned in his stead. And David said, "I will deal loyally (literally 'do chesed') with Hanun the son of Nabash as his father dealt loyally with me"' (cf. 2 Sam. xvi. 16). David was not going to take advantage of the change on the Ammonite throne. He would remain faithful to his treaty obligations. When used of God, 'chesed' points to that untiring and unwavering faithfulness in God's character upon which man may utterly rely. God had taken the initiative in making the covenant with Israel and, come what may, he would never prove faithless. The translators of the R.S.V. pondered long over an adequate meaning for this word when used of God's attitude to men. 'Steadfast love' is what they happily offer us. This translation serves to underline at one and the same time that element of fidelity which is there in 'chesed', and also points to that which alone keeps God faithful to us who are so often faithless, the mystery of divine love. 'Chesed' is often, indeed, used in close connection with another word which, having no covenant connection, means 'tenderness' or 'compassion'.

> 'For the LORD will not
> cast off for ever,
> but though he cause grief he will have compassion,
> according to the abundance of his steadfast love.'
>   (Lam. iii. 31–32; cf. Exod. xxxiv. 7; Ps. cxlv. 8)

The Book of the prophet Hosea is perhaps the best commentary on the meaning of God's 'chesed'. Hosea lived in the Northern Kingdom of Israel not long before its overthrow by the Assyrians in 721 B.C. He married Gomer, the daughter of Deblaim. She proved to be unfaithful. This is still the most probable interpretation of chapters i. and iii. 1–3. Hosea discovered that he could not blot the image of Gomer out of his heart. He loved her still in spite of her infidelity. But if he thus continued to cherish Gomer beyond all her deserving, what of God's attitude to Israel? Hosea was under no illusions about his people's past record or present behaviour. Israel had shamelessly played the harlot (Hosea ii); she had been faithless to the LORD who had brought her out of Egypt. Discipline was much needed; dire punishment was assuredly coming.

> 'Set the trumpet to your lips,
> for a vulture is over the house of the LORD,
> because they have broken my covenant
> and transgressed my law.
> To me they cry,
> My God, we Israel know thee.

Israel has spurned the good;
the enemy shall pursue him.'
                    (viii. 1–3; cf. chapters viii and ix)

But could this be God's last word? Though the nation's 'chesed'
towards God had been

'like a morning cloud,
like the dew that goes early away.'
                                (vi. 4)

God could not finally renounce his people.

'How can I give you up, O Ephraim!
How can I hand you over, O Israel!
How can I make you like Admah![1]
How can I treat you like Zeboim!
My heart recoils within me,
my compassion grows warm and tender.
I will not execute my fierce anger
I will not again destroy Ephraim;
for I am God and not man,
the Holy One in your midst,
and I will not come to destroy.'
                    (xi. 8–9; cf. xii. 16–20)

Such is God's 'chesed', his steadfast love.

Never were some people more certain that God's 'chesed' had
failed than in the dark days of the sixth century B.C. when Jerusalem
lay in ruins, her people exiled to Babylon. To such people this word
was spoken:

'Fear not, for you will not be ashamed;
be not confounded for you will not be put to shame;
for you will forget the shame of your youth,
and the reproach of your widowhood you will remember
    no more.
For your Maker is your husband

[1] Admah and Zeboim were among the cities of the plain traditionally destroyed
along with Sodom and Gomorrah. Cf. Gen. xix. 24 ff.

the LORD of hosts is his name;
and the Holy One of Israel is your Redeemer,
the God of the whole earth he is called.
For the LORD has called you
like a wife forsaken and grieved in spirit,
like a wife of youth when she is cast off,
says your God.
For a brief moment I forsook you
but with great compassion I will gather you.
In overflowing wrath for a moment
I hid my face from you,
but with everlasting love I will have compassion on you
says the LORD, your Redeemer.
For this is like the days of Noah to me;
as I swore that the waters of Noah
should no more go over the earth,
so I have sworn that I will not be angry with you
and will not rebuke you.
For the mountains may depart
and the hills be removed,
but my steadfast love shall not depart from you,
and my covenant of peace shall not be removed,
says the LORD who has compassion on you.'

(Isa. liv. 4-10)

Truly this is 'The LORD, the LORD, a God merciful and gracious, slow to anger and abounding in steadfast love and faithfulness, keeping steadfast love for thousands' (Exod. xxxiv. 6–7). Small wonder then that one of the shortest Psalms in the Psalter issues this invitation:

'Praise the LORD all nations!
Extol him all peoples!
For great is his steadfast love toward us;
and the faithfulness of the LORD endures for ever.
Praise the LORD!'

(Ps. cxvii)

This emphasis upon the sure, unswerving, utterly dependable love of God may be seen in many of the metaphors used by the Old Testament writers to describe God's relationship with Israel.

God is Father, *Israel His son*

Moses is ordered to go to Pharaoh and say, 'Thus says the LORD, "Israel is my firstborn son and I say to you, Let my son go, that he may serve me . . ." ' (Exod. iv. 22 f.). The prophet Hosea depicts God as saying:

> 'When Israel was a child I loved him,
> and out of Egypt I called my son.'
> > (Hos. xi. 1; cf. Isa. lxiii. 16)

There is here no general statement about the universal fatherhood of God. Israel is God's son because of what happened at the Exodus. Through this mighty act of deliverance, God established the father-son relationship, and upon such a father a son may utterly depend.

God is Shepherd,[1] *Israel his flock*

In Eastern lands the shepherd walks before his flock. The sheep follow, knowing that he, their protector, will lead them to fresh pasture or home to the safety of the fold. Hence Psalm lxxviii, recalling the deliverance from Egypt, says that God

> 'led forth his people like sheep,
> and guided them in the wilderness like a flock.
> He led them in safety, so that they were not afraid;
> but the sea overwhelmed their enemies.'
> > (Ps. lxxviii. 52–53; cf. Ps. lxxx. 1)

> 'Know that the LORD is God!
> It is he that made us and we are his;
> we are his people and the sheep of his pasture.'

proclaims Psalm c. 3 and ends:

[1] 'Shepherd' is a familiar epithet for 'King' in the Near East. Since the 'King' guarantees 'justice' to his people, we have here another sign of the link between 'justice' and steadfast love.

F

'For the LORD is good;
his steadfast love endures for ever,
and his faithfulness to all generations.'

(verse 5; cf. Ps. xcv. 7)

The prophet Ezekiel, speaking against the sombre backcloth of national disaster, attributes part of the reason for that disaster to the poor leadership the nation enjoyed. The flock of Israel had been scattered, had been a prey for wild beasts because of self-indulgent, careless shepherds (Ezek. xxxiv. 1–6). But there is hope for the future. Israel has a true shepherd, 'For thus says the LORD God; Behold I, I myself will search for my sheep, and will seek them out. As a shepherd seeks out his flock when some of his sheep have been scattered abroad, so will I seek out my sheep; and I will rescue them from all places where they have been scattered on a day of clouds and thick darkness. And I will bring them out from the peoples, and gather them from the countries, and will bring them into their own land; and I will feed them on the mountains of Israel, by the fountains, and in all the inhabited places of the country. I will feed them with good pasture and upon the mountain heights of Israel shall be their pasture; there they shall lie down in good grazing land, and on fat pasture they shall feed on the mountains of Israel. I myself will be the shepherd of my sheep, and I will make them lie down, says the LORD God. I will seek the lost and I will bring back the strayed, and I will bind up the crippled, and I will strengthen the weak, and the fat and the strong I will watch over; I will feed them in justice' (Ezek. xxxiv. 11–16).

Nowhere perhaps has this quiet confidence, rooted in the steadfast love of God, found more moving expression than in the famous 'Shepherd' Psalm.

'The LORD is my shepherd, I shall not want;
he makes me lie down in green pastures.
He leads me beside still waters;
he restores my life.
He leads me in right paths
for his name's sake.

Even though I walk through the valley of deep darkness,
I fear no evil;
for thou art with me;
thy rod and thy staff,
they comfort me.

Thou preparest a table before me
in the presence of my enemies;
thou anointest my head with oil,
my cup overflows.
Surely goodness and mercy (chesed) shall follow me
all the days of my life;
and I shall dwell in the house of the LORD
for ever.'

(Ps. xxiii)

God is Redeemer

Ancient Hebrew social custom was firmly rooted in the solidarity of the family. If, for example, a member of the family was murdered it was the duty of his nearest kinsman to avenge his death by killing the slayer[1] (cf. the story of Joab and Abner in 2 Sam. ii. and iii). Again, if a member of a family was compelled, through poverty, to sell part of the family property, 'then his next of kin shall come and redeem [i.e. buy back] what his brother has sold' (Lev. xxv. 25; cf. Ruth iii. 11–12; iv. 1–6; Jer. xxxii. 6 ff.). If dire circumstance forced a man to sell himself into debt slavery 'then after he is sold he may be redeemed; one of his brothers may redeem him, or his uncle or his cousin may redeem him, or a near kinsman belonging to the family may redeem him' (Lev. xxv. 48). This kinsman who acts as 'avenger of blood', restorer of family property, or rescuer of his brother from slavery, is called in Hebrew 'go'el', Redeemer. In their attempts to explain the wonder of deliverance from Egypt, Old Testament writers describe the LORD as the Go'el, the Redeemer of Israel. 'The LORD . . . redeemed you from the house of bondage, from the hand of Pharaoh, king of Egypt' (Deut. vii. 8; cf. xiii. 5; xv. 15; xxi. 8).

[1] Cf. Num. xxxv. 6–21 which seeks to control this ancient custom of blood revenge by drawing a distinction between intentional and accidental homicide.

'Who is like thee, O LORD, among the gods?
Who is like thee, majestic in holiness,
terrible in glorious deeds, doing wonders?
Thou didst stretch out thy right hand,
the earth swallowed them.
Thou hast led in thy steadfast love
the people whom thou hast redeemed.'

(Exod. xv. 11–13)

When in the course of the passing centuries the people again
found themselves enslaved, in exile in Babylon, one of the favourite,
hope-inspiring titles given to God by the author of Isaiah xl-lv. is
'Redeemer':

'Fear not, you worm Jacob,
you men of Israel!
I will help you, says the LORD;
your Redeemer is the Holy One of Israel.'

(Isa. xli. 14; cf. xliii. 14; xlvii. 4; xlviii. 17; xlix. 7; liv. 5)

... that is to say, God, the Holy one of Israel, standing in covenant
relationship with His people, can be relied upon to fulfil the function
of the Go'el. He will rescue His people from bitter exile and restore
them to their family homeland.

Such is God's steadfast love which Israel believed was demonstrated throughout her national history, in good times and in bad,
and which, she came to believe, was the great reality undergirding
the whole universe. Listen to the Psalmist inviting us to share this
faith as with unwearying joy he extols the steadfast love of God.

'O give thanks to the LORD, for he is good,
for his steadfast love endures for ever.
O give thanks to the God of gods,
for his steadfast love endures for ever.
O give thanks to the lord of lords,
for his steadfast love endures for ever
to him who alone does great wonders,
for his steadfast love endures for ever;

to him who by understanding made the heavens,
for his steadfast love endures for ever;
to him who spread out the earth upon the waters,
for his steadfast love endures for ever;
to him who made the great lights,
for his steadfast love endures for ever;
the sun to rule over the day,
for his steadfast love endures for ever;
the moon and stars to rule over the night,
for his steadfast love endures for ever;

to him who smote the first-born of Egypt,
for his steadfast love endures for ever;
and brought Israel out from among them,
for his steadfast love endures for ever;
with a strong hand and an outstretched arm,
for his steadfast love endures for ever;
to him who divided the Red Sea in sunder,
for his steadfast love endures for ever;
and made Israel pass through the midst of it,
for his steadfast love endures for ever;
but overthrew Pharaoh and his host in the Red Sea,
for his steadfast love endures for ever;
to him who led his people through the wilderness,
for his steadfast love endures for ever;
to him who smote great kings,
for his steadfast love endures for ever;
and slew famous kings,
for his steadfast love endures for ever;
Sihon, king of the Amorites,
for his steadfast love endures for ever;
and Og, king of Bashan,
for his steadfast love endures for ever;
and gave their land as a heritage,
for his steadfast love endures for ever;
a heritage to Israel his servant,
for his steadfast love endures for ever.

It is he who remembered us in our low estate,
for his steadfast love endures for ever;
and rescued us from our foes,
for his steadfast love endures for ever;
he who gives food to all flesh,
for his steadfast love endures for ever.

O give thanks to the God of heaven,
for his steadfast love endures for ever.'

(Ps. cxxxvi; cf. Ps. cxi)

It cannot be too strongly emphasized that the steadfast love of God is not in opposition to His righteousness. God is not, as it were, torn by two conflicting emotions, the one demanding, 'Let us exact our pound of flesh', the other whispering, 'No, let us be forgiving'. Since righteousness refers to the way in which God acts in the world to establish His sovereignty, steadfast love is of the very essence of this righteousness. Nowhere is this more clearly seen than in Isaiah xl-xlv, where there is a close link between 'righteousness' and 'salvation' or deliverance. After a section in which he hails Cyrus of Persia, the new political star in the East, as the agent in the fulfilment of God's purposes for His people, the author breaks into a lyrical interlude called forth by the thought of coming deliverance:

'Shower, O heavens, from above,
and let the skies rain down righteousness;
let the earth open that salvation may sprout forth,
and let it cause righteousness to spring up also;
I the LORD have created it.'

(Isa. xlv. 8)

We may paraphrase as follows: 'God, through His active intervention (righteousness), in the affairs of men is about to bring to His exiled people deliverance (salvation) and victory (righteousness)'. The second 'righteousness' is slightly different from the first in form in the Hebrew original, and probably emphasizes the result of

God's activity, that is to say, victory for His people. So to this same poet-prophet God is 'a righteous God *and* a Saviour' (Isa. xlv. 21). It is a convincing demonstration of His righteousness that in the international situation of the day He comes to deliver His people (cf. Isa. liv. 1).

Who can stand before this holy God?—holy, holy in righteousness, holy in steadfast love.

4

The People of God

The faith of the Old Testament is essentially a community faith. The covenant is between God and a people. From this people there is demanded a grateful obedience to God's Torah, i.e. instruction, the kernel of which we find in the 'Ten Words' (Exod. xx. 2–7).

Two principles appear in these Ten Words.

1. The demand for an exclusive loyalty to a jealous God. This loyalty was often severely tested. The settlement in Canaan brought with it the lure of the agricultural gods of Canaan. Israel's political situation often tempted her politicians to worship at the shrine of power politics. Elijah in the ninth century B.C. and Isaiah in the eighth remind the people of the meaning of loyalty.

2. True response to God implies a moral obedience demonstrated in daily living and in the right ordering of society.

The 'Book of the Covenant' (Exod. xxi. 1 ff.) gleans material from different sources yet stamps it with a peculiarly Hebraic ethos. Categorical demands are made upon the community as the will of God. When kingship arose in Israel, king as well as commoner was bound by these demands. Furthermore, the known character of God becomes decisive for the kind of obedience required. 'As the LORD . . . so shall you.' Thus the 'righteousness' expected of the nation, because it is a reflection of God's righteousness, is shot through with a deep concern for the helpless, as the prophets of the eighth and seventh centuries B.C. insist.

The prophets vehemently attack 'Religion without Morals'.

DURING World War II the late C. E. M. Joad wrote an amusing satire called *The Adventure of a Young Soldier in Search of the Better World*. In search of that better, happier world for which the politicians assured him he was fighting, the young soldier sets out on a lonely pilgrimage. From cynical old soldier to Oxford Grouper, from distinguished, if somewhat despairing, church dignitaries to rabid Socialists he journeys, to meet at last a philosopher who suggests to him that one of the signposts on the road to a better world will be a revival of man's spiritual life. 'But,' he adds, 'if you ask me how that is to be brought about, I have not the faintest idea.'[1]

We have fallen into the habit of regarding religion as the Adventure of the Human Soul in search of God; and it is a 'lonely' adventure. We may seek advice of course, but in the end, whether we are 'religious' or not is a purely personal, private decision, a leap into the dark which each one of us must make for himself. This is a dangerous half truth. Whatever the Bible is, it cannot be adequately described as 'The Adventure of the Human Soul in Search of God'; nor does it describe a lonely pilgrimage. If one side of the Covenant coin in the Old Testament bears the imprint 'this holy God', the other side is stamped, not 'the individual human soul', but 'Israel, the people of God', a community. This emphasis upon 'a people', 'a community', is not an unfortunate hangover from primitive ideas of tribal solidarity to be found in the earliest strands of the Old Testament. It is there in the latest, as well as in the earliest, portions of the Old Testament, and, as we shall see,[2] it is as characteristic of the New Testament as of the Old.

The Old Testament is not devoid of great personalities, nor lacking in descriptions of intensely personal religious experiences. We need but mention the call of Moses (Exod. iii.), Isaiah (Isa. vi.), Jeremiah (Jer. i. 4–10), the confessions of Jeremiah (e.g. Jer. xii. 1–6; xv. 15 ff.; xvii. 5 ff.), the visions of Ezekiel (Ezek. i, viii., xxxvii), the laying bare of the soul of Hosea. The stress, however, upon the people of God serves to place such religious experience in its proper context. There is no renunciation of the world in pursuit of some private beatific vision, no thought of cultivating personal religion as an end in itself. The vision at the burning bush summons Moses to be the instrument whereby God will lead His people out of the hand of the Egyptians (Exod. iii. 8). All the mighty energy of his personality

[1] C. E. M. Joad, op. cit., p. 123.
[2] Cf. chapter 10.

is bent on establishing and sustaining the life of this people whom the LORD delivered and with whom He chose to make His covenant. When, many centuries later, national ruin and disaster were descending upon this people, the bitter fruit of their own folly, the prophet Jeremiah stakes all his hope for the future not on the thought of personal salvation, but on the conviction that God will make a *new* covenant ushering in the day when, 'I will be their God and they shall be my people' (Jer. xxxi. 33). The Old Testament is the story of God and a people.

In the thought of the Old Testament, the covenant, as we have seen,[1] is not a bargain struck between God and the people. It is far more truly described as God's gift to the people. The initiative throughout belongs to God. From the outset, however, the people had to realize that this holy God was no beneficent Father Christmas handing out free gifts with an indulgent smile. God's initiative was intended to evoke from the people a response of gratitude which would find expression in a glad obedience to the demands of God. In the story of the ratification of the covenant in Exodus xxiv, after Moses had sprinkled some blood upon the altar, sign of God's participation in the covenant, we hear that 'he took the book of the covenant and read it in the hearing of the people and they said, "All that the LORD has spoken we will do and we will be obedient" ' (Exod. xxiv. 7). Thus would the people demonstrate their 'chesed', their faithfulness to the covenant. The covenant people are a people under instruction. They must give heed to the 'teaching' (Torah, usually translated Law) of their God. 'We will be obedient'—in this one word, for it is one word in the original Hebrew, there is writ large the glory and the tragedy of the people of God in the Old Testament.

The Books of Exodus, Leviticus, Numbers and Deuteronomy present us with an imposing edifice of instructions covering the whole of life, from slavery (Exod. xxi. 1–7) to sanitation (e.g. Lev. xiv. 33 ff.), from perjury (e.g. Exod. xxiii. 1 ff.) to jealousy (e.g. Num. v. 11 ff.), from the great festivals of the religious year (Exod. xxxiv. 18 ff.; Deut. xvi. 1–17; Lev. xxiii) to care of widows and orphans (e.g. Exod. xxii. 22; Deut. xxiv. 17). If God be the architect, then His

[1] Cf. pp. 77.

labourer, according to the Biblical narrative, was the lawgiver, Moses, who, after years of guiding a not always co-operative people, died on the very borders of the promised land, but not before he had seen the final coping stone of the Law placed in position. The picture which modern scholarship presents to us is very different, though no less impressive. Instead of a sanctuary, completed in every detail during the feverish activity of a lifetime, we are asked to gaze upon a venerable cathedral, incorporating into its fabric the workmanship of many generations; partially destroyed and rebuilt time and again; gathering diverse styles of architecture into a harmonious whole. The finished structure is not the record of the life's work of a law-giver of genius, but the abiding monument to a people seeking mid the ever-changing circumstances of their national life to translate into reality their promise, 'We will be obedient'. Moses, however, did preside at the laying of the foundation stone when the people accepted the covenant at Mount Sinai. In the tradition of the 'Ten Words', which, there is little reason to doubt, go back in essentials to Moses, we may see 'the fundamentals of community life under the rule of God'.[1] The 'Ten Words' are recorded for us in two slightly different forms in Exod. xx. 2–17 and Deut. v. 6–21, both of which may be expansions of a shorter original. We may attempt to reconstruct that original as follows:

The 'Ten Words' are introduced by a reminder of God's gracious initiative which is the very foundation of the people's existence. 'I am the LORD your God who brought you out of the land of Egypt, out of the house of bondage.' There follows the series of ten unconditional demands:

1. You shall have no other gods before me.
2. You shall not make yourself a graven image.
3. You shall not take the name of the LORD your God in vain.
4. Remember the Sabbath day to keep it holy.
5. Honour your father and mother.
6. You shall not kill.
7. You shall not commit adultery.
8. You shall not steal.

[1] M. Buber, *Moses*, p. 124.

9. You shall not bear false witness against your neighbour.
10. You shall not covet your neighbour's house.[1]

Within these 'Ten Words' are two principles intended to be decisive for the life of the people of God, principles which had to be restated and fought for again and again in the history of this people.

I

The people of God are committed to an *exclusive loyalty* to the LORD, the one invisible God who, having delivered His people from Egypt, has entered into covenant relationship with them. Such is the theme of the first three words, no 'other gods', no 'graven images', no 'taking the name of the LORD in vain'. Other gods, other divine powers may be worshipped by other tribes, but for this people, for whom the LORD has done great things, there can be only one loyalty. There is evidence in the Old Testament to suggest that what had happened once at Mount Sinai was solemnly relived from time to time in the people's worship on great religious occasions. 'The LORD our God made a covenant with us at Horeb. Not with our fathers did the LORD make this covenant, but with us who are all of us here alive this day' (Deut. v. 2–3; cf. Deut. xxvii. 9). Whenever we find the covenant thus relived and renewed, one theme is inevitably heard. The God who deals with Israel demands an exclusive loyalty. He is a *'jealous God'*, a phrase which, far from being an unfortunate relic of barbarity, has a central place in the Biblical witness.

Thus the recital of all that the LORD has done for His people in Joshua xxiv[2] culminates in the people's response, 'we will serve the LORD, for he is our God' (Joshua. xxiv. 18). But Joshua bids the people think twice. Do they fully realize to what, in the enthusiasm of the moment, they are committing themselves?

'But Joshua said to the people, "You cannot serve the LORD; for

---

[1] 'House' for the Hebrew includes all that a man possesses, wife, children, servants, cattle, etc. Cf. Exod. xx. 17; Deut. v. 21.

[2] Cf. chapter 2, pp. 42–43.

he is a holy God; he is a jealous God; he will not forgive your transgressions or your sins. If you forsake the LORD and serve foreign gods, then he will turn and do you harm, and consume you, after having done you good" ' (Joshua. xxiv. 19–20). In the Book of Deuteronomy we find this warning given to the people, 'Take heed to yourselves, lest you forget the covenant of the LORD your God, which he made with you and make a graven image in the form of anything which the LORD your God has forbidden you. For the LORD your God is a devouring fire, a jealous God' (Deut. iv. 23–24). 'I, the LORD your God am a jealous God'—these very words occur in that form of the second of the 'Ten Words' which is recorded in Exodus xx. 5 and Deuteronomy v. 9, while in another very ancient complex of laws dealing in the main with regulations concerning worship we read 'you shall worship no other god, for the LORD whose name is Jealous, is a jealous God' (Exod. xxxiv. 14).

We have come to regard tolerance as high on the list of religious virtues. So in general did the ancient world. At least there was seldom much difficulty in finding room for another god or goddess in most divine households. It merely involved working out some suitable family relationship. Yet in the God of Israel there is a ruthless streak of intolerance. Having laid His hand upon this people He brooks no rival in their affections. He demands an exclusive loyalty.

We are not suggesting that the Old Testament presents us with a picture of a people fired with zeal to demonstrate to an admiring world an unshakable loyalty to the LORD. The Old Testament is far too honest a book for that. Indeed, according to the narrative in Exodus xxxii, the covenant at Mount Sinai was no sooner ratified than trouble began. 'When the people saw that Moses delayed to come down from the mountain, the people gathered themselves together to Aaron and said to him, "Up, make us gods who shall go before us; as for this Moses, the man who brought us up out of the land of Egypt, we do not know what has become of him." And Aaron said to them, "Take off the rings of gold which are in the ears of your wives, your sons and your daughters and bring them to me." So all the people took off the rings of gold which were in their ears and brought them to Aaron. And he received the gold at their

hand, and fashioned it with a graving tool and made a molten calf;
and they said, "These are your gods, O Israel, who brought you up
out of the land of Egypt" ' (Exod. xxxii. 1–4). Even if, as many have
suggested, the narrative is strongly coloured by events which happened centuries later[1] it loses none of its significance. It reveals to us
a people who never found it easy to give this total allegiance which
was demanded. Much of the Old Testament is the sombre record
of a people who drifted through one disloyalty after another into
ultimate disaster.

The first crisis in the people's pledged loyalty to the LORD came
with the settlement of the tribes in Canaan. There they found a
religion ideally suited to the kind of life which now perforce they
had to adopt, the life of the peasant farmer. Moreover, it was a
religion which claimed to pay substantial dividends since it centred
on the worship of various local 'Baals', the mysterious 'owners' of
the land. These Baals were essentially gods of fertility who, if worshipped with appropriate rites, and satisfied by appropriate gifts,
could be relied upon to bless the farmer's labour. The modern
farmer expects fertilizers to increase his yield per acre—his ancient
counterpart expected no less from his gods. The Israelite settler was
in a dilemma. To be sure, the LORD had delivered His people from
Egypt. He had proved effective as the God of the warrior hosts
of Israel, but what could this God, whose abode was a mountain
in the wilderness, know about agriculture? Could the Israelite
farmer afford to slight the gods who so obviously helped his
Canaanite neighbour to prosper? Was it not better to play safe, to
take out, as it were, a Comprehensive Religious Insurance Policy?
The LORD would remain, of course, as the bond uniting His people;
He would always be gratefully remembered as the God who had
called the nation into being; but in the everyday labour of wresting
a living from the soil, it was surely only prudent to acknowledge the
power of the gods of the good earth, the gods of the life-giving
showers, the Baals. The prophet Hosea in the eighth century B.C.
complains that the people, like a faithless wife, say, 'I will go after
my lovers, who give me my bread and my water, my wool and my
flax, my oil and my drink' (Hos. ii. 5).

[1] Cf. 1 Kings xii. 25–30.

A little over a century later, Jeremiah, in an illuminating 'flash-back', spotlights what went wrong when the people exchanged the austere life of the desert for that of the peasant farmer.

'Hear the word of the LORD, O house of Jacob and all the families of the house of Israel. Thus says the LORD:

'What wrong did your fathers find in me
that they went far from me,
and went after worthlessness and became worthless?
They did not say, Where is the LORD
who brought us up from the land of Egypt,
who led us in the wilderness,
in a land of deserts and pits,
in a land of drought and deep darkness,
in a land that none passes through,
where no man dwells?
And I brought you into a plentiful land
to enjoy its fruits and its good things.
But when you came in you defiled my land
and made my heritage an abomination.
The priests did not say, "Where is the LORD?"
Those who handle the law did not know me;
the rulers transgressed against me;
the prophets prophesied by Baal,
and went after things that do not profit.
Therefore I still contend with you, says the LORD,
and with your children's children I will contend.
For cross to the coasts of Cyprus and see,
or send to Kedar and examine with care;
see if there has been such a thing.
Has a nation changed its gods,
even though they are no gods?
But my people have changed their glory
for that which does not profit.
Be appalled, O heavens, at this,
be shocked, be utterly desolate, says the LORD. .
for my people have committed two evils;

> they have forsaken me,
> the fountain of living waters,
> and hewed out cisterns for themselves,
> broken cisterns
> that can hold no water.'
>
> (Jer. ii. 4–13)

The tragedy of this disloyalty is stressed in the vivid pictures in the last verse where the LORD is likened to a 'fountain of living water', bubbling up unceasingly from the ground, ever available to slake the thirst of weary traveller or tired beast, while the Baals are depicted as 'broken cisterns', storage tanks cracked, broken and hence utterly unfitted for their purpose. The LORD, Who had demonstrated His power in the mighty deeds which had called Israel into being as a nation, is the God who likewise controls all the forces of nature. The Baals are powerless nonentities, 'worthless', 'no gods'. Yet, strangely, in view of her pledge of exclusive loyalty, Israel

> '—did not know
> that it was I who gave her
> the grain, the wine and the oil,
> and who lavished upon her silver
> and gold which they used for Baal.'
>
> (Hos. ii. 8)

We, standing within a Jewish-Christian tradition which has long taken for granted the existence of one God, and one god only, Who is the source of all life and power, may be tempted to regard with an indulgent smile of superiority, the folly of such Israelite farmers. We would be better employed in asking ourselves whether we do not similarly departmentalize life. A field of growing grain may suggest no rival to 'Our Father in heaven', but what of a hydrogen bomb?

We are perhaps on more familiar, though no less uncomfortable, ground when we consider the other source from which Israel's exclusive loyalty to the LORD was directly challenged. No sooner had Israel established her right to national sovereignty than she found herself involved in the power politics of the Ancient Near East. Even at their greatest, under David and Solomon in the tenth century B.C., the Hebrews formed a comparatively small nation, a terror, perhaps, to some of the lesser peoples on her borders, but otherwise maintaining a somewhat precarious foothold in a world of ambitious imperialism. When, after the death of Solomon, the nation, split into two, the plight of these two often quarrelling kingdoms was perilous. The shadow of Assyria, one of the most ruthlessly militaristic states the world has witnessed, began to fall ominously upon the petty kingdoms of the Near East. The LORD may have demonstrated His power and sovereignty in the affairs of men once long ago by delivering His people from Egypt, but to many an anxious politician in the ninth, eighth and seventh centuries B.C. it must have seemed as if the sovereignty of the LORD was an exploded myth. To attempt to maintain the balance of power by politically expedient alliances, therein lay the only hope of security. The price Israel had to pay for such alliances was the granting of some recognition to the gods of her allies.

King Ahab, who ruled the Northern Kingdom from about 869–850 B.C., faced an immediate threat from the Syrian tribes on his northern borders. To offset this menace he contracted a diplomatic alliance with Jezebel, a Tyrian princess who brought with her into Israel the cult of Baal Melkart, the god of Tyre. So we read in the Book of Kings that Ahab 'took for wife Jezebel the daughter of Ethbaal king of the Sidonians, and went and served Baal and worshipped him. He erected an altar for Baal in the house of Baal which he built in Samaria. And Ahab made an Asherah' (1 Kings xvi. 31–33)—an Asherah being a wooden symbol of Asherah the goddess of fertility, who was frequently associated with Baal. What now of the people's exclusive loyalty? There were two gods being worshipped in Israel, the LORD and Baal Melkart of Tyre, and the cult of the latter had the backing of the palace. At this point there steps forward one of the great figures of the Old Testament, Elijah the Tishbite, a prophet vehemently opposed to Ahab and his aggressive wife.

'When Ahab saw Elijah, Ahab said to him, "Is it you, you

G

troubler of Israel?" And he answered, "I have not troubled Israel; but you have, and your father's house, because you have forsaken the commandments of the LORD and followed the Baals. Now therefore send and gather all Israel to me at Mount Carmel, and the four hundred and fifty prophets of Baal and the four hundred prophets of Asherah who eat at Jezebel's table! So Ahab sent to all the people of Israel and gathered the prophets together at Mount Carmel. And Elijah came near to all the people, and said, "How long will you go limping with two different opinions? If the LORD is God, follow him; but if Baal, then follow him" ' (1 Kings xviii. 17–21).

The people must choose. Elijah proposes a contest on Mount Carmel to prove once and for all which god wields power. The devotees of Baal are to take a bull, cut it into pieces and lay it upon a pile of wood. Elijah will do likewise. The respective gods are then to be summoned to send down fire from heaven to kindle the wood under their worshippers' sacrifice. The scene is vividly portrayed. The prophets of Baal whip themselves up into a fury of religious enthusiasm. They whirl round their altar in a cultic dance, gashing themselves with swords and lances, uttering weird, unintelligible cries—typical expression of the orgiastic worship of a fertility god. Elijah, with calm indifference, mocks their efforts. 'Cry aloud for he is a god; either he is musing, or he has gone aside, or he is on a journey, or perhaps he is asleep and must be awakened' (1 Kings xviii. 27). Their efforts prove vain. Elijah thereupon takes twelve stones, one for each of the tribes of Israel, builds an altar, places thereon the wood and the bull, bids the people for good measure drench the altar and its offering three times with water, then prays, ' "O LORD, God of Abraham, Isaac and Israel, let it be known this day that thou art God in Israel, and that I am thy servant, and that I have done all these things at thy word. Answer me, O LORD, answer me, that this people may know that thou, O LORD, art God, and that thou hast turned their hearts back." Then the fire of the LORD fell, and consumed the burnt offering, and the wood and the stones and the dust, and licked up the water that was in the trench. And when all the people saw it they fell on their faces; and they said, "The LORD, he is God; the LORD he is God " ' (1 Kings xviii. 36–39). 'The LORD, he is God'—thus do the people renew their

allegiance to the LORD and to him alone. But the same battle had to
be refought in the changing political circumstance of every age.

One hundred and fifty years after Elijah's act of faith, the
political scene is vastly different. The Northern Kingdom Israel has
disappeared, crushed ruthlessly by the Assyrian juggernaut. Only
the tiny Kingdom of Judah remains, her people trembling at the
thought of what may happen when the Assyrians strike once more.
Where lies safety in this hour of crisis? The politicians have no
doubt as to the answer—Egypt. Hurriedly envoys are sent to the
Pharaoh of Egypt to conclude a military alliance. A prophet has no
doubt as to the answer—and it is not Egypt!

> 'Woe to the rebellious children, says the LORD,
> who carry out a plan, but not mine;
> and who make a league, but not of my spirit,
> that they may add sin to sin;
> who set out to go down to Egypt
> without asking for my counsel,
> to take refuge in the protection of Pharaoh,
> and to take shelter in the shadow of Egypt!
> Therefore shall the protection of Pharaoh turn to your
>   shame,
> and the shelter in the shadow of Egypt to your humil-
>   iation.'
>
> (Isa. xxx. 1–3)

> 'Woe to those who go down to Egypt for help
> and rely on horses,
> who trust in chariots because they are many
> and in horsemen because they are very strong,
> but do not look to the Holy One of Israel
> or consult the LORD!
> And yet he is wise and brings disaster,
> he does not call back his words,
> but will arise against the house of the evildoers,
> and against the helpers of those who work iniquity.
> The Egyptians are men and not God;

and their horses are flesh and not spirit.
When the LORD stretches out his hand,
the helper will stumble and he who is helped will fall,
and they will all perish together.'

(Isa. xxxi. 1–3)

To invoke the help of Egypt is sin. It reveals a tragic failure in trust and loyalty. The issues of human history are not decided by the big battalions. Naked power does not rule the world. To rely upon the Egyptians is to put trust in men, 'men not God'; their vaunted chariotry is but 'flesh', weak, fragile, transitory, not 'spirit', not the power of the LORD. The only hope of safety lies in a renewal of trust in Him who alone shapes and directs the course of events—the LORD. 'You shall know no other gods before me', not even 'Power', that fatal seducer whose shrines were never more crowded than they are today in our world of H-bombs and the 'nuclear deterrent'.

II

Of the ten unconditional demands laid upon the people of God at Mount Sinai, no less than six are concerned not with the attitude of man to God, but with the attitude of man to his fellow man within the community. Respect within the family, the right of every man to life, marriage, property, social honour, the prohibition of covetousness, which, cancer-like, eats at the very vitals of harmonious community life (Exod. xx. 12–17; Deut. v. 16–21)—all this is fundamental to the religious life of the people of God. There could be no response to the LORD, the God who is 'holy in right-eousness' which was not a response in righteousness, that is to say, in right dealings with one's neighbours. In the covenant the people of God were committed to a *moral obedience*.

'When a man leaves a pit open, or when a man digs a pit and does not cover it, and an ox or an ass falls into it, the owner of the pit shall make it good; he shall give money to its owner, and the dead beast shall be his' (Exod. xxi. 33–34).

'You shall take no bribe, for a bribe blinds the officials, and subverts the cause of those who are in the right' (Exod. xxiii. 8).

'You shall not curse the deaf or put a stumbling block before the blind' (Lev. xix. 14).

What, we may ask at first sight, have such regulations to do with religion? The answer is everything, since they are concerned with a man's relationships with his fellows.

The general moral direction which the obedience of the covenant people is to take is outlined in six of the ten commandments. But this was not enough. The practical outworking of such an obedience in terms of the right ordering of society was a task which the people of God had to undertake anew from age to age in the light of changing circumstances. A society may pay lip service to high moral principles, but its sincerity will be tested by the extent to which it can transfer these ideals into practical politics. In the so-called Covenant Code (Exod. xxi. 1–xxiii. 33) which may date from the early period of the settlement in Canaan we find one of the first attempts of the people of God to do this. A curious mixture of civil and criminal law, and regulations concerning worship, the Covenant Code did not drop directly from heaven, nor was it placed personally by God himself into the hands of Moses. It draws upon Canaanite social custom; it preserves some of the traditional customs of the wandering desert tribes; but from whatever source it draws, it stamps its material with a peculiar emphasis; it gathers it up into the covenant relationship between the LORD and His people.

One hundred years ago, such Old Testament laws towered above the landscape of the Ancient Near East like some lone peak solitary in moral grandeur. Today the lone peak is but one feature in a mountain range. Assyrian, Babylonian, Hittite, Egyptian codes are known to us; yet the distinctive contours of the Old Testament peak remain. For our purposes, one of the most interesting of these codes is the Code of Hammurabi, King of Babylon in late eighteenth and early seventeenth centuries B.C., interesting because Babylonian influence was for long strong in Canaan, and there are striking similarities between the Covenant Code and Hammurabi's code. The differences, however, are instructive. To be sure, Hammurabi's Code presupposes a more complex commercial society with a different scale of values concerning life and property; but there is a greater difference. Both codes are given a religious setting, yet in the one case the religious element is formal, exercising no marked influence upon the content of the code, while in the other there is a vital and indissoluble link between faith and the right ordering of society.

At the top of the famous diorite stele on which Hammurabi's Code is inscribed, the king is depicted as receiving a command to establish the laws from Shamash the Sun god, the god of justice. Likewise in the Epilogue to the Code we read, 'I Hammurabi am the king of justice to whom Shamash committed law.'[1] Within the body of the laws, however, Shamash receives never a mention. What we are given is purely a codification of the customary law of the people in the light of the needs of society in Hammurabi's day. Religion serves solely to give added authority to the law. The violator of the law must reckon not only with the state but with the god of justice.

In the Covenant Code the situation is very different. For one thing there is a type of law found within the Covenant Code which is unparalleled throughout the customary law of the Ancient Near East.

'You shall not revile God nor curse a ruler of your people. You shall not delay to offer from the fulness of your harvest and from the outflow of your presses. The first-born of your sons you shall give to me. . . . You shall not utter a false report. You shall not join hands with a wicked man, to be a malicious witness. You shall not follow a multitude to do evil; nor shall you bear witness in a suit, turning aside after a multitude so as to pervert justice; nor shall you be partial to a poor man in his suit' (Exod. xxii. 28–xxiii. 3; cf. Exod. xxii. 18, 21; xxiii. 6 ff.).

This categorical 'you shall not', 'you shall', reminiscent of the 'Ten Words', calls our attention to the fact that certain things are demanded from the people of God for no other reason than that the LORD so wills. To belong to the people of God means accepting God's directives. This applied to the highest and to the lowest in the land, to the king as well as to the poorest peasant farmer. In the eleventh century B.C. the tribes of Israel faced a determined and

[1] Pritchard, *Ancient New Eastern Texts*, p. 163, col. 6.

sustained onslaught from their neighbours from over the seas, the Philistines. Hitherto the tribes had relied upon the hour of crisis calling forth an acceptable leader. Once the crisis was over, however, the tribes went their separate ways, and the leader or 'judge' (cf. The Book of Judges) resumed his ordinary vocation.

The severity of the Philistines' threat convinced the people that there was urgent need for a stable, effective central authority. You may read in 1 Samuel xi how Saul was chosen to be their first king. Many a king in Israel, from Saul onwards, was tempted to play the typical oriental monarch, assuming that might is right, that his word would go unquestioned in the land; only to find to his cost that this could not be so in Israel. Nowhere is this more vividly illustrated than in the stormy relationship between King Ahab and Elijah the prophet. Ahab wished to extend the palace vegetable garden. Unfortunately there stood in the way a small vineyard owned by an insignificant farmer, Naboth. Ahab tried to be reasonable with Naboth:

' "Give me your vineyard that I may have it for a vegetable garden, because it is near my house; and I will give you a better vineyard for it; or if it seems good to you, I will give you its value in money." But Naboth said to Ahab, "The LORD forbid that I should give you the inheritance of my fathers." And Ahab went into his house, vexed and sullen because of what Naboth the Jezreelite had said to him; for he had said, "I will not give you the inheritance of my fathers." And he lay down on his bed and turned away his face, and would eat no food' (1 Kings xxi. 2–4).

Ahab knew that in the light of the traditions of his people, Naboth was within his rights in refusing. The land was not his. It belonged to the family and he had it in trust for future generations. Jezebel, Ahab's Tyrian wife, is mystified by her husband's sulky acceptance of Naboth's refusal. 'Do you now govern Israel? Arise and eat bread and let your heart be cheerful; I will give you the vineyard of Naboth the Jezreelite' (verse 7). Brought up in Tyrian court circles, where it would be accepted that the king's word was law, she did not hesitate for a moment. She had Naboth arrested, condemned on a trumped-up charge—it was as well to give the appearance of legality—and stoned to death. She then presented her

husband with a *fait accompli*. 'Arise, take possession of the vineyard
of Naboth the Jezreelite, which he refused to give you for money,
for Naboth is not alive, but dead' (verse 15).

Naboth was dead, but the prophet Elijah was very much alive.
When Ahab went down to take possession of the vineyard, he
found himself face to face with the man he already had good reason
to call his enemy. 'Ahab said to Elijah, "Have you found me, O
my enemy?" He answered, "I have found you, because you have
sold yourself to do what is evil in the sight of the LORD. Behold, I
will bring evil upon you; I will utterly sweep you away, and will cut
off from Ahab every male, bond or free, in Israel. . . . And of Jezebel,
the LORD also said, The dogs shall eat Jezebel within the bounds of
Jezreel" ' (1 Kings xxi. 20–21, 23). To belong to the people of
God, even as its King, meant accepting God's directives.

But even more significant, we see in the Covenant Code how the
kind of obedience demanded is influenced by the known character
of the LORD. For example, we read, 'You shall not wrong a stranger
or oppress him, for you were strangers in the land of Egypt' (Exod.
xxii. 21). This is echoed by the so-called Holiness Code in Leviticus: 'When a stranger sojourns with you in your land, you shall
not do him wrong. The stranger who sojourns with you shall be to
you as the native among you, and you shall love him as yourself;
for you were strangers in the land of Egypt: I am the LORD your
God' (Lev. xix. 33–34; cf. Deut. xxvii. 19).

Behind this injunction there lies the memory of how the LORD
had acted towards His people, once strangers in Egypt. He had
stretched out a helping hand. In like manner must the people act
to the stranger in their midst. Again Exodus xxii. 26–27 insists, 'If
ever you take your neighbor's garment in pledge, you shall restore
it to him before the sun goes down; for that is his only covering; it
is his mantle for his body; in what else shall he sleep? And if he cries
to me I will hear, for I am compassionate.' The large outer wrap
was the nomad's sole protection against the biting cold of the
desert night. To deprive him of it at night was virtually to sign his
death warrant. To inflict such a penalty for what may well have been
a trifling debt was to act in a way quite contrary to the way in which
the LORD acted. The LORD was compassionate as His people had

good reason to know. Now they are called to show a like compassion.

This insistence upon the quality of the people's obedience being brought into line with the known character of the LORD becomes of ever-increasing importance in the Old Testament. There is an ancient social custom concerning debt slavery preserved in Exodus xxi. 2 ff. If a man were unable to pay a debt, he might sell himself into slavery to work off the debt. A limit of six years, however, was placed on the length of time which such a debt slave might serve. In the seventh year he was to be given back his freedom.[1] In the Book of Deuteronomy, which reflects a later development of many of the regulations in the Covenant Code, this regulation appears in the following form. 'If your brother, a Hebrew man, or a Hebrew woman, is sold to you, he shall serve you six years, and in the seventh year you shall let him go free from you. And when you let him go free from you, you shall not let him go empty-handed; you shall furnish him liberally out of your flock, out of your threshing floor and out of your wine press; as the LORD your God has blessed you, you shall give to him. You shall remember that you were a slave in the land of Egypt, and the LORD your God redeemed you; therefore I command you this today' (Deut. xv. 12–15). Notice the reason now given for release. Because the LORD had once acted as the redeemer (go'el)[2] of his people, so must the people now act towards an enslaved brother. Furthermore, the released slave is not to go out empty-handed; 'as the LORD your God has blessed you, you shall give' (verse 14). '*As the Lord—so you.*' Here is a people summoned to reflect in their attitude to one another God's attitude to them.

Since 'righteousness' in the Old Testament is a description of how God acts, the righteousness which is demanded from the people has a distinctive flavour. It is a righteousness which no coldly equalitarian concept of justice can adequately describe. This righteousness is shot through with mercy, a righteousness revealing a marked concern for, if not a bias in favour of, the helpless. In an age of rapid social change, when many a poor peasant farmer became

---

[1] Cf. Hammurabi § 117, where the limit is *three* years.
[2] Cf. pp. 83 f.

hopelessly enmeshed in debt, when judges expected a bribe, when a new commercial class valued money more than human brotherhood, the prophet Amos demanded:

> 'let justice roll down like waters,
> and righteousness like an ever-flowing stream.'
>
> (v. 24)

But what means this righteousness? It means rooting out from the life of society conditions under which men

> 'sell the righteous (i.e. the innocent) for silver
> and the needy for a pair of shoes
> —trample the head of the poor into the dust of the
>   earth
> and turn aside the way of the afflicted.'
>
> (Amos ii. 6–7; cf. v. 12)

To protect the poor and the needy, this is to do righteousness. Isaiah stressing the same theme, bids the people:

> 'Wash yourselves; make yourselves clean;
> remove the evil of your doings from before my eyes;
> cease to do evil, learn to do good;
> seek justice, correct oppression;
> defend the fatherless, plead for the widow.
>
> (Isa. i. 16–17)

Bitterly he complains:

> 'Your princes are rebels and companions of thieves.
> Everyone loves a bribe and runs after gifts.
> They do not defend the fatherless,
> and the widow's cause does not come to them.'
>
> (i. 23)

In some of the most biting words ever directed against an oriental monarch, Jeremiah denounces Jehoiakim, King of Judah,

from 609–598 B.C., contrasting him unfavourably with the true ideal
of Hebrew kingship exemplified by his father Josiah.

> 'Woe to him who builds his house by unrighteousness,
> and his upper rooms by injustice;
> who makes his neighbor serve him for nothing,
> and does not give him his wages;
> who says, "I will build myself a great house
> with spacious upper rooms,"
> and cuts out windows for it,
> paneling it with cedar
> and painting it with vermilion.
> Do you think you are a king
> because you compete in cedar?
> Did not your father eat and drink
> and do justice and righteousness?
> Then it was well with him.
> He judged the cause of the poor and needy;
> then it was well.
> Is not this to know me?
> says the LORD.'
>
> (Jer. xxii. 13–16)

'To judge the cause of the poor and the needy . . . is not this to
know me, says the LORD.' The author of the Book of Job certainly
thought so. Witness the way in which he made his hero defend his
integrity:

> 'If I have withheld anything that the poor desired,
> or have caused the eyes of the widow to fail,
> or have eaten my morsel alone,
> and the fatherless has not eaten of it,
> if I have seen anyone perish for lack of clothing,
> or a poor man without covering;
> if I have raised my hand against the fatherless,
> because I saw help in the gate;
> then let my shoulder blade fall from my shoulder.'
>
> (Job xxxi. 16, 17, 19, 21)

Such is the characteristic flavour of the moral obedience demanded from the people of God since 'the LORD your God is God of gods and Lord of lords, the great, the mighty, and the terrible God, who is not partial and takes no bribe. He executes justice for the fatherless and the widow, and loves the sojourner, giving him food and clothing. Love the sojourner therefore; for you were sojourners in the land of Egypt. You shall fear the LORD your God; you shall serve him and cleave to him, and by his name you shall swear. He is your praise; he is your God, who has done for you these great and terrible things which your eyes have seen' (Deut. x. 17–21).

As the LORD . . . so you: 'You shall be holy; for I the LORD your God am holy' (Lev. xix. 2).

'When you reap the harvest of your land, you shall not reap your field to its very border, neither shall you gather the gleanings after your harvest. And you shall not strip your vineyard bare, neither shall you gather the fallen grapes of your vineyard; you shall leave them for the poor and for the sojourner: *I am the LORD your God.* You shall not steal, nor deal falsely, nor lie to one another. And you shall not swear by my name falsely, and so profane the name of your God: *I am the LORD.* You shall not oppress your neighbour or rob him. The wages of a hired servant shall not remain with you all night until the morning. You shall not curse the deaf or put a stumbling block before the blind, but you shall fear your God: *I am the LORD.* You shall do no injustice in judgement; you shall not be partial to the poor or defer to the great, but in righteousness shall you judge your neighbor. You shall not go up and down as a slanderer among your people, and you shall not stand forth against the life of your neighbor: *I am the LORD.* You shall not hate your brother in your heart, but you shall reason with your neighbor, lest you bear sin because of him. You shall not take vengeance or bear any grudge against the sons of your own people, but you shall love your neighbor as yourself: *I am the LORD*' (Lev. xix. 9–17).

In the Old Testament there can be no thought of 'Morals without Religion', because it is what is known about the LORD which is decisive for conduct. But equally, there can be no 'Religion without Morals', though 'Religion without Morals' was familiar

enough to the ancient world and more than once proved seductive
to the people of God. 'If the LORD is God, follow him, but if Baal,
then follow him' (1 Kings xviii. 21). Such was Elijah's challenge to
the people. We may be tempted to say, 'What's in a name?' 'Does
it matter what we call God, provided we worship?' But Elijah knew
that this was a struggle to the death between two different kinds of
religion. The religion of the Baals was a fertility cult. Provided the
correct offerings were brought, the correct ritual performed, the
gods could be relied upon to give fertility to land and people. There
is no essential connection here between religion and daily conduct.
Indeed, there were repulsively immoral features in such a religion.
At the sanctuaries there was a recognized class of 'holy women', i.e.
sacred prostitutes, to have intercourse with whom was an act of
piety since, by a process of sympathetic magic, such an act would
help the god to fulfil his function. Such was religion. Too easily did
the Israelites take over the sanctuaries where once the Baals had
been worshipped and reconsecrate them to the worship of the
LORD, but without changing the character of the worship. It was
the greatness of the Old Testament prophets that they saw that
immorality, in any shape or form, was utterly inconsistent with the
worship of the LORD who demanded from His people a moral
obedience. There was no lack of religion in Amos' day. The temples
were thronged, lavish offerings and sacrifices abounded, pilgrim-
ages to the great religious centres were popular. With it all, 'a
man and his father go in to the same maiden'—an act of piety? Not
at all, insists Amos, in the name of the LORD:

> 'A man and his father go in to the same maiden
> so that my holy name is profaned.'
>
> (Amos ii. 7)

'Come to Bethel', a famous royal sanctuary, cries Amos, come and
worship? No:

> 'Come to Bethal and transgress;
> to Gilgal, and multiply transgression:
> bring your sacrifices every morning,
> your tithes every three days;

offer a sacrifice of thanksgiving of that which is leavened,
and proclaim freewill offerings, publish them;
for so you love to do, O people of Israel!
says the LORD God.'

(Amos iv. 4–5)

Another prophet protests:

'What to me is the multitude of your sacrifices?
says the LORD;
I have had enough of burnt offerings of rams
and the fat of fed beasts;
I do not delight in the blood of bulls,
or of lambs or of he-goats.
When you come to appear before me,
who requires of you
this trampling of my courts?
Bring no more vain offerings
incense is an abomination to me.
New moon and sabbath and the calling of assemblies—
I cannot endure iniquity and solemn assembly.
Your new moons and your appointed feasts
my soul hates;
they have become a burden to me,
I am weary of bearing them.
When you spread forth your hands,
I will hide my eyes from you,
even though you make many prayers,
I will not listen;
your hands are full of blood.'

(Isa. i. 11–15)

'Your hands are full of blood'—there is the rub. Plenty of religion,
but little true religion. Abundant sacrifices and offerings, but piti-
fully little justice and righteousness. Yet 'in the day that I brought
them out of the land of Egypt, I did not speak to your fathers, or
command them concerning burnt offerings and sacrifices. But this

command I gave them, 'Obey my voice, and I will be your God, and you shall be my people; and walk in all the way that I command you, that it may be well with you!' (Jer. vii. 22–23). Here is a people committed to a moral obedience to the LORD. Without such an obedience, elaborate religious ritual is but a facade; without such a moral response, sacrifice is but a smoke-screen coming between the LORD and His people (cf. Ps. li. 15–19).

As Hosea reminded the people, the God whose very nature is steadfast love (chesed) demands from His people:

> '. . . steadfast love and not sacrifice,
> the knowledge of God rather than burnt offerings.'
>
> (Hos. vi. 6)

If we ask further, 'What is this knowledge of God?' a very famous passage in the Book of Micah gives us the answer:

> With what shall I come before the LORD,
> and bow myself before God on High?
> Shall I come before him with burnt offerings,
> with calves a year old?
> Will the LORD be pleased with thousands of rams,
> with ten thousands of rivers of oil?
> Shall I give my first-born for my transgression,
> the fruit of my body for the sin of my soul?
> He has showed you, O man, what is good;
> and what does the LORD require of you
> but to do justice and to love kindness,
> and to walk humbly with your God?'
>
> (Mic. vi. 6–8)

The Old Testament speaks of the people of God united to God by a bond of His making. In return they found themselves pledged to an exclusive loyalty to the LORD, a loyalty which could only be adequately realized in a society whose life reflected the known moral demands of this holy God. In every age, the summons to the people of God was to be:

'Hear, O Israel; the LORD our God is one LORD; and you shall love the LORD your God with all your heart, and with all your soul, and with all your might. And these words which I command you this day shall be upon your heart; and you shall teach them diligently to your children, and shall talk of them when you sit in your house, and when you walk by the way, and when you lie down, and when you rise' (Deut. vi. 4–7).

The people never found it easy to give either that exclusive loyalty, or such a moral obedience, but then, if we are honest, neither do we.

5

The Reason Why

Why did God choose Israel to be His people? The Old Testament itself is certain that no material greatness or genius for religion among the Hebrews prompted the choice.

The reason must be in the heart of God, in a mystery of divine love which is wholly unmerited. This love of God is a purposive love, wishing to use Israel to fulfil God's purposes in the world. Israel is intended to be the nucleus of a new humanity.

When Israel fails to bring forth the response for which God is looking, then to be chosen means to be judged and punished—as the prophet Amos (mid-eighth century B.C.) insists—so that in the end she may be made fit for her vocation.

Israel is to be 'a priestly nation' (Exod. xix. 6) bringing God to man and man to God. Her faith is to be universal, her God recognized by all peoples; only then will there dawn the age of peace for which men yearn (Isa. ii. 2–4). This missionary consciousness reaches its climax in Isaiah xl–lv, in the portrait of Israel as 'The Servant of the Lord', gladly accepting suffering on behalf of others in fulfilment of her mission.

After the exile (586–538 B.C.), Judaism often regarded itself as a 'saved' rather than a 'saving' community. But the spirit of the Servant lived on, notably in the Book of Jonah.

Israel exists only for the sake of the world, and the furtherance of God's purposes therein.

'WHY' is a stubborn little word; one of the words a toddler early learns to use, much to the perplexity of his parents; a word we must never cease to use if we think at all seriously about life. There are abiding mysteries in life in face of which even the wisest, wonderingly or defiantly, ask 'why?' Perhaps only a vague familiarity with the Bible prevents us from realizing that there is something breathtaking in the thought, central to all that the Bible has to say, that God, the Creator of all, the sovereign lord of the universe, entered into a unique relationship at one particular time in human history, with one particular nation, and that, humanly speaking, an insignificant one. It is either breathtaking, or it is so fantastic that it is not worth giving it a second thought. Is it not grossly unfair of God to make fish of one and fowl of the other nations of the world? When the Old Testament speaks of the Jews as 'the chosen people', is not this simply a reflection of Jewish nationalism, a people's perverted egotism? Why should God choose *one* people? Why indeed! It is, of course, all part of the fun of human life that in every age we ask questions, searching questions, we think, only to find that they were asked and answered long before we were born. The Old Testament itself is well aware that it was 'odd of God to choose the Jews'. The people of Israel may originally have accepted without question that God, having delivered them out of Egypt, had chosen them to be His people, but soon they were to ask, and ask more than once, 'Why has God done this?'

Certain answers were ruled out of court. There is a frank recognition that no might or greatness in the people of Israel could explain this God's choice.

'You are a people holy to the LORD your God; the LORD your God has chosen you to be a people for his own possession, out of all the peoples that are on the face of the earth. It was not because you were more in number than any other people that the LORD set his love upon you and chose you, for you were the fewest of all peoples' (Deut. vii. 6–7). If God had possessed a millionaire mentality, he would never have given Israel a second thought. He could have found in the world of the Ancient Near East, Egypt, Assyria, Babylon, the Hittites, all immeasurably superior to Israel in political power and cultural achievement.

Was it then that Israel, unhampered by the snare of material greatness, evinced a peculiar genius for true religion? Psalm cvi gives us the answer. It celebrates the 'steadfast' love of the LORD and the anything but steadfast love of the people. Right from the beginning, and throughout their history, claims this Psalm, the people showed a remarkable resistance to the LORD, and an astonishing failure to understand wherein true religion lay.

> 'Both we and our fathers have sinned:
> we have committed iniquity, we have done wickedly.
> Our fathers, when they were in Egypt,
> did not consider thy wonderful works;
> they did not remember the abundance of thy steadfast
>   love,
> but rebelled against the Most High at the Red Sea'
>
> > (verses 6–7)

and so it continues: 'they soon forgot' (verse 13).

> 'they had a wanton craving in the wilderness'
>
> > (verse 14)

> 'they made a calf in Horeb
> and worshipped a molten image,
> they exchanged the glory of God
> for the image of an ox that eats grass,
> they forgot God their Saviour,
> who had done great things in Egypt'
>
> > (verses 19–21).

they had 'no faith in his promise'

> > (verse 24).

> 'they provoked the LORD to anger with their doings'
>
> > (verse 29)

> 'they sacrificed their sons
> and their daughters to the demons;
> they poured out innocent blood,
> the blood of their sons and daughters
> whom they sacrificed to the idols of Canaan'
>
> > (verses 37–38)

'they were rebellious in their purposes'

(verse 43)

It reads rather like the story of a people with a genius for infidelity. Passage after passage in the Old Testament reiterates that *this* is the story of Israel (cf. Ps. lxxviii 17 ff.; Micah vi.; Amos iv; Hosea ix-x).

I

Why then did God choose this forgetful and rebellious people? There is a mystery here, a wonder which can only find explanation in the heart of God. 'It was not because you were more in number than any other people that the LORD set his love upon you and chose you, for you were the fewest of all peoples; but it is because the LORD loves you, and is keeping the oath which he swore to your fathers, that the LORD has brought you out with a mighty hand, and redeemed you from the house of bondage, from the hand of Pharaoh, king of Egypt' (Deut. vii. 7-8).

He set His love on you . . . because He loves you; we seem to be going round in a circle, but it is an inevitable circle whenever we talk about love. 'I love him . . . well, because I love him.' It is not very logically satisfying, but it is true to life's experience—which is perhaps just as well for many of us!

It is because the LORD loves you. But verse 8 goes on to say, 'and is keeping the oath which he swore to your fathers'. Such a promise we find God giving to Abraham in Genesis xii. 2–3: 'And I will make of you a great nation, and I will bless you and make your name great, so that you will be a blessing. I will bless those who bless you, and him who curses you I will curse, and by you all the families of the earth will bless themselves.' This but takes us one step further back to ask, 'Why did God make such a promise to Abraham?' We return to the same answer.

'Behold, to the LORD your God belong heaven and the heaven of heavens, the earth with all that is in it; yet the LORD set his heart in love upon your fathers and chose their descendants after them, you above all peoples, as at this day' (Deut. x. 14-15).

It is because the LORD loves you. The word here translated 'love' is not the word 'chesed', 'steadfast love'. There is no suggestion in it of steadfastness to a covenant bond. It takes us back beyond the covenant to that in the heart of God which led Him to take the initiative in coming to His people. Nothing that Israel was or had done could account for God's action. It must be the expression of a freely given, unmerited love.

> 'When Israel was a child, I loved him,
> and out of Egypt I called my son.
> The more I called them,
> the more they went from me;
> they kept sacrificing to the Baals,
> and burning incense to idols.
> Yet it was I who taught Ephraim to walk.
> I took them up in my arms;
> but they did not know that I healed them.
> I led them with cords of compassion,
> with the bands of love,
> and I became to them as one
> who eases the yoke on their jaws,
> and I bent down to them and fed them.'
>
> (Hos. xi. 1–4)

Side by side with the waywardness of the people, this passage places two pictures of God. The first is of a fond father, teaching a young toddler to walk, catching whenever the unsteady legs give way; the other is of a considerate farmer, easing the yoke on his oxen, making sure that they are well fed. Both underline the love and care in the heart of God which account for all His dealings with His people.

Another prophet can say of this people:

'Your origin and your birth are of the land of the Canaanites; your father was an Amorite and your mother a Hittite. And as for your birth, on the day you were born your navel string was not cut, nor were you washed with water to cleanse you, nor rubbed with salt, nor swathed with bands. No eye pitied you, to do any of these things to you out of compassion for you; but you were cast out on the open field, for you were abhorred on the day that you were born. And when I passed by you, and saw you weltering in your blood, I said to you in your blood, "Live and grow up like a plant of the field." And you grew up and became tall and arrived at full maidenhood; your breasts were formed and your hair had grown; yet you were naked and bare' (Ezek. xvi. 3*b*–7). . . . Israel, the unwanted, untended baby, exposed to die in the desert, only to be succoured by God's compassion.

> 'He found him in a desert land,
> and in the howling waste of the wilderness;
> he encircled him, he cared for him,
> he kept him as the apple of his eye.'
>
> (Deut. xxxii. 10)

The sex may have changed but not the attitude of the LORD. This is the point from which any understanding of God's choice of Israel must begin, in the care, compassion and love of God.

II

This love of God is none the less a purposive love. He has an end in view in choosing this people. They are to be His agents in the fulfilment of His purposes in and for the world. Return for a moment to Psalm cvi. After stressing the callous rebelliousness of the people, the Psalm continues:

> 'Yet he saved them for his name's sake,
> that he might make known his mighty power.'
>
> (verse 8)

The recollection of God's continuing goodness leads the Psalmist to his plea for the present, a plea probably coming from the time immediately after the exile.

> 'Save us O LORD our God,
> and gather us from among the nations,

that we may give thanks to thy holy name
and glory in thy praise.
Blessed be the LORD, the God of Israel,
from everlasting to everlasting!
And let all the people say, "Amen!"
Praise the LORD.'

(verses 47-48)

'*For his name's sake* . . . that we may give thanks to *thy holy name*.' So the prophet Jeremiah, at a time when severe drought was causing untold distress, makes this appeal:

'Though our iniquities testify against us,
act, O LORD, for thy name's sake.
Do not spurn us, for thy name's sake;
do not dishonour thy glorious throne;
remember, and do not break thy covenant with us.
Are there any among the false gods of the nations that
    can bring rain?
Or can the heavens give showers?
Art thou not he, O LORD our God?
We set our hope on thee,
for thou doest all these things.'

(Jer. xiv. 7, 21–22)

The prophet Ezekiel is particularly fond of describing God as acting 'for his name's sake'. Severely tempted to wash His hands of this people, God yet restrains Himself, 'But I acted for the sake of my name, that it should not be profaned in the sight of the nations, in whose sight I had brought them out' (Ezek. xx. 14).

Behind this frequent appeal to the name of God, there may lurk an ancient, naïve belief that if a god did not have in the world a people to honour his name, then he could not truly be said to exist, or to have any share in the affairs of men. The thought of many Old Testament passages, however, ranges far from this humble beginning. One and all, the prophets taught the people to believe that national disaster was God's just judgement upon their sinfulness. But disaster was not the end. The author of Isaiah xl-lv. bids the people lift up their hearts.

> 'For my name's sake I defer my anger,
> for the sake of my praise I restrain it for you,
> that I may not cut you off.
> Behold I have refined you, but not like silver;
> I have tried you in the furnace of affliction.
> For my own sake, for my own sake I do it,
> for how should my name be profaned?
> My glory I will not give to another.'
>
> (xlviii. 9–11)

In other words, the LORD has *some purpose of His own* in view in all His dealings with Israel, and not even national disaster, deserved though it be, can thwart His purpose. It is the frank recognition that Israel exists to serve God's purposes that lies behind the recurring reference to 'His name' and 'for His name's sake'.

The prophet Jeremiah once stood watching a potter working with a lump of clay upon his wheel. Skilled hands fashioned and refashioned the clay till the potter was satisfied that the finished article expressed what he had in mind.

'Then the word of the LORD came to me: "O house of Israel, can I not do with you as this potter has done?" says the LORD. Behold, like the clay in the potter's hand, so are you in my hand, O house of Israel' (Jer. xviii. 5–6). The people of God existed to be fashioned and refashioned till they expressed what was in the mind of the Divine Potter.

But what is this purpose of God? It is no accident that the myths in Genesis i–xi, with their underlying theme of man gone wrong, are immediately followed in Genesis xii with the story of God's call to Abraham, the forbear of the people of God. This is the point of God's entry into the wilderness of self-centred humanity, there to establish a new, revitalized community of men, wherein the sin of Adam and Eve (self at the centre of life) and the sin of Cain (enmity towards a fellow man) will be overcome.

Thus the story of the people of God[1] is the story of a people called to an exclusive loyalty and a moral obedience, a community, in other words, in which God's sovereignty, and His alone, will be recognized, a community in which, man's self-assertiveness overcome, there will be true brotherhood.

Precisely because Israel is called to be this kind of community, and can fulfil God's purpose only by so being, the note of *judgement* sounds again and again in the Old Testament. The people of the Northern Kingdom of Israel in Amos' day, circa 750 B.C., had a lively sense of being God's chosen people. Moreover, they had strong views as to what this meant. They were the apple of the LORD's eye. He was their private patron saint, existing to promote the peace, power and prosperity of His people, and to deal deadly destruction to all her enemies. To be sure, all was not yet well in Israel's world, but there was coming a 'Day of the LORD', a day of joy and gladness, when Israel would be given her rightful place in the universe. Thus thought the people; but thus spoke the prophet Amos:

'Are you not like the Ethiopians to me
O people of Israel? says the LORD.
Did I not bring up Israel from the land of Egypt,
and the Philistines from Caphtor (i.e. Crete)
and the Syrians from Kir?' [i.e. probably somewhere
in North Mesopotamia]

(ix. 7)

Far from being the private possession of Israel, the LORD controlled the destiny of all peoples. Not only so, but the LORD, the *moral* sovereign of the world, holds all peoples responsible for their actions. One by one, the nations surrounding Israel are summoned to the bar of divine judgement to be condemned for wartime atrocities, brutal indifference to human life, and flagrant disregard of solemn pledges (cf. i. 3–ii. 5). No doubt Amos' fellow countrymen heartily approved. There was little love lost between Israel and these peoples.

[1] Cf. chapter 4.

Now comes the shock. The burden of Amos' biting invective is directed, not against these heathen neighbours, but against the people of God. Fearlessly he exposes the social injustices (e.g. ii. 6); the irresponsible luxury (iv. 1; vi. 4); the corruption in the administration of the law (v. 10 and 12); the travesty of true religion (ii. 7; v. 21, 24–25); the false complacency (vi. 1) rampant among his own people. 'A day of the LORD'? 'Certainly' says Amos, but:

> 'Woe to you who desire the day of the LORD!
> Why would you have the day of the LORD?
> It is darkness and not light;
> as if a man fled from a lion,
> and a bear met him;
> or went into the house and leaned with his hand against
>   the wall,
> and a serpent bit him.
> Is not the day of the LORD darkness and not light?
> and gloom with no brightness in it?'
>
> (v. 18–20)

To be chosen by the LORD does not mean to be His pampered favourites; far from it. 'Hear this word that the LORD has spoken against you, O people of Israel, against the whole family which I brought up out of the land of Egypt:

> "You only have I known
> of all the families of the earth;
> therefore I will punish you
> for all your iniquities." '
>
> (iii. 1–2)

Far from siding with Israel in the conflicts of the age, the LORD will use her enemies to punish her.

> 'An adversary shall surround the land,
> and bring down your defences from you,
> and your strongholds shall be plundered.'
>
> (iii. 11)

Israel had to learn that, in the words of a New Testament writer, 'It is a fearful thing to fall into the hands of the living God' (Heb. x. 31).

The life of the nation, as Amos knew it, had to collapse, not because the LORD, having lost His temper with His people, wished to relieve His own feelings by hurling a divine thunderbolt, but because only thus could the people be delivered from the dangerous delusions which prevented them from being serviceable to the LORD.

Only beyond judgement could there be hope, hope of a people taught by tragedy, set free to resume its task of building the community God desires.

III

We must, however, go further. God did not choose Israel simply to create an island of sanity in an insane world. In various strands of the Old Testament, and in different ways, there is expressed the belief that the people of God is in the world for the sake of the world; in the world with a mission to the world; in the world to be the nucleus of a new humanity.

The Book of Exodus records this word as given to Moses: 'Thus you shall say to the house of Jacob, and tell the people of Israel: You have seen what I did to the Egyptians, and how I bore you on eagles' wings and brought you to myself. Now therefore, if you will obey my voice and keep my covenant, you shall be my own possession among all peoples; for all the earth is mine, and you shall be to me a kingdom of priests, and a holy nation' (Exod. xix. 3b–6a).

By grateful obedience the people are to be God's own people, a distinctive community (i.e. a holy nation), but also a 'kingdom of priests'. The functions and organization of the priests in Israel may have varied from age to age, but always, basic to their existence, is the fact that they are a 'community within the community', set apart to be the link between God and the people. They instruct the people in the correct approach to God; they operate the sacrificial system, a system which, at its best, was recognized to be God's gift to the people, a means of conveying His blessings to them. As the priest in Israel, so Israel is in the world, a community set apart to bring the world to God, and God to the world.

When Abraham is summoned to leave the life he knows for a venture into the unknown, the LORD gives him this promise: 'I will make of you a great nation, and I will bless you and make your name great, so that you will be a blessing. I will bless those who bless you and him who curses you I will curse; and by you all the families of the earth will bless themselves' (Gen. xii. 2–3). This same promise, 'by you shall the families of the earth bless themselves' is solemnly repeated to Abraham (Gen. xviii. 18), to his son Isaac (Gen. xxii. 18; xxvi. 4) and to his grandson Jacob (xxviii. 14). The Authorized Version is misleading in its translation, 'by you shall all the families of the earth be blessed'. The words need imply no more than that one day other peoples will think of no higher blessing to wish for themselves than the blessing given by God to Abraham and his descendants. 'As you blessed Abraham, so bless me' will be their prayer to God. But let us not underestimate the significance of this. The call of Abraham and his descendants is here linked to the destiny of other peoples. The blessing God bestows upon Abraham is seen to be the desire of all nations.

There is a prophetic oracle popular in the eighth century B.C., since it is preserved for us both in Isaiah and Micah, which stresses the same theme.

> 'It shall come to pass in the latter days
> that the mountain of the house of the LORD
> shall be established as the highest of the mountains,
> and shall be raised above the hills;
> and all the nations shall flow to it,
> and many peoples shall come and say:
> Come, let us go up to the mountain of the LORD,
> to the house of the God of Jacob;
> that he may teach us his ways
> and that we may walk in his paths!
> For out of Zion shall go forth the law,

and the word of the LORD from Jerusalem.
He shall judge between the nations,
and shall decide for many peoples;
and they shall beat their swords into ploughshares
and their spears into pruning hooks;
nation shall not lift up sword against nation,
neither shall they learn war any more.'

(Isa. ii. 2-4 = Mic. iv. 1-3)

There is no false humility here, no tentative suggestion that Israel may perhaps have something to offer to the new world-faith of the future. There is the unshakable conviction that Israel's faith is the true faith, Israel's God the true God, and that one day this will be recognized by other peoples who will gladly flock to Mount Zion, the centre of the worship of the LORD, there to learn His ways and to walk in His paths. There is no easy optimism here. Only when men and nations have been drawn out of their self-centred isolationism into a community lost in the wonder of true worship, can there be lasting human brotherhood, the hideous nightmare of war banished for ever. The false gods must vanish, the LORD, the one true God must reign. This is Israel's mission.

'O LORD, my strength and my stronghold,
my refuge in the day of trouble,
to thee shall the nations come
from the ends of the earth and say:
"Our fathers have inherited nought but lies,
worthless things in which there is no profit,
Can man make for himself gods?
Such are no gods".

Therefore behold, I will make them know, this once I will make them know my power and my might, and they shall know that my name is the LORD' (Jer. xvi. 19-21).

The Psalmist has no doubt that

'There is none like thee among the gods, O LORD,
nor are there any works like thine,

> All the nations thou hast made shall come
> and bow down before thee, O LORD,
> and shall glorify thy name.
> For thou art great and doest wondrous things,
> thou alone art God.'
>
> (Ps. lxxxvi. 8–10)

It is in Isaiah xl–lv., however, that the missionary consciousness
of the Old Testament reaches its climax. The political fortunes of
the people of God had never been worse. Jerusalem was in ruins;
most of her people languished in exile in Babylon. This is the
LORD's doing, fit recompense for a nation's folly.

> 'Who gave up Jacob to the spoiler,
> and Israel to the robbers?
> Was it not the LORD, against whom we have sinned,
> in whose ways they would not walk,
> and whose law they would not obey?
> So he poured upon him the heat of his anger
> and the might of battle;
> it set him on fire round about, but he did not under-
>   stand;
> it burned him, but he did not take it to heart.'
>
> (Isa. xlii. 24–25)

But the LORD has not washed His hands of this people. Nowhere in
the Old Testament is there so certain a conviction that Israel, even
in tragedy, is the LORD's chosen people.

> 'But you, Israel, my servant,
> Jacob whom I have chosen,
> the offspring of Abraham, my friend;
> you whom I took from the ends of the earth,
> and called from its farthest corners,
> saying to you, "You are my servant,
> I have chosen you and not cast you off";
> fear not, for I am with you,

be not dismayed, for I am your God;
I will strengthen you, I will help you,
I will uphold you with my victorious right hand.'
(Isa. xli. 8–10)

Israel the *Servant of the LORD*—this is the people's true destiny, traceable right back to the beginning of the nation's story, to Abraham, to Jacob, who live still in their descendants, the people of God in the world as the agent of the LORD's purposes. It is undoubted that in many passages in Isaiah xl–lv. the Servant of the LORD is Israel the nation. To the passage quoted we may add:

'But now hear, O Jacob my servant,
Israel whom I have chosen!
Thus says the LORD who made you,
who formed you from the womb and will help you:
"Fear not, O Jacob my servant,
Jeshurun[1] whom I have chosen".'
(Is. xliv. 1–2; cf. xliii. 10; xlix. 3)

Yet in xlix. 5, the Servant is said to have been created by the LORD:

'to be his servant,
to bring Jacob back to him,
and that Israel might be gathered to him.'

In other words the Servant has here a mission *to* Israel. Furthermore, in certain passages, notably the four so-called Servant Songs (xlii. 1–4; xlix. 1–6; l. 4–9; lii. 13–liii. 12), the Servant is depicted in such vividly personal terms that an impressive array of scholars believe that we must here think not in terms of a nation but of an individual. As to the possible identity of the individual, there is no agreement. We must not, however, be misled by western ways of thinking. The oriental mind is highly imaginative, given to making daring personifications, particularly in poetic passages. The Book

[1] Jeshurun is a diminutive of endearment from a Hebrew root meaning 'upright'.

of Lamentations abounds in them. Nor is this merely poetic fancy. The Hebrew drew far less sharp a distinction than we do between the individual and the group or community of which he is a member. In his thinking he often jumps disconcertingly from the one to the other. Traditionally Jewish thought has identified the Servant with Israel, and so it still seems best to do, though in xlix. 5 we must perhaps think rather of a faithful minority within Israel remaining true to Israel's mission.[1]

But what is the mission of the Servant of the LORD?

> 'Behold my servant, whom I uphold,
> my chosen in whom my soul delights;
> I have put my spirit upon him,
> he will bring forth justice to the *nations*.'
>
> (xlii. 1–2)

Unobtrusively, persistently, he is to continue:

> 'Till he has established justice in the earth;
> and the coastlands wait for his law.' [i.e. instruction]
>
> (verse 4)

Israel, in spite of her faults and failings—and they are never ignored, cf. xlii. verses 18 and 19 where the Servant is described as 'deaf' and 'blind'—is to be:

> 'a covenant to the people,
> a light to the nations,
> to open the eyes that are blind,
> to bring out the prisoners from the dungeon,
> from the prison those who sit in darkness.'
>
> (verses 6–7)

Even in xlix. 5 f, where the Servant has a mission *to* Israel, the thought ranges out into the wider world.

[1] For an excellent discussion of the 'Servant' cf. J. Muilenberg in Interpreter's Bible, Vol. 5, pp. 406–414.

'It is too light a thing that you should be my servant
to raise up the tribes of Jacob
and to restore the preserved of Israel;
I will give you as a light to the nations,
that my salvation may reach to the end of the earth.'

(verse 6)

Israel is not in the world to save her own soul, but to spread the light of true faith, and bring God's blessing to the very ends of the earth. To nothing less than this is she called by the LORD.

The prophets who tried to keep Israel true to the LORD had no easy task. Misunderstanding, insult, persecution, even martyrdom were their lot. Israel's mission to the world is no less hazardous. The Servant is disfigured (lii. 14), outcast (liii. 3), persecuted to the bitter end (liii. 8). Uncomplaining, silently, he endures it all (liii. 7). He suffers, and behind all his suffering there stand the purposes of God. Looking at his agony, others will be led to confess:

'Surely he has borne our griefs
and carried our sorrows;
yet we esteemed him stricken,
smitten by God and afflicted.
But he was wounded for our transgressions,
he was bruised for our iniquities;
upon him was the chastisement that made us whole,
and with his stripes we are healed.
All we like sheep have gone astray;
we have turned every one to his own way:
and the LORD has laid on him
the iniquity of us all.'

(liii. 4–6)

The Servant offers himself as a 'guilt offering' (liii. 10), a type of sacrifice which, in the Old Testament, normally accompanied the act of making amends for some wrong done, a sacrifice designed to take away the guilt incurred by the evil action. Through the Servant's mission of suffering, the nations of the world, disobedient

I

to, and ignorant of the LORD, can have their guilt removed, and enter into a new at-one-ment with Him who 'made the earth and created man upon it' (xlv. 12). Chosen by the LORD, chosen to suffer and through suffering, to unite the world in allegiance to the one true God—such is Israel's vocation.

It would be misleading to suggest that the Jews who returned from exile in Babylon returned fired with the vision of a world mission. At least, if they did, the vision soon faded. The returned exiles had to struggle hard to rebuild their homeland, in face of local jealousy and opposition (cf. Neh. iv. ff.). Deeply conscious of the teaching of the prophets that sin brought inevitable judgement and national ruin, the leaders of the new community sought to reconstruct a national life which would be truly holy, truly obedient, to the instructions of the LORD. We are told in Nehemiah viii, how Ezra, the scribe, brought 'the book of the law of Moses which the LORD had given to Israel' (viii. 1) and read it to the assembled people. In response, the people made a 'firm covenant' with the LORD (Neh. ix. 38). Unfortunately, the means taken to preserve the purity of the people was a policy of rigid exclusiveness. Salvation was to be sought in social and religious apartheid. Outside help was scathingly rejected; disciplinary measures were taken to eradicate mixed marriages from the community (Ezra x). Even where foreigners are thought of as being admitted to the new God-created community, their place is often firmly defined.

> 'Aliens shall stand and feed your flocks,
> foreigners shall be your ploughmen and vine-dressers;
> but you shall be called the priests of the LORD,
> men shall speak of you as the ministers of our God;
> you shall eat the wealth of the nations,
> and in their riches shall you glory.'
>
> (Isa. lxi. 5–6)[1]

For others, the menial tasks in life; for the Jews the priestly life of worship and instruction, not to mention the wealth of nations. The

[1] Isa. lvi ff. are later than Isa. xl–lv, and come probably from an author or authors belonging to the Isaianic group of disciples.

author of Zechariah xiv depicts a day when 'the LORD will become king over all the earth', but only as the outcome of violent warfare between Jerusalem and the nations of the world, the LORD, naturally, smiting with a plague all Jerusalem's enemies; 'their flesh shall rot while they are still on their feet, their eyes shall rot in their sockets, and their tongues shall rot in their mouths' (Zech. xiv. 12). As for the survivors, unless they are prepared to make a yearly pilgrimage to Jerusalem, dire will be their lot (cf. Zech. xiv. 16 ff.). The fever of nationalism, particularly religious nationalism, is not easily purged from the human system.

But the vision of Isaiah xl–lv was not entirely lost. For proof of this we need look no further than the Book of Jonah, probably written in protest against the spiritual and racial 'iron curtain' which the post-exilic community was erecting. This little book, an example of religious fiction, must be read as a story, not as a solemn chronicle of events. It is one of the greatest apologies in the Old Testament for the world mission of the people of God. Once a man called Jonah, so the story begins, was called upon by the LORD to undertake a strange mission. 'Arise, go to Nineveh, that great city, and cry against it, for its wickedness has come up before me' (i. 2). 'But LORD,' we can almost hear Jonah say, 'Nineveh is the capital of the Assyrian Empire, the home of the ruthless oppressors of Israel; anywhere else, but surely not Nineveh, even to pronounce a word of doom upon it.' You might as well have asked a rabid anti-communist to conduct an evangelistic campaign in Moscow. Jonah tries to escape by running away to sea, but in vain. A storm overtakes the tiny boat. Jonah is held to be responsible for the turbulent elements expressive of God's anger. Overboard he goes, from ship to monster fish, then after a strange sojourn in the fish, back again to dry and, to hear for the second time the word of the LORD. 'Arise go to Nineveh, that great city, and proclaim to it the message that I tell you (iii. 2). So Jonah went, no doubt with a bad grace, determined, at least, to make the most of his opportunities, to call down hell fire upon the hated Ninevites. To his horror, the people of Nineveh repent at his preaching, and, worse still, God grants them a reprieve. Jonah had obviously feared that this might happen, since he angrily rounds on the LORD, 'I pray thee, LORD, is not this what I said when

I was yet in my country? That is why I made haste to flee to Tarshish; for I knew that thou art a gracious God and merciful, slow to anger and abounding in steadfast love, and repentest of evil' (iv. 2).

In high dudgeon, Jonah stamps off. Death would have been preferable. That he should live to see the Ninevites enjoying God's favour! As Jonah sat, moodily contemplating the future of Nineveh, God—so the story goes—caused a great plant to grow up to shelter him from the blazing heat of the day. Jonah's pleasure turns to anger when, next day, the plant withers and dies, leaving him to the mercy of the sultry east wind and the pitiless sun.

'But God said to Jonah, "Do you do well to be angry for the plant?" And he said, "I do well to be angry, angry enough to die." And the LORD said, "You pity the plant for which you did not labour, nor did you make it grow, which came into being in a night, and perished in a night. And should not I pity Nineveh, that great city, in which there are more than a hundred and twenty thousand persons who do not know their right hand from their left, and also much cattle?" (iv. 9–11).

Thus the story ends on the note of God's compassion for the misguided people of Nineveh; not to mention their cattle.

Without a doubt, Jonah represents Israel, Israel reluctant to hear God's call to mission out with its own borders. But for the people of God there can be no escape, from such world mission, since it is rooted in the compassionate concern of God for all men, a compassion which embraces within its healing purposes, even the enemies of Israel.

The people of God neither existed for its own sake, nor for the selfish enjoyment of what God had given. This is a people chosen to witness to the far ends of the earth, and to be used by God in the fulfilment of His gracious purposes for all mankind. If Israel never fully dedicated all her energies in response to this vision, who are we to stand in judgement?

6

God Will Act

The Old Testament looks forward in confidence, because it looks back in faith. Because God has acted, so He will act. For a people disobedient to God, the 'Day of the LORD' means judgement (Amos). Beyond judgement, there is seen to be hope of reconstruction, of a new beginning for the people of God (Isa. xl; Hos. ii. 14–15; Jer. xxx–xxxi). Isaiah of Jerusalem (circa 750–700 B.C.) talks of a 'faithful remnant' surviving disaster to become the nucleus of a new people of God.

As a whole, the Old Testament's hope for a better future in the purpose of God centres upon:

1. A Coming Ruler. *The vital part played by kingship in the life of the community and the repeated disappointment of the great expectations roused by kingship, led to the hope that one day God would send a true king, fully endowed by God's spirit, to inaugurate a new era of righteousness and prosperity (Isa. ix. 6–7; xi. 1–5).*

2. The New Covenant. *Bitter experience taught Jeremiah that only a radical change of will among God's people would make them faithful. This must be God's doing. He looks for a 'New Covenant' with God's law written not on tablets of stone, but in the hearts of the people. Ezekiel witnesses to the same hope.*

3. A New Age. *Man and 'Nature' are indissolubly linked for weal and woe in the thought of the Old Testament, therefore there is hope of a day when disharmony of every kind will be banished from the universe.*

The Old Testament is thus an unfinished story. The New Testament claims to bring the story to fulfilment.

> 'Still thou art blest, compar'd wi' me!
> The present only toucheth thee:

But, och! I backward cast my ee
On prospects drear,
An' forward tho' I canna see,
I guess, an' fear.'

SO WROTE Burns, contrasting himself with a mouse, whose carefully built nest had been ruthlessly destroyed by the plough-
share. The Old Testament outlook is exactly the opposite. It casts
its eye backwards, not 'on prospects drear', but on 'the mighty acts
of God', and it faces the future with an unshakable conviction. As
God had acted, so one day He will act, finally and decisively. This is
no mere flight into fantasy. It is neither dope, injected into exploited
men to keep them content with their miserable lot, nor is it irresponsible optimism based on the belief that man is getting better and
better as age succeeds age, and that in the end, with the help of a
dash of enlightenment, all will be well. The Old Testament outlook
upon the future springs from the tension between what faith rooted
in past events knows to be true, and what is, in fact, true in the
present. God has acted, yet the world refuses to live in the light of
His activity. The people of God, called to an exclusive loyalty,
dither from one betrayal to the next; called to a moral obedience, are
riddled with corruption and social injustice; called to a world
mission, develop an 'iron curtain' mentality, keeping the world at
arm's length. Does this mean that God's purposes must be for ever
frustrated? No, God will act.

Psalm cxxvi was one of the songs sung by pilgrims as they made
their way to Jerusalem. Nowhere does faith more joyfully look
back, in this case to God's mighty act in delivering His people
from exile in Babylon, and nowhere does faith more confidently call
upon God to act again.

'When the LORD restored the fortunes of Zion,
we were like those who dream.
Then our mouth was filled with laughter,
and our tongue with shouts of joy;
then they said among the nations,
"The LORD has done great things for them!

The LORD had done great things for us;
we are glad.
Restore our fortunes, O LORD,
like the water-courses in the Negeb!
May those who sow in tears
reap with shouts of joy!
He that goes forth weeping,
bearing the seed for sowing,
shall come home with shouts of joy,
bringing his sheaves with him.'

(Ps. cxxvi)

'The LORD *had done* great things for us. . . . *Restore* our fortunes, O LORD.' The memory of the past is the hope of the future. There is in the Old Testament an eager 'forward' look rooted in past certainties, fixing its eye ultimately upon the time when

'. . . The earth will be filled
with the knowledge of the glory of the LORD
as the waters cover the sea.'

(Hab. ii. 14; cf. Isa. xi. 9)

This 'forward look' expresses itself in an embarrassingly rich variety of ways. The details of the future hope vary from writer to writer, and from age to age. Certain themes, however, predominate.

I

The Day of the LORD. As we have seen,[1] the people of Israel and the prophet Amos had a lively, if somewhat different, sense of a coming 'Day of the LORD'. 'The day of the LORD', 'The day', 'That day', 'days are coming', 'the latter days', such phrases occur frequently in the prophetic books of the Old Testament, and always

[1] pp. 121 ff.

the reference is not merely to a future day in the calendar, but to a 'day' often regarded as imminent when God will act decisively on the stage of human history. Inevitably for the people of God, far from being responsibly the people of God, this day brings judgement.

> '. . . on that day, says the LORD God,
> I will make the sun go down at noon,
> and darken the earth in broad daylight.
> I will turn your feasts into mourning,
> and all your songs into lamentation;
> I will bring sackcloth upon all loins,
> and baldness on every head;
> I will make it like the mourning for an only son,
> and the end of it like a bitter day.'
>
> (Amos viii. 9–10)

For the pampered rich, callously indifferent to the LORD's demand for social brotherhood, it is a day of reckoning.

'In that day the LORD will take away the finery of the anklets, the headbands and the crescents; the pendants, the bracelets and the scarfs; the headdresses, the armlets, the sashes, the perfume boxes and the amulets; the signet rings and nose rings; the festal robes, the mantles, the cloaks and the handbags; the garments of gauze, the linen garments, the turbans and the veils.

> Instead of perfume there will be rottenness;
> and instead of a girdle, a rope;
> and instead of well-set hair, baldness;
> and instead of a rich robe, a girding of sackcloth;
> instead of beauty, shame.'
>
> (Isa. iii. 18–24; cf. Amos iv. 1–3)

As for the priests who ought steadfastly to have instructed the people in the LORD's ways, and the prophets who ought to have troubled the nation's conscience:

'from prophet to priest,
every one deals falsely.
They have healed the wound of my people lightly,
saying "Peace, peace"
when there is no peace.
Were they ashamed when they committed abomination?
No they were not at all ashamed;
they did not know how to blush.
Therefore they shall fall among those who fall;
at the time that I punish them,
they shall be overthrown, says the LORD.'

(Jer. vi. 13–15)

But the day of reckoning is not confined to the people of God.
The Book of Amos opens with all the surrounding nations being
summoned one by one, to the bar of the LORD's judgement—
Syrians, Philistines, Phoenicians, Edomites, Ammonites, Moabites,
called to account for brutal atrocities in wartime, for ruthless violation of treaties, for savage treatment of non-combatants, for deeds of
impiety (Amos i. 3–ii. 3). It reads like a catalogue of war crimes of
the nations of the twentieth century. For such deeds, says the
LORD, 'I will not revoke the punishment' (i. 3 ff.—literally 'I will
not turn it back', a sentence ominous in its very vagueness). Similarly, Isaiah depicts the day of the LORD as a day when all human
pretension and pride will be humbled.

'For the LORD of hosts has a day
against all that is proud and lofty,
against all that is lifted up and high;
against all the cedars of Lebanon,
lofty and lifted up;
and against all the oaks of Bashan;
against all the high mountains,
and against all the lofty hills;
against every high tower,
and against every fortified wall;
against all the ships of Tarshish;

and against all the beautiful craft.
And the haughtiness of man shall be humbled,
and the pride of men shall be brought low;
and the LORD alone will be exalted in that day.'

(Isa. ii. 12–17)

It will be a day, furthermore, when the false religions which have misled men will be utterly destroyed.

'In that day men will cast forth
their idols of silver and their idols of gold,
which they made for themselves to worship,
to the moles and to the bats,
to enter the caverns of the rocks
and the clefts of the cliffs,
from before the terror of the LORD
and from the glory of his majesty,
when he rises to terrify the earth.'

(Isa. ii. 20–21)

In dark and sombre terms of foreboding, Zephaniah depicts the impending day of the LORD as a day of judgement upon all the peoples of the earth.

'The great day of the LORD is near,
near and hastening fast;
the sound of the day of the LORD is bitter,
the mighty man cries aloud there.
A day of wrath is that day,
a day of distress and anguish,
a day of ruin and devastation,
a day of darkness and gloom,
a day of clouds and thick darkness,
a day of trumpet blast and battle cry
against the fortified cities
and against the lofty battlements.
I will bring distress on men,

so that they shall walk like the blind,
because they have sinned against the LORD
their blood shall be poured out like dust,
and their flesh like dung.
Neither their silver nor their gold
shall be able to deliver them
on the day of the wrath of the LORD.
In the fire of his jealous wrath
all the earth shall be consumed;
for a full, yea sudden end
he will make of all the inhabitants of the earth.'
(Zeph. i. 14–18; cf. Obad. i. 15)

God's purpose in judgement is not, however, destructive, but liberating. The people of God must pass through the fire of affliction so that, purified and penitent, they may emerge to serve God's purposes. The self-centred pride and delusive religion of men must be destroyed to open the way for a humble, self-forgetting adoration of the true God. The author of Isaiah xl-lv., who never tires of proclaiming the new restoration that God is about to accomplish for His people, prefaces His message of hope with the assurance that judgement has taken place, that the nation has paid the penalty of its folly.

'Comfort, comfort my people,
says your God.
Speak tenderly to Jerusalem,
and cry to her
that her warfare is ended,
that her iniquity is pardoned,
that she has received from the LORD's hand
double for all her sins.'

(Isa. xl. 1–2)

Across the threshold of judgement the people pass into God's new world. Many and varied are the pictures of this glorious, God-given future. A prominent feature is the thought of the people of God reconstituted on the other side of disaster. The entry of the people of Israel into Canaan had been marred by the tragic story of Achan, whose greed led him and his family to disaster and brought trouble upon the people. Joshua vii. concludes its narrative of the punishment meted out to Achan by saying, 'Therefore to this day the name of that place is called, the Valley of Achor.' The Valley of Achor [i.e. trouble] seems to have become a byword for tragedy. The prophet Hosea, certain of inexorable judgement upon his people, but convinced that in the last analysis, such judgement is within the purpose of God's 'steadfast love', looks beyond disaster to a new beginning for the people. Back to the desert they shall go, but this time, there shall be no tragedy.

> 'Therefore I will allure her [i.e. Israel]
> and bring her into the wilderness,
> and speak tenderly to her.
> And there I will give her her vineyards,
> and make the valley of Achor a door of hope.
> And there she shall answer as in the days of her youth,
> as at the time when she came out of the land of Egypt.'
> (Hos. ii. 14–15)

An interesting incident in the career of Jeremiah stresses the same hope. The last hour has come for the Kingdom of Judah. The Babylonians are besieging the city. On all sides there is panic and gloomy foreboding. Jeremiah himself is in prison, accused of high treason. His cousin Hanamel comes to request him to exercise his duty as kinsman, to purchase a piece of property which is in danger of passing out of the hands of the family. It is not exactly the moment for sound business deals, particularly in land, but Jeremiah solemnly completes the deed of purchase and says:

'Thus says the LORD of hosts, the God of Israel: Take these deeds, both this sealed deed of purchase and this open deed, and put them in an earthenware vessel that they may last a long time. For thus says the LORD of hosts, the God of Israel: Houses and fields and vineyards shall again be bought in this land' (Jer. xxxii. 14–15).

In the darkest hour of his nation's life, the prophet, who had insistently proclaimed that the LORD's purposes demanded the destruction of the nation, looks soberly beyond destruction to the beginning of a new life.

Chapters xxx–xxxi of the Book of Jeremiah, which stand out sharply from the surrounding chapters, have often been described as 'A Book of Comfort' or 'A Book of Hope'. The material in these chapters is varied; its dating has been much disputed.[1] Some of it may not come from Jeremiah, but date and authorship are comparatively unimportant, inasmuch as the various sections in this Book of Comfort stress certain familiar features of the Old Testament hope for the future. The opening verses of chapter xxx state the theme:

'Behold, days are coming, says the LORD, when I will restore the fortunes of my people, Israel and Judah, says the LORD, and I will bring them back to the land which I gave to their fathers, and they shall take possession of it' (xxx. 3; cf. xxx. 10; xxxi. 10 ff.; xxxi. 17). Notice how essentially historical is this restoration. Against the background of the people scattered in exile, the hope is for a return to the land of their fathers. It is characteristic of the Old Testament, with its repeated emphasis on the God Who acts in history, that its hope for the future is no flight from the world, but a restoration of the fortunes of God's people in the world. Later and more perplexing times tended to transfer the hope out of this world into a heavenly sphere, or to demand an utterly 'new heaven and new earth' as the scene for God's triumphs.

A future for God's people is certain because of how God has acted in the past. 'At that time, says the LORD, I will be the God of all the families of Israel, and they shall be my people.

> Thus says the LORD:
> The people who survived the sword
> found grace in the wilderness;
> when Israel sought for rest,
> the LORD appeared to him from afar.
> I have loved you with an everlasting love;
> therefore I have continued my faithfulness to you.

[1] Cf. Interpreter's Bible, Vol. 5, pp. 1022 ff.

> Again I will build you and you shall be built,
> O virgin Israel!
> Again you shall adorn yourself with timbrels,
> and shall go forth in the dance of the merrymakers.
> Again you shall plant vineyards
> upon the mountains of Samaria;
> the planters shall plant
> and shall enjoy the fruit.
> For there shall be a day when watchmen will call
> in the hill country of Ephraim:
> "Arise, and let us go up to Zion,
> to the LORD our God".'
>
> (Jer. xxxi. 1–6)

The covenant relationship between God and His people will be renewed. God's past faithfulness is the assurance of an ever greater and more joyful future, when the people will once again answer the summons to worship the LORD in His temple in Jerusalem (cf. xxxi. 10–14; 23–24).

Destruction and ultimate restoration—these two facets of the 'Day of the LORD' are linked together in certain strands of the Old Testament by the thought of the *REMNANT*. It was early recognized that the people of God, as a whole, failed lamentably. But always there was the faithful minority, the 'true Israel' within Israel. In a mood of frustration and despair, the prophet Elijah complained, 'the people of Israel have forsaken thy covenant, thrown down thy altars and slain thy prophets with the sword; and I, even I only, am left; and they seek my life, to take it away' (1 Kings xix. 14). He was unduly pessimistic. There were seven thousand within Israel who had kept their loyalty to the LORD (1 Kings xix. 18). The very fact that the teaching of the prophets has come down to us across the centuries is proof that their words struck a responsive chord in some hearts. Even in the darkest days a minority kept the faith. In the thought of the prophet Isaiah, this minority, the Remnant, becomes supremely important.

Hebrew parents were accustomed to give their children meaningful names. Thus Hosea inflicted upon an unsuspecting child a name recalling a dark deed of shame in his people's past; and upon other two, the names 'Not pitied' and 'Not my people', indicating the LORD's terrible judgement upon His people. Isaiah called one of his children Shear-yashub, i.e. 'a remnant will return'. When disaster overtakes the deep-seated corruption of the nation, there is to come a minority of faithful people who will return to the LORD in true repentance.

'In that day the remnant of Israel and the survivors of the house of Jacob will no more lean upon him that smote them, but will lean upon the LORD, the Holy One of Israel, in truth. A remnant will return, the remnant of Jacob, to the mighty God' (Isa. x. 20–21).

When the nation totters to destruction, the remnant will survive to become the nucleus out of which God will create a new people.

'And the surviving remnant of the house of Judah shall again take root downward, and bear fruit upward; for out of Jerusalem shall go forth a remnant, and out of Mount Zion a band of survivors. The zeal of the LORD of hosts will accomplish this' (Isa. xxxvii. 31–32 = 2 Kings xix. 30–31).

High hopes seem to have been entertained that such a remnant, holy, faithful to the LORD, would emerge from among those who returned from exile in Babylon to rebuild Jerusalem (cf. Ezra ix. 8; 15). But it was not to be.

II

The stress upon a faithful remnant reminds us that, though the Old Testament hope for the future is firmly based on what has happened in the past, it can never mean simply 'putting the clock back'. There was no point in going back to the beginning, only to repeat the same round of dubious loyalty and uncertain obedience. That would be to invite renewed disaster. God will act, and His act will mark a decisive change for His people and for the world. Into the uncertain mists of the future, the Old Testament at this point sends three shafts of light. There will be a *Coming Ruler*, a *New Covenant*, a *New Age*.

A

The Coming Ruler. For a time after their settlement in Canaan, the scattered Hebrew tribes were content to rely upon each crisis in their fortunes to bring to the fore a natural leader. Once the crisis was over, the leader returned to his normal life. Pressure of external events, and doubtless the example of their neighbours, led them to see advantages in a stable, permanent kingship. Kingship was a far more important institution to the ancient world than it is even to the most royalist-minded amongst us. In Egypt, the ruling monarch was the god incarnate; in Sumeria, he was the indispensible link between God and people. Upon the king and upon the part he played in the yearly religious ritual, the total well-being of the community depended. There has been considerable discussion in recent years[1] as to the extent to which Israelite kingship shared in the typical oriental pattern. Certainly the king in Israel was regarded as divinely appointed. He was the LORD's 'anointed' (cf. Ps. ii, 2; 1 Kings i. 34). He was regarded as being endowed to an especial degree with 'the spirit of the LORD' (cf. 1 Sam. x. 6); his person was regarded as sacrosanct (cf. 1 Sam. xxvi. 9); he had certain priestly privileges and functions (cf. 1 Kings iii. 15). There is, however, no evidence that the king in Israel was ever identified with the LORD, or even accorded divine honours. Fulsome eulogy abounds, but the old idea of tribal chieftainship where the chief is but a first among equals, and a religion which enthroned the LORD and the LORD alone, kept the Israelite monarch with his feet firmly on the ground.

Great things, none the less, were expected from the king as may be seen in the Royal Psalms. The king was expected to embody in his own person, and to guarantee to his people, the true Israelite ideal of righteousness, ruling in accordance with the 'justice' of the LORD, and in the light of Israelite custom.

> 'Give the king thy justice, O God,
> and thy righteousness to the royal son!

[1] Cf. S. Mowinckel, *He that Cometh* (E.T. by G. W. Anderson), chapter 3.

May he judge thy people with righteousness,
and thy poor with justice!'

(Ps. lxxii. 1–2)

'May he defend the cause of the poor of the people,
give deliverance to the needy,
and crush the oppressor!'

(verse 4)

The true king

'. . . delivers the needy when he calls,
the poor and him who has no helper.
He has pity on the weak and the needy,
and saves the lives of the needy.
From oppression and violence he redeems their life;
and precious is their blood in his sight.'

(verses 12–14)

Through him the community expected protection from, and indeed
triumph over, all their foes:

'May he have dominion from sea to sea,
and from the River to the ends of the earth!
May his foes bow down before him,
and his enemies lick the dust
May the kings of Tarshish and of the Isles
render him tribute,
may the kings of Sheba and Seba bring gifts!
May all kings fall down before him,
all nations serve him!'

(verses 8–11)

Upon him depends the entire good fortune of the community in-
cluding abundant harvests and material well-being.

'May he be like rain that falls on the mown grass,
like showers that water the earth!'

(verse 6)

K

'May there be abundance of grain in the land;
on the tops of the mountains may it wave;
may its fruit be like Lebanon;
and may men blossom forth from the cities
like the grass of the field!'

(verse 16)

All that the Old Testament means by 'shalom', 'peace', is linked with the reigning monarch. 'Shalom' means far more than absence of strife or warfare. It indicates a condition in which the community, freed from all oppressing limitations, physical as well as spiritual, will achieve its maximum fulness and richness of life. Upon a king ruling in righteousness did such 'shalom' depend.

'In his days may righteousness flourish,
and peace abound till the moon be no more!'

(verse 7)

Great expectations—but the reality tended to be far other. King after king failed to live up to the eager hopes which greeted his coronation, and were kept alive in the liturgy of the Temple. Only David, shrewd in statesmanship, gracious and generous, though by no means perfect in character, was considered to come anywhere near the ideal. Since in the person of king, so much was at stake for the community, the conviction grew that one day the LORD would send a king after His own heart.

When a coalition of northern states attempted to coerce King Ahaz of Judah into joining an anti-Assyrian front, he panicked. Instead of heeding the words of the prophet Isaiah to put his trust in the LORD, he made overtures for Assyrian help. If you find it difficult to have faith in the LORD in such a situation, said Isaiah to the king, ask for any sign you like and the LORD will grant it. But Ahaz would have none of it. Cloaking his lack of faith with pious cant, he said, 'I will not ask, and I will not put the LORD to the test' (Isa. vii. 12).

But even the disobedience of the king cannot thwart God's purposes.

'Therefore the LORD himself will give you a sign. Behold, a

young woman[1] shall conceive and bear a son, and shall call his name Immanuel' (vii. 14).

The identity of the young woman and the child have been vigorously discussed. The young woman *may* be Ahaz' wife, the queen; in which case the child will be the heir to the throne. The question of identity, however, is of minor importance compared with the significance of the name to be given to the child. Immanuel, i.e. 'God with us'. Within a few short years, 'before the child knows how to refuse the evil and choose the good, the land before whose two kings you are in dread will be deserted' (verse 16). The two kings referred to are the leaders of the northern coalition. Ahaz has refused to trust, but he will soon have reason to know that such a trust would have been justifiable. The promise in the name 'Immanuel' will come true. The people will be able to say, as they watch their enemies scattered, 'God is with us'. The northern coalition will be shattered, but Ahaz, having played with fire, will be severely burned. 'The LORD will bring upon you and upon your people and upon your father's house such days as have not come since the days that Ephraim departed from Judah[2]—the king of Assyria' (verse 17). 'The king of Assyria' may be an addition to the text in the light of later events, but the threat is there, and the Assyrians in whom Ahaz fondly trusted were to execute it.

This incident stresses the shortcomings, the lack of faith of the reigning monarch. Two other oracles of Isaiah focus our attention upon the character and qualities of the true king that is to be. Both may have been sung at the coronation or the anointing of a new king, but both witness to expectations which no human king could bring to fulfilment. Joy and freedom from oppression are to be the lot of the people.

> 'For to us a child is born,
> to us a son is given;
> and the government will be upon his shoulder,
> and his name will be called
> Wonderful Counselor, Mighty God,
> Everlasting Father, Prince of Peace.

[1] Not 'Virgin'. The original simply indicates a young woman of marriageable age.
[2] I.e. the tragic days of the break up of the Old United Kingdom.

Of the increase of his government and of peace
there will be no end
upon the throne of David, and over his kingdom,
to establish it and to uphold it
with justice and with righteousness
from this time forth and for evermore.
The zeal of the LORD of hosts will do this.'

(Isa. ix. 6–7)

'There shall come forth a shoot from the stump of
  Jesse,
and a branch shall grow out of his roots.
And the Spirit of the LORD shall rest upon him,
the spirit of wisdom and understanding,
the spirit of counsel and might,
the spirit of knowledge and the fear of the LORD.
... He shall not judge by what his eyes see,
or decide by what his ears hear;
but with righteousness he shall judge the poor,
and decide with equity for the meek of the earth;
and he shall smite the earth with the rod of his mouth,
and with the breath of his lips he shall slay the wicked.
Righteousness shall be the girdle of his waist,
and faithfulness the girdle of his loins.'

(Isa. xi. 1–5)

In such portraits of this ideal king, there are certain recurring features.

(*i*) This 'Ruler' will be a legitimate member of the royal house which traces its descent from David. He is to be 'a shoot from the stump of Jesse' (David's father); he will sit 'upon the throne of David'. In Micah v. 2, Bethlehem, the home of David, is spotlighted as the home town of the coming Ruler.

David had been for his people the epitome of real Kingship. The coming Ruler must be true to this type of kingship. In 2 Samuel vii, when the prophet Nathan comes to tell David that he is not the man God has chosen to build the Temple at Jerusalem, the blow is softened by a promise. 'Your house and your kingdom shall be made sure for ever before me; your throne shall be established for ever' (vii. 16). This promise is to find its fulfilment.

(*ii*) The coming Ruler will be endowed with the Spirit of the LORD.[1] No king could truly reign unless the Spirit of the LORD rested upon him. In the 'last words of David', recorded in 2 Samuel xxiii. 2–4, we read:

> 'The Spirit of the LORD speaks by me,
> his word is upon my tongue.
> The God of Israel has spoken,
> the Rock of Israel has said to me:
> When one rules justly over men
> ruling in the fear of God,
> he dawns on them like the morning light,
> like the sun shining forth upon a cloudless morning,
> like rain that makes grass to sprout from the earth.'

Only as the Spirit of the LORD worked through the king could he rule justly, and thus bring blessing upon his people.

The Spirit of the LORD is in the Old Testament, the source of all supra-normal gifts or activity. The strength of Samson (Judges xiv. 19); the outstanding skill of the craftsman (Exod. xxxi. 3); the weird, excited behaviour of the groups of prophets (1 Sam. x. 10 ff.). What other than a plentiful endowment of this same Spirit of the LORD could enable this Coming Ruler to live up to the names he is given, 'Wonderful Counselor', truly guiding the affairs of his people; 'Mighty God', that is to say, divine in might; 'Everlasting Father' (literally Father of years) unchanging in his care for the community; 'Prince of Peace', one whose rule will be marked by true fulness of life for his people.

(*iii*) There is an unwearied insistence upon 'justice' and 'righteousness' as the twin essentials in the reign of this coming King; that typical Old Testament justice and righteousness, which reveals itself in its especial concern for the rights of the 'poor' and the 'meek', and in its detestation of wickedness and tyranny. Might and

[1] Cf. p. 25.

power are never enough in themselves. They must be harnessed to that true ordering of society which God wills. What the people knew to be true of the LORD, what they looked for, often in vain, from the ruling monarch, they expected to find in the Ruler to come.

If the hope of a Coming Ruler was born in the tension between the ideal of kingship and the far from ideal men who sat upon the throne, it was fostered by the collapse of the national life in the Babylonian conquest of 586 B.C. and the virtual disappearance thereafter of the Jews as an independent nation with their own native dynasty. The darker the times, the more eager the expectation of the people becomes that one day the LORD 'will set up over them one shepherd, my servant David, and he shall feed them; he shall feed them and be their shepherd. And I, the LORD, will be their God, and my servant David shall be prince among them; I the LORD have spoken' (Ezek. xxxiv. 23–24).

This is the 'Messianic hope' of the Old Testament—that, one day, God will send to His people an earthly ruler who, fulfilling the true ideal of kingship, will inaugurate a new era of peace and prosperity. Our word 'Messiah' is simply the Hebrew word 'anointed', 'the LORD's anointed' the King.

B

A New Covenant. '. . . In those days, says the LORD, they shall no more say, "The ark of the covenant of the LORD." It shall not come to mind, or be remembered or missed; it shall not be made again' (Jer. iii. 16). The 'ark of the covenant'.[1] had been the visible sign of the presence of the LORD with His people. After a somewhat chequered history, the ark finally disappeared; when, it is difficult to say. But no matter, says this passage, it need not be missed. Something greater is coming than the covenant based on the Exodus from Egypt, and the gathering at Mount Sinai. For all to be well with the people of God, something more than a future ideal king was needed. Had not the people themselves proved disloyal to their obligations even before kingship was known among them? The

[1] Cf. pp. 63 f.

bitter experience of a lifetime taught the prophet Jeremiah what this 'more' was.

As a young man, Jeremiah witnessed a national religious reformation, backed by the full authority of the church and state. When repairs were being undertaken to the Temple in Jerusalem, there was found a copy of a 'book of the law' which troubled the conscience of the people. One memorable day, to the people assembled in the Temple, King Josiah 'read in their hearing all the words of the book of the covenant which had been found in the house of the LORD. And the king stood by the pillar and made a covenant before the LORD, to walk after the LORD and to keep his commandments and his testimonies and his statutes, with all his heart and all his soul, to perform the words of this covenant that were written in this book; and all the people joined in the covenant' (2 Kings xxiii. 2*b*–3).

At first Jeremiah may have given the reformation his support, but he was to be sadly disillusioned. As old abuses were eliminated, new and even more dangerous ones crept in to take their place. There seemed to be a strange perversity in the heart of the people.

> 'The heart is deceitful above all things,
> and desperately corrupt;
> who can understand it?'
>
> (Jer. xvii. 9)

And the heart, for the Old Testament, is the centre not of the emotion, but of the will. Time and again Jeremiah returns to 'the stubborn evil will' rife among his people (e.g. xvi. 12; xxiii. 17). It looked as if the people were incapable of responding fully to the LORD. The old covenant failed, not because God had been found wanting, but because the people had utterly failed to fulfil their obligations. Yet even the mulish obstinacy of the people could not, in the end, veto God's purposes.

'Behold the days are coming, says the LORD, when I will make a new covenant with the house of Israel and the house of Judah, not like the covenant which I made with their fathers when I took them by the hand to bring them out of the land of Egypt, my covenant which they broke, though I was their husband, says the

LORD. But this is the covenant which I will make with the house of Israel after those days, says the LORD: I will put my law within them and I will write it upon their hearts; and I will be their God and they shall be my people. And no longer shall each man teach his neighbour, and each his brother saying, "Know the LORD", for they shall all know me from the least of them to the greatest, says the LORD; for I will forgive their iniquity, and I will remember their sin no more' (Jer. xxxi. 31–34).

There is to be a *new covenant*. Once again the initiative is God's. Instead of confronting His people with a series of moral demands, 'You shall', and 'You shall not'; demands hurled at them, as it were, from without, his 'teaching' (law) will be within them, written not on stone tablets, as were the original Ten Words, but on their hearts. The gulf between what God demands and what the people can give is to be bridged—*by God*. Only thus could there be true fellowship between God and His people, a fellowship rooted in that intimacy implicit in 'knowing the LORD'. Jeremiah was by no means the only Old Testament prophet to realize the need for a radical renewal of the people as the basis for a future of promise. When the fortunes of His people were at a low ebb, Ezekiel looked for a day of restoration and even greater glory for the people of God. But first there is an essential condition to be fulfilled by God. 'A new heart I will give you, and a new spirit I will put within you; and I will take out of your flesh the heart of stone and give you a heart of flesh. And I will put my spirit within you, and cause you to walk in my statutes and be careful to observe my ordinances' (Ezek. xxxvi. 26–27; cf. xi. 19; xviii. 31). Instead of stony hardness, there is to be a people impressionable, responsive, directed by the spirit of the LORD.

Sad experience of the people's obstinacy did not lead the Old Testament prophets to despair. Their hope is firmly founded on God. If one path proved to be a dead end, God would open up another. There is to be a 'new covenant' in terms of which, the fatal perversity of the people being a thing of the past, it may truly be said, 'I will be their God and they shall be my people.'

C

A New Age. We cheated in our quotation of the passage about the Coming Ruler in Isaiah xi, cheated to the extent of stopping short in the middle of the vision. After depicting the ideal, coming King of the lineage of David, ruling in justice and righteousness, the passage continues:

> 'The wolf shall dwell with the lamb,
> and the leopard shall lie down with the kid,
> and the calf and the lion and the fatling together,
> and a little child shall lead them.
> The cow and the bear shall feed;
> their young shall lie down together;
> and the lion shall eat straw like the ox.
> The sucking child shall play over the hole of the asp,
> and the weaned child shall put his hand on the adder's
>   den.
> They shall not hurt or destroy
> in all my holy mountain:
> for the earth shall be full of the knowledge of the LORD
> as the waters cover the sea.'
>
> (Isa. xi. 6–9)

Nature no longer 'red in tooth and claw', a babe at the breast fearlessly fondling venomous snakes, true harmony in the world of nature as well as in the world of men—this is part of the Old Testament hope for the future.

The 'world of nature' and the 'world of men'—the fact that we speak thus of two sharply separated worlds shows how far we are from the outlook of the Bible. The Old Testament has no word for 'Nature'. It never regards the world around us as an impersonal system working according to its own unalterable laws.[1] Both 'Nature' and 'Man' are part of God's creating, wholly dependent upon, and pliable in, the hands of God, and linked to one another.

[1] Cf. H. W. Robinson, *Inspiration and Revelation in the O.T.*, pp. 1–33.

Linked to one another? In the myth of the Garden of Eden in Genesis iii the upshot of the self-centred rebellion against God of Everyman and Everywoman is that a curse falls upon the tempting serpent. There is to be henceforth

> '. . . enmity between you and the woman,
> and between your seed and her seed;
> he shall bruise your head,
> and you shall bruise his heel.'
>
> (Gen. iii. 15)

Not only so, but Adam is informed

> 'cursed is the ground because of you;
> in toil you shall eat of it all the days of your life;
> thorns and thistles it shall bring forth to you;
> and you shall eat the plants of the field.'
>
> (Gen. iii. 17b–18)

Because man is at sixes and sevens, so is the world in which he lives. That is why Jeremiah, appalled by the callousness and perversity of the society in which he lived, can say:

> 'I looked on the earth, and lo, it was waste and void;
> and to the heavens, and they had no light.
> I looked on the mountains and lo they were quaking,
> and all the hills moved to and fro.
> I looked, and lo, there was no man,
> and all the birds of the air had fled.
> I looked, and lo, the fruitful land was a desert,
> and all its cities were laid in ruins
> before the LORD, before his fierce anger.'
>
> (Jer. iv. 23–26)

This is no flight of poetic fancy. It is wholly realistic to the mind of the Old Testament. The chaos in human society is reflected by chaos in the 'natural' world. In Deuteronomy xxviii, we find among the penalties for disobedience to the commandments of the LORD, '... cursed shall you be in the field. Cursed shall be your basket and your kneading trough. Cursed shall be the fruit of your body, and the fruit of your ground, the increase of your cattle and the young of your flock' (verses 16*b*–18).

'You shall carry much seed into the field and shall gather little in; for the locust shall consume it. You shall plant vineyards and dress them, but you shall neither drink of the wine nor gather the grapes; for the worm shall eat them. You shall have olive trees throughout all your territory, but you shall not anoint yourself with the oil; for your olives shall drop off' (verses 38–40).

Perhaps we who today anxiously ponder the possible consequences of testing nuclear weapons may be able to give a more sympathetic understanding to this outlook than was possible in a past age.

The opposite also holds good. When the day comes on which the people give a whole-hearted obedience to the LORD, then all will be well, even in the natural world. A new harmony will bind together the whole of creation. There will be universal peace. Men shall

> 'beat their swords into ploughshares,
> and their spears into pruning hooks;
> nation shall not lift up sword against nation,
> neither shall they learn war any more.'
>
> (Mic. iv. 3; Isa. ii. 4)

The Spirit of the LORD hitherto seen at work in the chosen few, the mighty, the skilful, the king and the prophet, will be the common possession of all.

> 'And it shall come to pass afterward,
> that I will pour out my spirit on all flesh;
> your sons and your daughters shall prophesy,
> your old men shall dream dreams,
> and your young men shall see visions.

> Even upon the menservants and maidservants
> in those days, I will pour out my spirit.'
>
> (Joel ii. 28–29)

And they will live in a world of abundance and paradisal fertility.

> 'Behold the days are coming, says the LORD,
> when the ploughman shall overtake the reaper
> and the treader of grapes him who sows the seed;
> the mountains shall drip sweet wine,
> and all the hills shall flow with it.'
>
> (Amos ix. 13)

In this day, water will freely flow in the treacherous water courses which the heat of summer normally turns into dry beds of sand (cf. Joel iii. 18). What more could the desert tribesman desire?

So God will act.

The story of the Old Testament is thus an unfinished story. It leaves us with a future hope. It is the startling claim of the New Testament that God *has* so acted, the long expected Ruler has come, the New Covenant is in being, the New Age has dawned.

PART TWO

The New Testament

7

God Was in Christ

The books of the New Testament are the product of a missionary movement, witnessing to Jesus of Nazareth. The early Christians claimed that all that happened in the life, death and resurrection of Jesus was 'in accordance with the scriptures'. They not only understood the life of Jesus in the light of the Old Testament, they saw in Jesus the key to all God's purposes outlined in the Old Testament. The form of their argument may be unconvincing, but the truth asserted remains.

(a) To the Jews, Christians claimed that in Jesus the long-expected Ruler had come. To the fact that, contrary to all Jewish thinking about the Coming Ruler, Jesus had died a shameful death on a cross, they replied:

(1) That Jesus was the 'Servant of the Lord',

(2) That His death had been dramatically reversed by His Ressurection to the place of supreme authority at God's right hand. 'Jesus is Lord' is one of the key notes of early Christian preaching.

(b) To non-Jews, Jesus is reinterpreted in terms of their own thought.

(1) He is the answer to man's age-long religious quest (cf. Acts xvii. 16 ff.).

(2) To the intelligent cosmopolitan He is the 'Word' made flesh.

We must face the issue posed by these astonishing claims.

IT IS the summer of A.D. 30. A new religious sect figures prominently in current 'talk of the town' in Jerusalem. The authorities, well aware that in this turbulent Roman province religious enthusiasm often goes hand in hand with political subversion, are keeping a watchful eye on events. The orthodox Jew is puzzled. On the one hand the behaviour of adherents of the new sect is highly commendable. They worship daily in the temple; they can hardly be faulted for their observance of the Jewish Law. On the other hand, they make outrageous claims about a certain Jesus of Nazareth, something of a seven days' wonder who had died, crucified by the Romans not many weeks previously. Rumour has it that, following a regrettable outburst of mass religious hysteria at the Feast of Pentecost (cf. Acts ii.), the new movement is making headway. As two of the leading lights in the new sect enter the temple courtyard a lame beggar asks for alms. 'And Peter directed his gaze at him, with John, and said, "Look at us". And he fixed his attention upon them, expecting to receive something from them. But Peter said, "I have no silver and gold, but I give you what I have; in the name of Jesus Christ of Nazareth, walk". And he took him by the right hand and raised him up; and immediately his feet and ankles were made strong' (Acts iii. 4–7).

A curious, excited crowd gathers. A word of explanation is obviously demanded. Peter gives it.

'Men of Israel, why do you wonder at this, or why do you stare at us, as though by our own power or piety we had made him walk? The God of Abraham and of Isaac and of Jacob, the God of our fathers, glorified His servant Jesus, whom you delivered up and denied in the presence of Pilate, when he had decided to release him. But you denied the Holy and Righteous One, and asked for a murderer to be granted to you, and killed the Author of life, whom God raised from the dead. To this we are witnesses. And His name, by faith in His name, has made this man strong whom you see and know; and the faith which is through Jesus has given the man this perfect health in the presence of you all' (Acts iii. 12–16). Jesus of Nazareth, according to Peter, is God's 'Servant', 'the Holy and Righteous One', 'the Author of life'. He died—everyone knew that —but, claims Peter, He has been raised by God from the dead. His 'name' now possesses power. This is dangerous, if not blasphemous talk about one who had been a village carpenter. The authorities act swiftly. Peter and John are interrogated after a night in the cells, and offered a conditional release. The authorities 'charged them not to speak or teach at all in the name of Jesus. But Peter and John answered them, "Whether it is right in the sight of God to listen to you rather than to God, you must judge; for we cannot but speak of what we have seen and heard" ' (Acts iv. 18–20).

This incident may serve as a convenient introduction to the New Testament. In the first place, it reminds us that our New Testament is the product of a missionary movement whose early stages we see here in Jerusalem. It is no haphazard collection of writings from the past, nor is it the reflections of a few men of religious genius. No less than twenty-one of its twenty-seven books are letters written by missionaries to their converts and friends in the faith. Of the others, one (Acts) might well have been commissioned by a Missionary Society, since it describes how, from insignificant beginnings in a second-rate province of the Roman Empire, this missionary faith comes to be firmly established in many parts of the Roman world, and indeed in Rome itself. Another (Revelation) is written to sustain the adherents of this faith in grim days of persecution. There remain the 'Four Gospels'. Contrary to first impressions, they are not well described as potted biographies of Jesus. In some respects they are the biographers' despair. The earliest of them, Mark, is introduced by the words, 'The beginning of the gospel (i.e. good news) of Jesus Christ, the Son of God' (Mark i. 1). The last of them, John, concludes by confessing that there is much more information about Jesus not in his book, 'but these are written that you may believe that Jesus is the Christ, the Son of God, and that believing, you may have life in his name' (John xx. 31).

We look in vain for the cold 'objectivity' of the uncommitted reporter. The Gospels are written by men of faith, to sustain the faith of an expanding missionary movement. This does not mean that the mists of religious bigotry and propaganda shroud for ever what once happened in Palestine. The Gospels select, the Gospels interpret; but as recent historical research has emphasized, so does every historical writing. May it not be that the life of Jesus *demands* the interpretation that the Gospels place upon it, and that no other interpretation is in the least adequate? Only a careful scrutiny of all the available evidence can help us to decide. The New Testament throughout is the product of a missionary faith.

L

But what is this missionary faith? Is it a new philosophy of life? Is it a new religion centred upon some key thought which, taught by a master mind, struck men with arresting freshness? No; listen— 'we cannot but speak of what we have seen and heard' (Acts iv. 20); 'we are witnesses' (Acts iii. 15) cries Peter. This is the authentic voice of all the New Testament writers. 'We are witnesses'; but witnesses to what? All point us not to 'ideas', but to a *man*, Jesus of Nazareth; not so much to His teaching, but to the man Himself, what happened in His life, death, and, so they assert, in His resurrection from the dead. The faith of the Old Testament is grounded in a series of events in which God was believed to be in action. The faith of the New Testament is likewise grounded in a series of events in which we are invited to see God in action, uniquely and decisively in action in Jesus of Nazareth. We shall approach the New Testament by looking at what the early Christian witnesses, preachers and writers, have to say about Jesus.

I

Jesus of Nazareth was a Jew. The first witnesses to Him were likewise Jews. The only Bible they knew was the Old Testament; and they were utterly convinced that what had happened in Jesus was a continuation of the story of the Old Testament. The examples of the early Christian preaching recorded in the Book of Acts are full of references to the Old Testament, tiresomely full we may be tempted to say. It was 'the God of Abraham, and of Isaac and of Jacob, the God of our fathers' (Acts iii. 13) who had now, according to Peter, acted in Jesus. When Paul (one of the greatest of the early missionaries), a Jew born in Tarsus, was invited to address his Jewish brethren in the synagogue at Antioch in Pisidia (now part of Asia Minor), he did not attempt to outline to them the characteristic features of the teaching of Jesus. He began with the Exodus, traced God's providential dealings with His people through their history and as the climax to this story claims that God has now 'brought to Israel a Savior, Jesus, as he promised' (Acts xiii. 23).

The claim is not simply that the New Testament continues the story of the Old; it does more than continue, it brings to fulfilment. In the eyes of the New Testament, the Old Testament is an unfinished book, unfinished not in the sense that it needed the addition of a few more pages, but unfinished in that it had been waiting for an ending which would gather together the different strands of its story, and show them in their true light. That ending was now known. Writing to the Christian community at Corinth in the midfifties of the first century of the Christian era, Paul reminds them of what he had preached to them, the traditional faith which he had received from others.

'For I delivered to you as of first importance what I also received that Christ died for our sins in *accordance with the scriptures*, that he was buried, that he was raised on the third day *in accordance with the scriptures*' (1 Cor. xv. 3–4). It had all happened 'in accordance with the scriptures' [i.e. the Old Testament], that was the considered verdict of the early Christian missionaries on all that they knew about Jesus of Nazareth. In the first Christian sermon recorded in Acts, we find Peter quoting Psalm xvi. 8–11 with its key phrase:

> 'Thou wilt not abandon my soul to Hades[1]
> nor let thy Holy One see corruption.'
>
> (Acts ii. 27)

—this in support of the Resurrection of Jesus.
Likewise Psalm cx. 1:

> 'The LORD says to my lord:
> "Sit at my right hand,
> till I make your enemies your footstool".'

by a somewhat tortuous argument is taken to substantiate the preacher's claim that Jesus now reigns in triumph (Acts ii. 34 ff.). Speech after speech in the Book of Acts features this same appeal to the Old Testament (cf. Acts iv. 25 ff.; viii. 26 ff.; xiii. 33–35, 41).

---

[1] Hades is the Greek equivalent of Hebrew Sheol, the shadowy abode of the departed.

The Gospels are equally instructive, particularly Matthew, which was written very much with a Jewish audience in mind. A glance at its opening chapters will suffice. Here is the story of the Virgin Birth of Jesus. 'All this took place to fulfil what the LORD had spoken by the prophet:

> "Behold a virgin shall conceive and bear a son,
> and his name shall be called Emmanuel".'
>
(Isa. vii. 14, quoted in Matt. i. 22–23)

Jesus was born in Bethlehem. Why? 'for so it is written by the prophet:

> "And you, O Bethlehem, in the land of Judah,
> are by no means least among the rulers of Judah;
> for from you shall come a ruler
> who will govern my people Israel".'
>
(Matt. ii. 5–6 quoting Mic. v. 2)

Mary, Joseph and the baby flee to Egypt to escape the anger of King Herod. Why Egypt? 'This was to fulfil what the Lord had spoken by the prophet "Out of Egypt have I called my son" ' (Matt. ii. 15 quoting Hos. xi. 1). So it continues throughout Matthew's Gospel.

This is all very perplexing to us, particularly when we approach such Old Testament passages with the tools provided for us by literary and historical criticism. Isaiah vii. 14 can hardly 'prove' the Virgin Birth since the word translated 'virgin' does not necessarily bear this meaning at all (cf. R.S.V. translation 'Behold a *young woman*'). Nor can Hosea xi. 1 be in any sense a foretelling of the flight into Egypt, since 'my son' is unquestionably Israel, the people of God, and the reference is to an event long past even in Hosea's day, the Exodus.

What can we say to this? Is this appeal to the Old Testament an evil necessity laid upon the early Christian missionaries when preaching to Jewish audiences who insisted upon having everything proved to them from the Old Testament; an irksome necessity which is now wholly irrelevant? Before so deciding we must try to understand what the New Testament witnesses to Jesus were claiming in this appeal to the Old Testament. They were not claiming merely that the Old Testament is the key to an understanding of Jesus, though that is in a real sense true. They were claiming that Jesus is the key to a true understanding of all that we find in the Old Testament of God's dealings with His people.

In Exodus xxxiv. 29 ff. we are told that when Moses came down from Mount Sinai after speaking with the LORD, his face shone with an unearthly radiance. The radiance remained while he told the people of the LORD's commandments.

'And when Moses had finished speaking with them, he put a veil on his face; but whenever Moses went in before the LORD to speak with him, he took the veil off until he came out; and when he came out and told the people of Israel what he was commanded, the people of Israel saw the face of Moses, that the skin of Moses' face shone; and Moses would put the veil upon his face again, until he went in to speak with him' (Exod. xxxiv. 33–35).

There is a very interesting reference to this incident in 2 Corinthians iii. 13 ff., where Paul claims that Moses had the veil over his face 'so that the Israelites might not see the end of the fading splendour'. Then he continues, referring to his fellow Jews who have not yet accepted the Christian faith, 'to this day, when they read the old covenant [i.e. what is recorded of God's dealings with his people in the Old Testament] that same veil remains unlifted, because only through Christ is it taken away. Yes, to this day whenever Moses is read a veil lies over their minds; but when a man turns to the Lord [i.e. Jesus] the veil is removed' (2 Cor. iii. 14–16).

In Jesus the veil has been removed from the Old Testament; its true glory can now be seen. A new light plays upon the story of God's dealings with His people. The Old and New Testaments hang together as surely as the acts of a well-constructed play. Omit the final act and the story so skilfully developed is left in mid-air. Of its characters and the relationship between them we can only say, 'the climax is yet to be'. Omit the early acts and the final act just does not make sense. The New Testament claims that 'its story is the continuation, the climax and the rightful interpretive centre for the previous story. If the claim is unfounded, then the Christian Gospel is quite without justification. It is an orphan in fact and a perjurer both about its ancestry and the nature of God's working.'[1]

II

We left the Old Testament looking forward to, among other things, a Coming Ruler. How the New Testament continues and brings to fulfilment the Old Testament story may be seen in what it says about this Coming Ruler.

The first recorded Christian sermon reaches its climax as Peter declares to a crowd gathered in the streets of Jerusalem, 'Let all the house of Israel therefore know assuredly that God has made him both Lord and Christ, this Jesus whom you crucified' (Acts ii. 36). God has made Jesus the 'Christ', which is the Greek form of the Hebrew word Messiah, 'the anointed one', the Coming Ruler. *The long-expected Ruler has come*; such is the repeated claim of the early church.

When persecution forced the followers of Jesus to flee from Jerusalem into the surrounding countryside, 'those who were scattered went about preaching the word. Philip went down to a city of Samaria and proclaimed to them the Christ' (Acts viii. 4–5). Philip was claiming, of course, that Jesus of Nazareth was the Christ. Saul of Tarsus, a persecutor turned missionary—his conversion story is vividly described in Acts ix. (cf. Acts xxii. 4–16; xxvi. 9–18)—'confounded the Jews who lived in Damascus by proving that Jesus was the Christ' (Acts ix. 22). Nearly twenty years after his conversion two of Paul's travelling companions rejoin him at Corinth in Greece, and find him 'occupied with preaching, testifying to the Jews that the Christ was Jesus' (Acts xviii. 5).

Jesus was the Coming Ruler; hence the New Testament witnesses are concerned to show how, in many ways, what was known of Jesus fitted in with the traditional portrait of that Ruler.[2] The Coming Ruler was expected to be a true offspring of Israel's ideal

---

[1] F. V. Filson, *The New Testament against its Environment*, p. 58.
[2] Cf. pp. 147 ff.

king, David. Jesus is described as 'of this man's [i.e. David's] pos-
terity' (Acts xiii. 23); 'descended from David according to the
flesh' (Rom. i. 3); 'the son of David' (Matt. i. 1).

The Coming Ruler would be generously endowed with the
Spirit of God. Jesus had been anointed by God 'with the *Holy Spirit*
and with power' (Acts x. 38); 'designated Son of God in power
according to the *Spirit of holiness* by his resurrection from the dead'
(Rom. i. 4). The Coming Ruler would be above all else a righteous
ruler. Jesus is described by Peter as 'the Holy and Righteous One'
(Acts iii. 14).

The Ruler had come. So commonplace did this revolutionary
assertion become that before long, particularly when the missionaries moved out from the Jewish world into the wider Graeco-
Roman world, 'Christ' lost all significance as a title, to become
merely part of a proper name. From the first century A.D. until the
present day, many a Christian has spoken of Jesus Christ without
giving a thought to the meaning of the word 'Christ'. Yet 'Jesus
Christ' became part of the Christian language only because from
the beginning, the witnesses to Jesus were convinced that He was the
Coming Ruler for whom God's people looked with eager anticipation.

This claim was vigorously contested. Paul usually began his
missionary activity in any town by visiting the local synagogue in
an attempt to convince his fellow Jews. We are told that at Thessalonica 'for three weeks he argued with them from the Scriptures,
explaining and proving that it was necessary for the Christ to
suffer and to rise from the dead, and saying, "This Jesus whom I
proclaim to you is the Christ" ' (Acts xvii. 2–3). Paul was no mean
debater; his knowledge of the Old Testament was extensive, but he
had a difficult brief. To the Jew, there was one apparently insur-
mountable 'stumbling block' (cf. 1 Cor. i. 23) in the way of accepting Jesus as the Coming Ruler. He was a 'gallows bird'. His death
had been that of a common criminal upon a Roman cross. The
Coming Ruler was expected to come victoriously to scatter the
enemies of God's people. Instead Jesus died at the hands of the
Roman occupation forces. From the outset, the witnesses to Jesus
were set the task of proving that one who had died on a cross could
yet be the Coming Ruler. In the first Christian sermon, Peter goes

out of his way to claim that the death of Jesus was within the purposes of God, 'this Jesus, delivered up according to the definite plan and foreknowledge of God' (Acts ii. 23). How did he know? How could Paul quote the faith of the church as declaring that 'Christ died for our sins *in accordance with the scriptures*' (1 Cor. xv. 3). Which Scriptures?

There is a story in the Book of Acts about Philip meeting an Ethiopian court official returning home after a visit to Jerusalem. The Ethiopian had cultivated the railway bookstall mentality. He is relieving the tedium of travelling by reading, reading, in this case, a passage from Isaiah liii., which describes the innocent suffering of the Servant of the LORD. 'Do you understand what you are reading?' says Philip. 'How can I unless someone guides me,' comes the reply. (The Bible has always been a puzzling book!) ' "About whom pray, does the prophet say this, about himself or about someone else?" Then Philip opened his mouth, and beginning with this scripture he told him the good news of Jesus' (Acts viii. 34–35).

Elsewhere in Acts we find Jesus described as the 'servant' (cf. Acts iii. 13, 26; iv. 27, 30). Jesus is at one and the same time the Coming Ruler and the Servant of the LORD. To all of which the pious Jew could hardly be expected to say 'Amen'. So far as we know, never before in Jewish thinking had the Coming Ruler been depicted in terms of the *suffering* Servant.[1] To the Jew, the Servant who suffers is essentially Israel, the people of God. In contrast the Coming Ruler is always a 'conquering hero' figure. We shall see later[2] whence the witnesses to Jesus derived this unorthodox interpretation of the Old Testament.

One other trump card remained. The cross had not been the end of Jesus. A broken body had been sealed in a tomb, but 'this Jesus God raised up, and of that we all are witnesses' (Acts ii. 32). The lame beggar, claims Peter before the Jewish religious authorities, has been cured 'by the name of Jesus Christ of Nazareth, whom you crucified, whom God raised from the dead' (Acts iv. 10; cf. x. 40; xiii. 30, 37; xvii. 3). It was said of Paul at Athens that 'he preached Jesus and the resurrection' (Acts xvii. 18). This is central to the

[1] Cf. H. H. Rowley, *The Servant of the Lord.*
[2] Cf. p. 193 ff.

preaching of all the witnesses to Jesus. With one voice they proclaim that Jesus, the long-promised Ruler, had triumphed. He had
been raised by God, victor over death and all the forces of evil which
had attempted to destroy Him. Is this the world's greatest hoax or is
it sober truth? To the first generation of Christians, at any rate, it
was sober, if exhilarating, truth. This certainty is poured into the
name they most frequently give to Jesus—Jesus is *Lord*. 'God has
made him both Lord and Christ, this Jesus whom you crucified'
(Acts ii. 36). It is the name they use when they pray to Jesus (cf.
Acts vii. 59; ix. 13; xxii. 19) and the very fact that these Jewish
witnesses, steeped in the tradition that there is only one God,
should pray to Jesus, ought to make us wonder. It is the name
which, in one form or another, occurs over two hundred times in
the missionary letters of Paul.[1] Two passages from these letters will
help us to understand the astonishing claims about Jesus contained
in this word 'Lord'.

Gods were ten a penny in the Graeco-Roman world of Paul's
day. Many of them were given the honorary title 'Lord'. Educated
people, if of a sceptical turn of mind, decided that this plethora of
deities was proof that religion was an illusion; if religious, they
concluded that the many gods were but different names for the
one divine reality pervading the universe. In his first letter to the
Corinthians, Paul has occasion to deal with a problem of conscience
raised by the existence of these pagan gods. Beginning from the
fundamental assumption of the Old Testament that 'there is no God
but one' he continues: 'For although there may be so-called gods in
heaven or on earth—as indeed there are many "gods" and many
"lords"—yet for us there is one God, the Father, from whom are all
things and for whom we exist, and one Lord, Jesus Christ, through
whom are all things and through whom we exist' (1 Cor. viii. 5–6).

For Christians, claims Paul, there is one God, the Creator (from
whom) and the Goal (for whom) of everything; and there is one
Lord, even Jesus Christ. But what is this that he is asserting about
one who was born into a carpenter's family and lived His life in the
Roman province of Judaea? He is the pivot upon which the whole
of creation turns (through whom are all things). He is the source

[1] Cf. V. Taylor, *The Person of Christ*, p.44.

of a new creation (this is the most probable meaning of 'through whom we exist'—the Christian community as the new creation). Notice that Paul does draw a distinction between God the Father and Jesus. The New Testament never obliterates that distinction. If, however, we were to divide the universe into 'things divine' and 'things human' is there any doubt, in the light of this passage, to which Paul would assign Jesus?

The Letter to the Philippians contains a famous passage about Jesus. It is all the more impressive inasmuch as it occurs, not in the course of a carefully constructed theological argument, but solely to support Paul's plea for a genuine spirit of humility to be demonstrated in the life of the Philippian Christians. It may even be that Paul is quoting the words of an early Christian hymn.

'Have this mind among yourselves, which you have in Christ Jesus, who, though he was in the form of God, did not count equality with God a thing to be grasped, but emptied himself, taking the form of a servant, being born in the likeness of men. And being found in human form, he humbled himself and became obedient unto death, even death on a cross. Therefore God has highly exalted him and bestowed on him the name which is above every name, that at the name of Jesus every knee should bow, in heaven and on earth and under the earth, and every tongue confess that Jesus Christ is LORD, to the glory of God the Father' (Phil. ii. 5–11). The tides of criticism have surged, and still surge, strongly around this passage. Particular phrases in it may be a matter of dispute, but the general drift of the passage is hardly in doubt. Jesus, claims Paul, is by nature and by right 'divine'. Willingly He laid aside His divine prerogatives to come to earth. His life was a life of service to all men. He died the shameful death of a common criminal. Yet the cross was the gateway to glory. His utter self-renunciation has been crowned by His triumph. He is now *Lord* of the whole universe. The closing section contains an echo of Isaiah xlv. 23, which looks forward to the day when the whole world will acknowledge the LORD, the God of Israel.

> 'To me every knee shall bow,
> every tongue shall swear.'

Notice how, without any sense of incongruity, a Christian writer can substitute Jesus in an Old Testament passage where the reference is to the LORD, the God of Israel. There are many instances of this in the New Testament. Indeed the Greek version of the Old Testament used by the early Christian church translates the Hebrew personal name for God by the word 'Kurios', Lord. That 'Jesus Christ is Kurios, Lord' (cf. Rom. x. 9), is one of the earliest Christian confessions of faith. In so confessing, and so worshipping Him, they were assigning to Him a key place in the universe, and attributing to Him an ultimate authority.

In Psalm cxviii, which celebrates the steadfast love of the LORD for His afflicted people, there is a verse:

> 'The stone which the builders rejected
> has become the chief corner-stone.' (verse 22)

The stone is Israel, despised by the surrounding nations, yet destined to be of vital importance in the purposes of God. Later Jewish thinking applied the text to the Coming Ruler, despised[1] by Israel's foes, yet destined to be the corner foundation stone, supporting the walls of a new glorious Israel. It is hardly surprising that, believing in One who had been rejected by His own people, crucified by the Romans, yet raised by God from the dead, the early Christians found this a convenient text in speaking to Jewish audiences. 'This is the stone which was rejected by you builders, but which has become the head of the corner' (Acts iv. 11; cf. 1 Pet. ii. 7). Jesus of Nazareth, village carpenter, gallows bird—yes; but passing through suffering to triumph, the long-expected Ruler—this was the message heard by many a first-century Jew.

III

The witnesses to Jesus, however, did not always address Jewish audiences. The Christian apologist found the title 'Lord' particularly useful since it was meaningful to both the Jew and the non-

---

[1] Not, however, suffering at their hands. He was to be, much to their surprise, triumphant over them.

Jew. When speaking to people to whom the Old Testament was an unknown book, it was no good claiming that the Ruler had come. Jesus had to be communicated to the Graeco-Roman world in language with which it was familiar; as He has to be interpreted and re-interpreted to each different age and culture. An unintelligible message is hardly likely to be effective, not even when couched in the most pious and hallowed of language. The New Testament witnesses were not afraid to reinterpret Jesus.

Athens, in Paul's time, was long past its heyday, but the glory of the past still haunted its streets. The unrivalled skill of Greek sculpture had populated the city with innumerable statues to innumerable gods and goddesses, to whom ordinary folk still paid a touching, if somewhat uncertain reverence. Rival schools of philosophy, each claiming to unravel the ultimate mysteries of life, sought to continue the tradition of Socrates and Plato. When Paul came to Athens, his first contacts were with the Jewish community. The novelty of his teaching attracted wider attention. Some of the intelligentsia dismissed him as a 'babbler', 'a picker up of odds and ends'; others described him as a 'preacher of foreign deities' (Acts xvii. 18). Given an opportunity to address a representative Athenian audience, Paul tries to meet them half way. 'Men of Athens, I perceive that in every way you are very religious. For as I passed along, and observed the objects of your worship, I found also an altar with this inscription 'To an unknown god'. What therefore you worship as unknown, this I proclaim to you' (Acts xvii. 22–23). All men, he continues, have been made for God, made to be His children—and he throws in a quotation from a Greek poet to underline his point. There has never been any real excuse for men believing that 'the God who made the world and everything in it, the Lord of heaven and earth . . . is like gold or silver or stone, a representation by the art and imagination of man' (verse 24 and verse 29)—a typically scornful Jewish attitude to idol worship. If ignorance be pleaded, then the age of ignorance is now past; God 'commands all men everywhere to repent, because he has fixed a day on which he will judge the world in righteousness by a man whom he has appointed, and of this he has given assurance to all men by raising him from the dead' (Acts xvii. 30–31).

Paul is here claiming that the age-long groping of the human soul for God, reflected both in popular religion and in the discussions of the philosophers, has now been met, 'by a man', that is to say, Jesus, proved to be Lord of all by His victory over death. Paul's speech does not seem to have made much impression upon his audience, but at least they would understand what he was asserting (cf. Gal. iv. 8–9).

The opening verses of John's Gospel provide us with another example. The last of the four Gospels to be written, the fruit of prolonged meditation upon the life of Jesus, it seeks throughout to draw forth the inner meaning and ultimate significance of all that happened in Jesus, and that with a very definite audience in mind. It is 'addressed to a wide public consisting primarily of devout and thoughtful persons . . . in the varied and cosmopolitan society of a great Hellenistic city.'[1]

In such a city, the educated Greeks would certainly be familiar with Stoic philosophy whose key idea was that of the '*Logos*', a Greek word which may be variously translated 'word', 'thought' or 'reason'. This 'Logos' is the ultimate divine reason pervading and ordering the whole created universe. This cosmic Logos, conceived of in quasi-materialistic terms, functions as the mind or soul of the universe; the 'soul' or 'reasoning faculty' in man being but a spark of this divine Logos. In such a city, the devout Jew would be well acquainted with the '*Word of God*' in the Old Testament, a 'word' which in certain passages seems, in terms of Hebrew thought, to take on an almost independent existence (cf. Isa. lv. 11). Likewise he would be familiar with the '*Wisdom*' of God which in Proverbs viii and in later Jewish writings, particularly the so-called 'Wisdom of Solomon', is strongly personified, existing with God before the foundation of the world, and after creation being regarded as the artificer and manager of all things. In such a city there would be devout educated Jews, attracted by the achievements of Greek culture, attempting, as did Philo in Alexandria in the first century A.D., to build a bridge between the faith of their fathers and the best in Greek philosophy, by identifying the creative Word of God and the Wisdom of God with the 'Logos' of the

[1] C. H. Dodd, *The Interpretation of the Fourth Gospel*, p. 9.

philosophers. Against this background, listen now to some verses from the prologue to John's Gospel.

'In the beginning was the Word [i.e. Logos], and the Word was with God, and the Word was God. He was in the beginning with God; all things were made through him, and without him was not anything made that was made. In him was life and the life was the light of men' (John i. 1–4).

The writer has the ear of his audience. What he has to say about the 'Word' reaches its climax, 'And the Word became flesh and dwelt among us, full of grace and truth' (verse 14). 'The Word became flesh'; in other words, all that the Greeks meant by the divine 'Logos', all that the Jews saw in the 'Word' and 'Wisdom of God', and indeed, all that men were looking for as the bridge between these two cultures, is to be found in the man, Jesus of Nazareth.

To the Jew it is blasphemy; to the cultured Greek, accustomed to look for God by stepping outside this changing world of sense and time, it must have sounded nonsensical; yet there were some, both Jews and Greeks who responded, to learn for themselves the truth declared by another New Testament writer, a Jew, thinking of the history of his own people.

'In many and various ways God spoke of old to our fathers by the prophets; but in these last days he has spoken to us by a Son, whom he appointed the heir of all things, through whom also he created the world. He reflects the glory of God and bears the very stamp of his nature, upholding the universe by his word of power' (Heb. i. 1–3a).

.   .   .   .   .

In Jesus, the long-expected Ruler has come. . . . Jesus is Lord. . . . in Him the unknown God is now known. . . . Jesus is the Logos . . . He is 'a Son . . . reflecting the glory of God, bearing the very stamp of his nature. . . .' Does it make sense to say such things about a Jew, born on the eastern fringe of the Roman Empire in the reign of the Emperor Augustus, a Jew who 'suffered under Pontius Pilate'? It is either arrant, irresponsible nonsense, or in literal truth, 'God was in Christ' (2 Cor. v. 19)—in this man, Jesus of Nazareth.

8

Reconciling the World

The New Testament is interested not only in who Jesus is, but in what God has done through Him. Jesus is presented as the answer to self-centred man, God's problem child. He died, it is claimed, 'for our sins'.

A barrier of language separates us from the New Testament witnesses at this point, since they use metaphors drawn from the world they knew in their attempts to explain.

1. From the realm of sacrifice once familiar to all, Jesus is described as our sacrifice, *or, according to the author of the Epistle to the Hebrews, our* high priest; *i.e. in Jesus, God acts to restore the full relationship between himself and man. Jesus is our way of 'at-one-ment' with God.*

2. Following upon the thought of Jeremiah, it is claimed that in Jesus the 'New Covenant' comes into being.

3. Paul draws upon the wider Graeco-Roman world for his metaphors.

(a) From the world of slavery, he speaks of Redemption.

(b) From the law-courts, he speaks of Justification.

(c) In terms more familiar to us, he speaks of Reconciliation.

All underline the fact that because of what God has done in and through Jesus, men are forgiven and brought back into true fellowship with God.

What basis is there for these claims in the life of Jesus?

THE New Testament writers show a remarkable interest in the identity of this Jesus of Nazareth, but, if anything, they are even more interested in what He does, or rather *what God does through Him*. In Jesus, they claim God has done something decisive for us and for the world.

The failure of the people to respond to God's initiative is a recurring theme in the Old Testament. Possessing God's Torah (instruction), they yet do not, seemingly they cannot, order their lives in the light of this instruction. The covenant founders on the rock of the people's stubborn evil will, outward sign of that 'self at the centre of life' attitude which the Bible describes as 'sin'. It is the claim of the New Testament that in the life, death and Resurrection of Jesus, God has acted to right this situation, has broken into the vicious circle of 'self' and destroyed the deadly grip of sin.

An essential feature in the portrait of the Servant of the LORD in Isaiah xl–lv is that the Servant undeservedly suffers, and His suffering, gladly borne, on behalf of others, brings new health and life to the nations as the witnesses of his humiliation and death confess.

> 'Surely he has borne our griefs
> and carried our sorrows;
> yet we esteemed him stricken,
> smitten by God and afflicted.
> But he was wounded for our transgressions,
> he was bruised for our iniquities;
> upon him was the chastisement that made us whole,
> and with his stripes we are healed.'
>
> (Isa. liii. 4–5)

Jesus, as we have seen, is thought of as the Servant. He dies—why? He 'died for our sins' (1 Cor. xv. 3).

'He himself bore our sins in his body on the tree' (1 Pet. ii. 24).

He 'dies for sins once for all' (1 Pet. iii. 18).

This does not mean simply that Jesus died, martyr-like, the innocent victim of the wickedness of His contemporaries. Indeed He was 'crucified and killed by the hands of lawless men' (Acts ii. 23). Jewish authorities, a Roman provincial governor, a fickle mob all had a hand in it. But this is not the whole truth about the death of Jesus. He was 'delivered up', claims Peter, 'according to the definite plan and foreknowledge of God' (Acts ii. 23). Paul, writing to Christians in Asia Minor, who were in no way connected with the series of events in Judaea which culminated on a cross, declared that

Jesus 'gave himself for our sins to deliver us from the present evil age according to the will of our God and Father' (Gal. i. 4).

Somehow or other the death of Jesus outside the walls of Jerusalem is regarded as being of universal significance. What can this mean? That Jesus died for *our* sins, ours in twentieth-century Europe, as much as in any other century in any other part of the globe—nothing is more central to the New Testament than this, yet nothing is more difficult for us to understand. Theologians will tell you that part of the difficulty today, as in any age, is that, being 'sinners', we do not want to understand. 'Self-centred' and 'self-reliant', we will try anything rather than face the fact that there is something that God, and God alone, must do for us if we are to be put right.

But that is only part of the difficulty. Between us and what the New Testament is here trying to say, there lies a barrier of language, vaguely familiar yet strangely 'out of this world' language. A few verses from Paul's letter to the Romans will make this clear. 'Since all have sinned and fall short of the glory of God, they are justified by his grace as a gift, through the redemption which is in Christ Jesus, whom God put forward as an expiation by his blood, to be received by faith' (Rom. iii. 23–25). Expiation ... redemption ... justification—such words, no longer common coinage, conceal rather than convey truth. Yet once they were living words, communicating the joyful certainty of Christian faith. If it is futile to bemoan the passing of such words, it is dangerous to ignore the truth they enshrine. We must seek to understand, and then to re-interpret in the language of our own day.

I

Twice in the first Epistle of John we find the word 'expiation' linked with Jesus.

'In this is love, not that we loved God but that he loved us and sent his Son to be the *expiation* for our sins' (1 John iv. 10).

Jesus is 'the *expiation* for our sins, and not for ours only, but also for the sins of the whole world' (1 John ii. 2).

M

Another New Testament writer has the same thing in mind when he says that Jesus 'appeared once for all at the end of the age to put away sin by the sacrifice of himself' (Heb. ix. 26; cf. x. 12).

We travel here into unfamiliar territory, yet every contour of this landscape is familiar to the New Testament writers, nourished in a world where animal sacrifice is a vital part of religion. To describe in detail, even to sketch in firm outline, the complete sacrificial system of the Old Testament, lies outwith our purpose. There is a rich variety of sacrifices in the Old Testament, not all of them by any means connected with 'sin'. Indeed, for deliberate, cold-blooded violations of the known commandments of God no sacrifices ever availed. Certain sacrifices, however, did apply to what are described as 'unwitting' sins, that is to say, inadvertent violations of some of the innumerable laws (cf. Num. xv. 24–29; Lev. iv.). This is a wholesome recognition that even inadvertent wrong-doing has a disruptive impact upon the relationship between a God, inexorable in His moral holiness, and the people of His choice. That being so, it is vitally important that there be a means of renewing the essential 'at-one-ment' between God and the people, an 'at-one-ment' upon which the whole welfare of the people depends. This is what God has provided in the sacrificial system. It cannot be too strongly emphasized that in the developed thought of the Old Testament, sacrifice is not a means of bribing or pacifying an outraged deity, but a God-given means of renewed at-one-ment. In many instances, the evil done is regarded as inflicting upon the offender a dangerous infection, which becomes a potential source of danger to the whole community. Sacrifice operates like a divine disinfectant, through the blood of an animal victim, provided and killed by the guilty party. Exactly how the blood was thought to operate has been disputed, but one thing is certain: it was not the death of the victim which was effective. Death was only a means to an end. To the primitive mind, blood is equated with *life*. As Leviticus xvii. 11 says, 'the life of the flesh is in the blood; and I have given it to you upon the altar to make atonement for your souls; for it is the blood that makes atonement by reason of the life'. What more natural than to think of blood as life, when blood pouring out of a gaping wound often meant the passing of life from the body?

This released life brought into the presence of God (i.e. sprinkled upon the altar by a priest) 'covers'—for that is probably the meaning of the technical term used—the forfeited life of the offender. The consequence of his sin being thus neutralized, he is again at one with God, within the community of God's people.

This is the background to the talk of 'expiation', i.e. 'covering' for our sins. Hence, too, the frequent mention in this connection of the *blood* of Christ, 'the *blood* of Jesus his [i.e. God's] Son cleanses us from all sin' (1 John i. 7).

'To him who loves us and has freed us from our sins by his *blood*' (Rev. i. 5; cf. v. 9; vii. 14; xii. 11).

This is the language of sacrifice. There is no evidence in the New Testament for regarding the death of Jesus on the Cross as a martyr death, so morally inspiring that henceforth men are enabled to live beyond themselves. But what do the witnesses to Jesus claim in applying to Him this language of sacrifice. Two things at least must be said. In the first place, the claim is here made that through Jesus, self-centred man has the consequences of his rebellion against God annulled, and finds renewed at-one-ment with God. Secondly *this is God's doing*. There is one vital distinction between the Old Testament sacrificial system and what is said in the New Testament. In the Old Testament, the guilty party must provide the victim, and slay it to release the blood which effects at-one-ment; in the New Testament, all is of God. He, in His love, sends Jesus His Son, to 'cover' our sins, to bring us again 'far ben' (to use a lovely Scottish phrase) to Himself. He Himself, in Jesus, bears the cost.

Another New Testament writer, the unknown author of the Epistle to the Hebrews,[1] uses a slightly different approach. He refers to Jesus again and again as 'the high priest'. No writer in the New Testament lays greater stress upon the bond linking Jesus and ourselves. He shared our human life to the full, knowing its extremities. 'In the days of his flesh, Jesus offered up prayers and supplications with loud cries and tears' (Heb. v. 7). Here is one 'who in every respect has been tempted as we are' (iv. 15), the only difference being that, unlike us, He did not succumb to temptation. But why

---

[1] Not Paul, as is stated in the A.V.

should this be if Jesus, as is asserted in the introductory verses, 'reflects the glory of God and bears the very stamp of his nature, upholding the universe by his word of power' (i. 3)? The author leaves us in no doubt. 'He had to be made like his brethren in every respect, so that he might become a merciful and faithful high priest in the service of God, to make expiation for the sins of the people' (ii. 17).

There is a passage in the letter where, after describing some of the furnishings in the Temple, the author concludes, 'Of these things we cannot now speak in detail' (ix. 5). We may adopt a similar attitude to his portrayal of Jesus as the true high priest.[1] Behind all that he says, however, there lies one of the great days in the Jewish religious year, *the* day, as it came to be known, the Day of Atonement, the coping stone of all that the Old Testament has to say about sacrifice and sin. On this day, and on this day alone, the high priest entered the 'holy of holies', i.e. the most holy place, the innermost sanctum divided from the rest of the Temple by a veil. Once the holy of holies had housed the ark;[2] but for many a long day it had been dramatically and mysteriously empty, the very abode of the invisible God. The ritual of this day, a ritual presupposing a time when the ark still stood within the 'holy of holies', is described in Leviticus xvi.

Sacrificing a bull on behalf of himself and his family, the high priest takes some of its blood with him into the holy of holies and sprinkles it before the so-called 'mercy seat', the covering of the ark. The people provide two goats. One of these, chosen by lot, is assigned to the LORD, the other to Azazel, probably originally a desert demon who became the symbol of evil. Taking the blood of the former, the high priest re-enters the holy of holies, to sprinkle some of it before the 'mercy seat' and afterwards upon the altar outside, where the daily animal sacrifices took place throughout the year. Thus he made 'atonement for the holy place, because of the uncleannesses of the people of Israel, and because of their transgressions, all their sins' (Lev. xvi. 16). Placing his hands upon the

---

[1] For an excellent summary of what the author has to say cf. Wm. Neil *The Epistle to the Hebrews* (The Torch Bible Commentaries).

[2] Cf. p. 63 f.

goat selected for Azazel he confessed over it 'all the iniquities of the people of Israel, and all their transgressions, all their sins; and he shall put them upon the head of the goat and send him away into the wilderness by the hand of a man who is in readiness. The goat shall bear all their iniquities upon him to a solitary land; and he shall let the goat go in the wilderness' (Lev. xvi. 21–22). Thus the high priest, using divinely appointed means, banished the sins of the people, and the full relationship between God and the people was restored.

The author of Hebrews sees two major flaws in this system. In the first place, only one person, the high priest, and he only once a year, is allowed into the very Presence of God (cf. ix. 7). In the second place, the whole system still applies only to unwitting sins, such as violations of the various ritual demands, 'food and drink and various ablutions, regulations for the body' (ix. 10). It does nothing, he claims, to 'perfect the conscience of the worshipper' (ix. 9). To the truly guilty conscience, troubled by the knowledge of past wrong-doing, it can speak no word of reassurance and forgiveness. Every relationship gone wrong implies at least one guilty party, troubled in conscience by his share in what has happened no matter how brazen a face he may put to the world; and only through forgiveness freely offered and received can the relationship be fully restored. In both of these respects, claims our author, the ritual of the Day of Atonement is but a dim 'shadow' of the 'reality' made known to men in Jesus. (The distinction between 'shadow' and 'reality' was a well-known feature of Platonic philosophy.) 'But when Christ appeared as a high priest of the good things that have come . . . he entered once for all into the Holy Place' (ix. 11–12). 'When he had offered for all time a single sacrifice for sins, he sat down at the right hand of God' (x. 12; cf. ix. 26; x. 20).

In other words, Jesus by His life and death has opened up for ever and for all of us a way into the very presence of God. Not only so, but when this high priest entered the Holy of Holies, he took with him not 'the blood of goats and bulls' dragged helplessly to the altar, but 'his own blood' freely and gladly offered (cf. ix. 13–14). If, then, the blood of such goats and bulls is regarded as effective in purifying the people from the infection of unwitting sins, 'how

much more shall the blood of Christ, who through the eternal
Spirit offered himself without blemish to God, purify your conscience from dead works to serve the living God' (ix. 14).

So through Jesus as His sacrifice, forgiveness comes to the conscience troubled by even the greatest sins and a right relationship is
restored between man and God. You may have noticed how the
author seems to change horses in mid-stream. One moment, Jesus is
the 'high priest', the next He is the 'victim'. He is both, because the
claim is being made that all that was dimly and imperfectly fore-
shadowed in the Old Testament sacrifices, has now perfectly and in
reality been given to us in Jesus. He is our way of 'at-one-ment'
with God.

II

Perhaps you have been finding the going rather hard in this unfamiliar terrain. We shall continue travelling for a moment in the
company of the author of Hebrews, but it will be by way of a return
visit to a district whose features ought by this time to be familiar.
We left the Old Testament looking forward to a day when God
would establish a 'New Covenant' with His people.[1] All that Hebrews says about Jesus as the new way of at-one-ment with God
pre-supposes that the New Covenant, spoken of in Jeremiah xxxi.
31–34[2] comes into being in Him. Jesus is 'the mediator of a new
covenant' (Heb. xii. 24; ix. 15); a new and better covenant
grounded on 'better promises' (viii. 6). The first covenant between
God and His people was ratified by blood sprinkled upon altar and
people.[3] Now, through the blood of Jesus, the long expected new
covenant is inaugurated, and the superiority of the new covenant
to the old is symbolized in the difference between the willing
sacrifice of Jesus, and the blood drawn from unwilling oxen.

The author of Hebrews has a distinguished 'fellow traveller'
among the New Testament witnesses. God, says Paul, 'has qualified
us to be ministers of a new covenant' (2 Cor. iii. 6). Paul likewise
provides us with our earliest documentary evidence of certain sig-

[1] Cf. pp. 150 ff.
[2] This whole passage is quoted in Heb. viii. 8–12.
[3] Exod. xxiv. 6–8.

nificant words and actions of Jesus which revolve round the thought of the new covenant. 'For I received from the Lord what I also delivered to you, that the Lord Jesus on the night when he was betrayed took bread, and when he had given thanks, he broke it and said, "This is my body which is for you. Do this is remembrance of me." In the same way also the cup, after supper, saying, "This cup is the *new covenant* in my blood. Do this as often as you drink it, in remembrance of me" ' (1 Cor. xi. 23–25).

It is enough for our present purpose to stress that here something that God had once promised to do for His people is now said to have been done, in Jesus.

III

To speak in terms of the Day of Atonement or the New Covenant served the witnesses to Jesus well, so long as they were talking to Jewish audiences or to people who had for long taken a sympathetic interest in the Jewish faith. Paul, a Jew from Tarsus, once a zealous persecutor of the followers of Jesus, had a revolutionary encounter with Jesus which convinced him that he had been chosen by God to take the 'good news' of Jesus to the non-Jewish world (cf. Gal. i. 13–15). But to explain what God had done in Jesus to non-Jews meant using word pictures which they would understand. The 'slave market' and the 'Law Courts', familiar features of life in the Graeco–Roman world, not only gave him what he needed, but proved particularly useful since they could be linked with ideas from the Old Testament which he knew so well.

A

No one in the Graeco–Roman world needed any introduction to the slave market. Slavery was the common fate of conquered peoples; men, women and children being sold to the highest bidder as we would sell cattle in an auction mart. Not that the lot of the slave was necessarily intolerable. Given a good owner he might rise to a position of considerable importance in his master's service.

More important still, he might one day be able to buy back his freedom, or even be given it by an act of generosity on the part of his master. Sometimes by a legal fiction the slave paid his 'freedom money' to a god [e.g. Apollo] in his temple to be henceforth no longer his owner's slave but the slave of the god.[1] This religious background no doubt encouraged Paul in his use of this metaphor, though the purely passive part played in the transaction by the god is utterly remote from his thought. In the New Testament we find the word 'redemption' with its allied verb, 'to redeem'. They refer to the recovery by a slave of his freedom, and may be used both where a cash payment, 'a ransom', is involved, and where emancipation is the free gift of the slave owner.

Consciously or unconsciously, Jewish thinking had tended to take the message of the Old Testament, and in one vital respect put the cart before the horse. So insistently had Jewish teachers stressed the importance of the people keeping God's law, that they tended to obscure one vital fact, central to the witness of the Old Testament, namely that the relationship between God and His people had been of God's making, and was based on His initiative. The keeping of the Law, instead of being regarded as the people's glad response to what God had done for them, came to be regarded, quite wrongly, as the very foundation stone of the relationship between God and His people. Consequently, a zealous, meticulous, often joyful yet in the last analysis impossible endeavour to keep every detail of the Law, and thus to ensure God's favour, came to be characteristic of the best in Jewish religion. Paul knew it to be impossible. He had tried this way to God, only to find: 'I do not do the good I want, but the evil I do not want is what I do. Now if I do what I do not want, it is no longer I that do it, but sin which dwells within me. So I find it to be a law that when I want to do right, evil lies close at hand. For I delight in the law of God, in my inmost self, but I see in my members another law at war with the law of my mind and making me captive to the law of sin which dwells in my members' (Rom. vii. 19–23).

The Law demands, and in the very act of making known God's demands reveals our moral weakness. We know what God

---

[1] A. Diessmann, *Light From the Ancient East*, pp. 322 ff.

would have us do, only to find that we cannot. We are left power-less, *slaves* in the grip of an exacting taskmaster, the Law.

'But when the time had fully come, God sent forth his Son, born of woman, born under the Law, to *redeem* those who were under the Law so that we might receive adoption as sons' (Gal. iv. 4–5).

Thus Paul argues when seeking to counter the propaganda of opponents who were trying to insist that a rigid observance of the Old Testament Law was necessary, even for non-Jewish Christians. But the same metaphor comes to his mind even when there is not this background. A non-Jew would understand what Paul meant by talking about 'slaves to sin' (e.g. Rom. vi. 17).

Elsewhere he describes Jesus as God's 'beloved Son in whom we have redemption, the forgiveness of sins' (Col. i. 14).

'In him, we have redemption through his blood, the forgiveness of our trespasses' (Eph. i. 7).

Notice in both these statements the close link between 'redemption' and 'forgiveness of sins'. That man is God's problem child needing to be forgiven, the slave to a diabolic preoccupation with self, is the background against which the whole story of the Bible is played out.[1] That he *is* forgiven, that he is set free (redeemed) from this enslavement, and that through Jesus of Nazareth, is the witness of the New Testament. Things have gone wrong between God and man, but 'there is one God, and there is one mediator between God and man, the man Christ Jesus, who gave himself as a ransom for all' (1 Tim. ii. 5–6).

Our uneasy world has become familiar in recent years with the figure of a 'mediator', appointed by the United Nations to use his good offices to bring a dispute to an end. But our modern analogy may mislead. For us an essential qualification for a mediator is that he be a neutral third party, with no personal interests in the dispute. But this 'mediator' comes from one of the parties involved in the quarrel. God was in Christ. Even more surprisingly, it is the of-fended party who, far from adopting an attitude of outraged inno-cence, takes the initiative and pays himself the price of man's re-demption. All true forgiveness is costly.

The language is the language of slavery, common coinage in

[1] Cf. pp. 34 ff.

Paul's day, but it has its roots in the Old Testament. God, you remember, is the great *Go'el*, redeemer of his people.[1] He wrought a mighty deliverance for His people by bringing them out of enslavement in Egypt, the house of bondage. Now in Jesus He accomplishes an even greater deliverance, bringing mankind out of enslavement to sin and self.

B

We turn to the Law Courts, from which Paul draws his favourite picture of what God does for men in Jesus. In the Old Testament, God is frequently depicted as a Judge.[2] Bring self-centred, rebellious man into the presence of this Judge. The charge sheet reads, 'All have sinned and fall short of the glory of God' (Rom. iii. 23). What must be the verdict? Guilty. Moreover, there is no point in putting the prisoner on probation, on condition that henceforth he keeps God's Commandments. This is precisely what his experience tells him he cannot do. To reduce all the commandments to the vital two, 'You shall love the Lord your God with all your heart, and with all your soul, and with all your strength and with all your mind; and your neighbour as yourself' (Luke x. 27), may help us to find our way among the hundred and one commandments in the Old Testament. But then to be told, 'Do this and you will live' (Luke x. 28) is still tantamount to passing the death sentence, if disobedience to God be a capital offence. Is there any possibility of acquittal? Not if we are to judge the prisoner on his merits, for we 'know that a man is not justified by works of the Law' (Gal. ii. 16); that is to say, no man can appear before the Divine Judge and claim acquittal with the words, 'I have kept on the right side of your Law.'

The word 'justify' is one of a series of words used by Paul—justify, justice, righteous, righteousness—all of them from the same root. We are hampered by the fact that in English there is no one root which will adequately translate these terms. We may go far wrong if we do not keep in mind the distinctive flavour that this series of words takes over from the Old Testament.[3] When used

[1] Cf. pp. 83 ff.
[2] E.g. Gen. xviii. 25.
[3] Cf. chapter 3, pp. 69 ff.

of God, 'righteousness' describes His activity, an essential part of which is righting wrongs, bringing deliverance to His people. The outcome of this righteous activity of God is 'justification', the putting of His people in the right, their acquittal, their deliverance from evil of every kind, their salvation.

There is no possibility of acquittal if, looking at the prisoner's record, we expect God to act as a 'just' judge administering an impartial standard of law. But—and here comes the shock to our way of looking at things—acquittal is handed out to the prisoner as a free gift from the Judge Himself. This is the supreme demonstration of God's 'righteousness'. 'This was to show God's righteousness . . . it was to prove at the present time that he is righteous' (Rom. iii. 25–26).

So God the Judge justifies, acquits, not because He likes the look of the prisoner, but because 'he himself is righteous and justifies *him who has faith in Jesus*' (Rom. iii. 26); 'a man is not justified by works of the Law, but by faith in Christ' (Gal. ii. 16).

'Therefore since we are justified by faith, we have peace with God through our Lord Jesus Christ' (Rom. v. 1).

Paul does not mean that, if only we can acquire a mysterious quality called 'faith', we can appear before God to claim acquittal. It is faith *in Jesus* which leads to acquittal, and the vitally important words are *in Jesus*. It is what God does for man in Jesus, claims Paul, which leads to our acquittal. There is now available 'the righteousness which is through faith in Christ, the righteousness from God that depends on faith' (Phil. iii. 9).

Faith is simply our saying 'yes' to an utterly unmerited and unmeritable gift which God offers us in Jesus.

'Since all have sinned and fall short of the glory of God they are justified by his [i.e. God's] grace as a gift' (Rom. iii. 24). Note that little word 'grace', a favourite word of Paul. For him it does not signify some likeable or attractive quality in us, but God's freely given love which comes to men beyond all their deserving in Jesus.

For Paul, the great example of true faith is Abraham, the pilgrim father of the Hebrew people (cf. Rom. iv. 1–25; Gal. iii. 6 ff.). Here is a man who relied on God and on God's faithfulness. The Christian follows in the footsteps of Abraham, relying wholly on what God, in His faithfulness, has done for us in Jesus, 'men of faith . . .

like Abraham who had faith' (Gal. iii. 9). Because Abraham thus relied on God and what God would do, 'it was reckoned to him as righteousness' (Gal. iii. 4; Rom. iv. 22). The verdict of the Divine Judge was 'Not guilty'. Likewise, says Paul, 'It will be reckoned to us who believe in him that raised from the dead Jesus our Lord, who was put to death for our trespasses and raised for our justification' (Rom. iv. 24; cf. 2 Cor. v. 2).

Because of what God has done for us in Jesus, in His death and resurrection, we leave the Divine Law Court acquitted by God Himself, though we are as guilty as sin. Is not this dangerous talk? Surely no human judge could act in this way without making a mockery of the Law? Paul intended us to be shocked, to be startled. He believed that in Jesus, God had done something for man which went far beyond what even the best of men could be expected to do, far beyond what they would consider right; something for which, in the last analysis, no metaphor drawn from the Law Courts can be wholly adequate.

'While we were yet helpless, at the right time Christ died for the ungodly. Why, one will hardly die for a righteous man—though perhaps for a good man one will even dare to die. But God shows his love for us in that while we were yet sinners Christ died for us' (Rom. v. 6–8).

IV

It requires an effort from most of us to feel at home in language drawn from the Old Testament sacrificial system, the slave market or even the Law Courts. But Paul has another word to describe what happened in Jesus, a word which ought to be readily understandable in a world of Industrial Arbitration and Marriage Guidance Councils. In international affairs, in the field of industry, in family life, we are only too sadly familiar with relationships at breaking point, with the need for bringing two parties together in reconciliation. Now listen to Paul:

'If while we were enemies we were reconciled to God by the death of his Son, much more, now that we are reconciled, shall we be saved by his life. Not only so, but we also rejoice in God through our Lord Jesus Christ, through whom we have now received our reconciliation' (Rom. v. 10–11).

The relationship between God and man had been stretched to breaking point by man's sinful preoccupation with self. God had every right to feel hurt. The fault was not His. Yet, far from standing on His offended dignity, 'God was in Christ, reconciling the world to himself, not counting their trespasses against them' (2 Cor. v. 19).

In a world where nations, political parties, different sides in industry, and ordinary people are so often concerned to justify themselves by underlining the faults and failings of the other party, is not this a great wonder? Because of what God has done in and through Jesus of Nazareth, men are forgiven, restored and brought back again into God's family circle. God and men are again at one. This is the witness of the New Testament.

.   .   .   .   .

If the previous chapter was mysterious in the things it said about the identity of Jesus, the present chapter, far from clearing up the mystery, deepens it. What right has anyone to say of a man who lived in a subject province of the Roman Empire over nineteen hundred years ago, that 'God was in him', and not only in him, but through him vitally affecting our whole relationship with God? It has been claimed that Jesus of Nazareth was no more than a gifted preacher and martyr, whose teaching can be summarized in the words, 'the fatherhood of God and the brotherhood of man'. Then came Paul, 'that unhappy man with his morbid sense of sin, a diabolically clever theologian to change this simple message into the story of some kind of dying and rising Saviour God—was not the Graeco-Roman world familiar with such stories? This theory, of course, will not do. The earliest examples of Christian preaching which we possess, and they go back beyond Paul's time—make astonishing claims about one who was merely 'a simple Galilean peasant'.[1] It is time we turned to the life of this Jesus of Nazareth, to see whether it has any light to throw on the assertion that in Him God was reconciling the world.

[1] Cf. E. Stauffer, *N.T. Theology*, p. 254.

9
This Jesus

Our sources for the life of Jesus give us a reliable summary of the out-standing events in His life.

1. At His Baptism we find the 'Coming Ruler' and the 'Servant of the Lord' uniquely linked in the thought of Jesus. This is confirmed by the Temptations when Jesus rejects one by one three short cuts to success. There remains for Him only the way of the 'Servant-Messiah' coming to His kingdom through suffering.

2. The burden of Jesus' early preaching is that the decisive hour for God's people is now, and is associated with Himself. In Him, God's kingdom or kingship is at hand, its power demonstrated in His 'mighty works', its challenge contained in His parables. People are summoned to 'repent' in response to the good tidings of God's fatherly love for all. This love Jesus demonstrated in His life, nowhere more clearly than in His concern for the outcasts of society. In this respect He parts company with the Pharisees.

3. The response to His witness and the mission of His disciples is disappointing. Though His popularity with the people is evident, the summons to repent is not heeded. Even His closest friends only partially understand Him, as is seen in Peter's confession and blunder at Caesarea Philippi. Deliberately challenging the opposition by His entry into Jerusalem, Jesus sees the cross as His Father's will, and the climax of His minstry as the Servant.

4. Jesus went to death convinced that it would be the gateway to triumph, the triumph of the 'Son of Man'. His death would inaugurate the 'New Covenant'.

The words from the cross are words of faith mid agony.

SOME thirty years ago, a New Testament scholar gave it as his personal opinion that 'we can now know almost nothing concerning the life and personality of Jesus, since the early Christian sources show no interest in either, are moreover fragmentary, and often legendary, and other sources about Jesus do not exist'.[1] If this be so, then the last two chapters may contain interesting examples of first-century religious speculation, but it is speculation suspended in mid-air, without any visible means of support. True, the early Christian sources do not display the professional biographer's interest in the life and personality of Jesus. The four Gospels are fragmentary. Some of the material in them undoubtedly circulated at first as separate units with no clear indication as to setting in the ministry of Jesus. Nor need we be surprised if legends gathered round Jesus. If but a fraction of the claims made about Him by the early Christian witnesses are true, it would be remarkable if there had been no legends. On the other hand, however, a considerable amount of information about Jesus of Nazareth may be gleaned from the preaching of the early witnesses and from the New Testament letters. As for the four Gospels, three of them, Mark, Luke and Matthew, stand together, looking at the life and ministry of Jesus from the same vantage point,[2] Luke and Matthew taking Mark's outline of events as the framework of their story. Of this Marcan outline, there is little reason to doubt that it gives us 'a convincing summary of the outstanding events in the life of Jesus'.[3] Furthermore, it is being increasingly recognized that in John's Gospel—so different in many respects from the other three—we are in touch with a genuine historical tradition which serves to supplement and, at points, correct the others. Legends there may be, in our sources, but the *essential* sobriety of the four Gospels may be clearly seen by comparing them with other pseudo Gospels, e.g. the Gospel of Peter, which circulated in the early church.[4] Need we ask for more than 'a convincing summary of the outstanding events in the life of Jesus'? In such outstanding events a man's character and inmost thoughts are most surely revealed.

---

[1] R. Bultmann, *Jesus and the Word*, p. 8.
[2] Hence they are called the 'Synoptic Gospels' from a Greek word meaning 'seeing together'.
[3] V. Taylor, *The Life and Ministry of Jesus*, p. 39.
[4] Cf. M. R. James, *The Apocryphal New Testament*.

I

Baptism and Temptation. The first outstanding event in the life of Jesus to claim our attention is His baptism by His kinsman John (Mark i. 9–11; Luke iii. 21–22; Matt. iii. 13–17). John the Baptist is a striking figure. He does not mince his words. With all the fire of an Old Testament prophet, he castigates the corruption of the age. 'Renounce your evil ways' is his cry. He was 'preaching a baptism of repentance for the forgiveness of sins. And there went out to him all the country of Judea, and all the people of Jerusalem; and they were baptised by him in the river Jordan, confessing their sins'. (Mark i. 4–5). But there is more here than a preacher of great moral earnestness. John is a herald, urgently proclaiming 'The Day of the Lord is nigh'. This is the hour of crisis, and crisis is but a Greek word meaning 'judgement'. 'Even now,' says John, 'the axe is laid to the root of the trees; every tree therefore that does not bear good fruit is cut down and thrown into the fire' (Luke iii. 9; Matt. iii. 10). Now is the time to 'Prepare the way of the Lord, make his paths straight.' (Is. xl. 3 quoted in Mark i. 3; Luke iii. 4; Matt. iii. 3). Great events are at hand. 'After me comes he who is mightier than I, the thong of whose sandals I am not worthy to stoop down and untie. I have baptised you with water, but he will baptise you with the Holy Spirit' (Mark i. 7–8; cf. Luke iii. 16 ff.; Matt. iii. 11 ff.). If God's Spirit is to be made freely available to the people, what can this mean, but that the New Age is dawning?[1] Who can this greater than John be, but the long expected Ruler? At this point we read: 'Jesus came from Nazareth of Galilee and was baptised by John in the Jordan. And when he came up out of the water, immediately he saw the heavens opened and the Spirit descending upon him like a dove; and a voice came from heaven, "Thou art my beloved Son; with thee I am well pleased" ' (Mark i. 9–11).

Why did Jesus join the crowds who came to John for baptism? Mark gives no reason. 'Matthew' declares that John hesitated to baptise Jesus. ' "I need to be baptised by you and do you come to me?" But Jesus answered him, "Let it be so now; for thus it is

[1] Cf. p. 155.

fitting for us to fulfil all righteousness" ' (Matt. iii. 14–15). 'To fulfil all righteousness'—an enigmatic saying; perhaps we ought to see Jesus here identifying Himself with God's people as the first step in His sharing in God's activity. What happened at the moment of Baptism? For Jesus, something decisive; a voice from heaven, the words, 'Thou art my beloved Son, with thee I am well pleased' (Mark i. 11; Luke iii. 22; cf. Matt. iii. 17). The words are deceptively simple, yet their meaning only becomes clear when we remember that Jesus' mind was steeped in the thought of the Old Testament. It is generally agreed that this sentence combines words from Psalm ii. 7 and Isa. xlii. 1; the former, coming originally from one of the Coronation Psalms of the King of Israel, had been long regarded as referring to the Coming Ruler; the latter is taken from one of the Servant Songs. This is surprise number one in the life of Jesus. The 'Coming Ruler' and the 'Servant of the Lord'? Hitherto, these two strands in the Old Testament had gone their own separate ways; the Servant, the people of God, experiencing humiliation and suffering in the service of God; the Coming Ruler, a conquering hero leading His people in triumph.[1] Here they are woven together in the mind of Jesus, with what consequences we shall see as we look at the story of the Temptations, the inevitable 'follow on' from the Baptism.

'The Spirit immediately drove him out into the wilderness. And he was in the wilderness forty days, tempted by Satan; and he was with the wild beasts; and the angels ministered to him' (Mark i. 12–13)—thus Mark briefly, leaving Matthew and Luke, or rather a common source, to fill in the picture.

There are three temptations, two of which begin significantly, 'If you are the Son of God . . .' Far from being the ordinary temptations of daily life, they are a truly devilish test of one who knows Himself to hold a unique place in God's purposes [i.e. the Coming Ruler], and hence to be in possession of unique power. But how is this God-given power to be used?

'If you are the Son of God, command this stone to become bread' (Luke iv. 3; Matt. iv. 3). In an enemy occupied country, where hunger and poverty were rife, how great a temptation this

[1] Cf. H. H. Rowley, *The Servant of the Lord*.

N

must have been for one whose life was to be characterized by a tireless concern for the needs of others. Was not the New Age expected to be an Age of plenty for all? Would this not be the royal road to popularity? All our Gospels record a story which seems, at first, to portray Jesus as yielding to this temptation, the story of the feeding of five thousand people (Mark vi. 32–44; Luke ix. 10–17; Matt. xiv. 13–21; John vi. 1–13). John concludes his account: 'When the people saw the sign which he had done, they said, "This is indeed the prophet who is to come into the world". Perceiving then that they were about to come and take him by force to make him king, Jesus withdrew again to the hills by himself' (John vi. 14–15). This was the kind of action the people understood. Five thousand loyalists were ready, there and then, to crown Jesus king, and to follow Him, if need be, to the death. But such was not the kingship Jesus coveted. The real hunger of men lay deeper. He takes His stand on a word from the Old Testament. 'It is written "Man shall not live by bread alone"' (Luke iv. 4; Matt. iv. 4, quoting Deut. viii. 3).

The second temptation (to follow Luke's order) depicts the devil giving Jesus a panoramic view of the kingdoms of the world and adding: 'To you I will give all this authority and their glory; for it has been delivered to me, and I will give it to whom I will. If you then will worship me, it shall all be yours' (Luke iv. 6–7; Matt. iv. 9–10). Take a short cut, a devilish short cut, to the establishment of God's kingdom among men. Surely the greatness of the prize will justify any means. Perhaps behind this temptation there lurks a course of action with which many people flirted, and which a few, the Zealots, openly advocated, a national religious uprising against the hated Roman imperialism. Was not the Coming Ruler expected to make short work of Israel's enemies? Why not a holy war against the infidel? 'Put your sword back into its place; for all who take the sword will perish by the sword' (Matt. xxvi. 52); these words of Jesus to one of His disciples (John's Gospel identifies him as Peter) who attempted to offer armed resistance to his master's arrest, are a fit commentary on the many abortive uprisings of Jewish religious nationalism against Roman imperialism. It was not, however, the possible bloody failure of such an uprising which deterred Jesus.

He was convinced that this was not God's way, and it was only in God's way that God's purposes in this world could be forwarded. 'It is written, "You shall worship the Lord your God and him only shall you serve" ' (Luke iv. 8; Matt. iv. 10, quoting Deut vi. 13).

So we turn to the topmost pinnacle of the temple, the imagined setting of the third temptation. 'If you are the Son of God, throw yourself down from here; for it is written, "He will give his angels charge of you, to guard you', and "On their hands they will bear you up, lest you strike your foot against a stone" ' (Luke iv. 9–11). There was a tradition (cf. Mal. iii. 1) that one day the LORD would appear suddenly in the temple at Jerusalem. Why should Jesus not use His power to make a dramatic entry, worthy of God Himself? Sooner or later, Jesus, if He were the Coming Ruler, would have to authenticate His claim. Why not dazzle people into believing by a spectacular sign? After all, there was scriptural warrant for it. Again Jesus refuses. Instead of serving God in God's way, in utter dependence upon God, this would be putting God to the test, attempting to force God's hand. 'It is written, "You shall not tempt the Lord your God" ' (Luke iv. 12; Matt. iv. 7, quoting, Deut. vi. 16). People did demand proof of Jesus' claims. He was later to say: 'This generation is an evil generation; it seeks a sign, but no sign shall be given to it except the sign of Jonah. For as Jonah became a sign to the men of Nineveh, so will the Son of man be to this generation' (Luke xi. 29–30; cf. Mark viii. 12). What did Jesus mean by 'the sign of Jonah'? Luke leaves us in no doubt.[1] Jonah himself, the man and the message on his lips, was the sign, the only sign given to the people of Nineveh, 'so will the Son of Man[2] be to this generation.' The only sign is to be Jesus Himself, the man and his message.

But if not the Welfare State in person, the instigator of political subversion or the spell-binding wonder worker, what? What kind of Coming Ruler is this? The answer is there in the words of the Baptism. This is a Ruler whose royal route is to be that of the Servant of the Lord. There is no easy way to establish *this* kingdom. The shadow of coming humiliation falls across even the early,

---

[1] A different interpretation in line with the author's well-known tendency to find exact parallels between Jesus and the O.T. is found in Matt. xii. 39 ff.

[2] 'Son of Man' is Jesus' favourite description of Himself, cf. pp. 210 ff.

apparently enthusiastic scenes of Jesus' ministry. He is noticeably
reticent in describing himself to other people as the Messiah, the
Coming Ruler. The reason is plain. Too many spurious hopes of
deluding grandeur and national glory clustered round the Coming
Ruler. Openly to have claimed to be the Coming Ruler would have
been to invite fatal misunderstanding. Jesus had no intention of
fitting Himself into popular expectations. He was to challenge men
to reinterpret all their expectations in the light of what they were to
learn from Him. It was the vision of the 'Servant of the Lord', fulfilling God's purposes through suffering, humiliation and death
which best fitted His intention.

II

The Decisive Challenge of the Kingdom

'The time is fulfiled and the kingdom of God is at hand; repent
and believe in the Gospel' (Mark i. 15).

Thus Mark summarizes the early teaching of Jesus. Every
phrase in that summary is a challenge, an intimation that men stand
in the hour of crisis.

A

The time is fulfilled (cf. Gal. iv. 4)—in other words, this is the
hour for the fulfilment of all God's purposes. The 'Day' for which
men have looked in fear and hope, is now. This is the threshold of
the New Age. Luke records a startling incident in Jesus' home town
of Nazareth. Jesus 'went to the synagogue, as his custom was, on
the sabbath day. And he stood up to read; and there was given to
him the book of the prophet Isaiah. He opened the book and found
the place where it was written,

"The Spirit of the Lord is upon me,
because he has anointed me to preach good news to the poor.
He has sent me to proclaim release to the captives

and recovering of sight to the blind,
to set at liberty those who are oppressed,
to proclaim the acceptable year of the Lord!"

And he closed the book and gave it back to the attendant, and sat down. And the eyes of all in the synagogue were fixed on him. And he began to say to them, "Today this scripture has been fulfilled in your hearing" ' (Luke iv. 16–21).

There is nothing unusual in Jesus being invited to read the lesson in the synagogue, and deliver a short discourse on the lesson to the people; but whereas the typical Jewish Rabbi (teacher) would attempt, after reading, to draw forth some spiritual or moral lesson from the passage, Jesus simply asserts, 'Today this scripture has been fulfilled in your hearing'. No wonder Mark records that the people of Capernaum, on a similar occasion, were 'astonished at his teaching, for he taught them as one who had authority, and not as the scribes' (Mark i. 22). With loving reverence, the scribes studied the 'Law' and sought, following distinguished predecessors whose opinions they revered, to interpret its demands to the people. 'It is written' was their ultimate authority. But here is one who says, 'You have heard that it was said [i.e. in the Law] . . . but I say' (e.g. Matt. v. 21, 27, 31, 33, 38, 43). A new decisive word is being spoken to God's people. The climax of all God's dealings with this people is *now* and is associated with Jesus. The time is fulfilled.

B

The Kingdom of God is at hand. The Kingdom of God;[1] saying after saying of Jesus centres upon the Kingdom of God. The theme of many of His challenge stories, the parables, is the Kingdom of God. 'The Kingdom of God is as if a man should scatter seed upon the ground' (Mark iv. 26); 'The Kingdom of God . . . is like a grain of mustard seed' (Mark iv. 30); 'The kingdom of heaven is like treasure hidden in a field' (Matt. xiii. 44); 'Again the kingdom of

[1] Matthew, reflecting the excessive Jewish reverence which hesitated even to mention the divine name, prefers 'the Kingdom of heaven'.

heaven is like a merchant in search of fine pearls' (Matt. xiii. 45);
'Again the kingdom of heaven is like a net which is thrown into the
sea' (Matt. xiii. 47). But what is the 'Kingdom of God'? When we,
for example, talk about the United Kingdom of Great Britain and
Northern Ireland, we think of a close-knit community with its
distinctive political organization, and at its head a monarch. All our
emphasis, however, is placed on the organized community, not
on the personal rule exercised by the monarch; the monarch may
possess very little real power. With Jesus and his contemporaries it
is different. The Kingdom of God means God's active kingly rule,
His personal sovereignty exercised among men. God's kingly rule
is 'at hand' claims Jesus (some would translate 'has come'[1]). This
is not the language of pious hope that some day, somehow, God's
kingship will be recognized by men. It is an uncompromising
declaration that God's kingship is now confronting men, and confronting them in the person of Jesus. John the Baptist was a herald,
but indeed a 'greater than John' is here.

'Being asked by the Pharisees when the kingdom of God was
coming, he answered them, "The kingdom of God is not coming
with signs to be observed; nor will they say 'Lo here it is', or 'There'
for behold, the kingdom of God is in the midst of you"' (Luke xvii.
20–21). No need to look for signs of a coming kingdom; God's
kingly rule is here now, in their midst, here in Jesus and His activity.
That the battle has been joined, decisively joined between God and
all the forces of evil, is the theme of the Gospels from the beginning. It is to be seen in the 'works of power', such is the
favourite description given in the Synoptics to the 'miracles' of
Jesus (e.g. Mark vi. 2, 5; Luke xix. 37; Matt. xiii. 54, 58). The first
chapter of Mark's Gospel describes three such 'mighty works'. In
the synagogue at Capernaum there is a man with an unclean spirit,
'and he cried out, "What have you to do with us, Jesus of Nazareth? Have you come to destroy us? I know who you are, the Holy
One of God!" But Jesus rebuked him, saying, "Be silent and come
out of him!" And the unclean spirit, convulsing him and crying
with a loud voice, came out of him' (Mark i. 24–26).

[1] Cf. C. H. Dodd, *The Parables of the Kingdom.* Contrast R. H. Fuller, *The Mission
and Achievement of Jesus.*

Simon Peter's mother-in-law is laid low with fever, 'And he came and took her by the hand and lifted her up, and the fever left her; and she served them' (Mark i. 31).

'And a leper came to him beseeching him, and kneeling, said to him, "If you will you can make me clean!" Moved with pity he stretched out his hand, and touched him, and said to him, "I will be clean"' (Mark i. 40–41).

Nearly a third of Mark's Gospel is concerned with such 'mighty works', explain them how you will. Jesus shares the view of His contemporaries, that many kinds of illness are attributable to evil spirits, demon possession. That Jesus possessed power over such evil spirits is the unanimous testimony of the Gospels (e.g. Mark v. 2 ff.; Matt. xii. 22 ff.; Luke ix. 37 ff.). When some of His opponents suggest that He must be in league with the devil to possess such power (Luke xi. 15), Jesus traces this power to 'the finger of God' or 'the spirit of God' (Matt. xii. 28). 'But if it is by the finger of God that I cast out demons, then *the kingdom of God has come upon you.* When a strong man, fully armed, guards his own palace, his goods are in peace; but when one stronger than he assails him and overcomes him, he takes away his armour in which he trusted and divides his spoil' (Luke xi. 20–22; cf. Matt. xii. 28–29). Evil is being assailed, nay is being overcome by the kingly power of God. The 'mighty works' are to Jesus demonstrations of the kingship of God in action *now*, in action through Himself.

As in His actions, so with His teaching. The art of story telling never had a more skilled exponent than Jesus (cf. Luke xv). Yet it would be wrong to think of Jesus' parables as mere stories, or indeed as homely illustrations of spiritual truths. In His parables, Jesus is throwing down the gauntlet, challenging men to decision in the light of God's kingship.

'The kingdom of God is as if a man should scatter seed upon the ground, and should sleep and rise night and day, and the seed should sprout and grow, he knows not how. The earth produces of itself, first the blade, then the ear, then the full grain in the ear. But when the grain is ripe, at once he puts in the sickle, because the harvest has come' (Mark. iv. 26–29).

The sting is in the tail. Harvest was a well-known symbol for the Kingdom of God. Harvest has come. God is putting in his sickle. Now is the hour of decision.

'And again he said, "To what shall I compare the kingdom of God? It is like leaven which a woman took and hid in three measures of meal, till it was all leavened" ' (Luke xiii. 20). The leaven is at work. Men are being challenged to face the fact that the ferment of the Kingdom in the world has begun. . . .

'The kingdom of heaven is like treasure hidden in a field, which a man found and covered up; then in his joy he goes and sells all that he has and buys that field' (Matt. xiii. 44). The treasure is *there* to be found. Ought not a man to sacrifice everything for the sake of the kingdom? 'His parables . . . are weapons of war, and his "mighty works" signs that the issue is being victoriously joined with the powers of evil.'[1]

C

The time is fulfilled . . . the kingdom of God is at hand . . . *Repent and believe the Gospel.* Repent! This is not an invitation to wring hands and feel sorry for the past; at least that is never the full flavour of the word. In the Old Testament prophets, the word 'repent' is closely linked with the word 'return' (cf. Jer. iv. 28; Ezek. xiv. 6; Joel ii. 14). This is a summons to do a right about turn, to change direction from a life centred in self to a life centred in God. The call to repent is a call to 'seek first God's kingdom and his righteousness' (Matt. vi. 33; Luke xii. 31). How does a man do this?

'And passing along by the Sea of Galilee, he saw Simon and Andrew the brother of Simon casting a net in the sea; for they were fishermen. And Jesus said to them, "Follow me and I will make you become fishers of men." And immediately they left their nets and followed him. And going on a little farther, he saw James, the son of Zebedee and John his brother, who were in their boat mending the nets. And immediately he called them; and they left their father Zebedee in the boat with the hired servants, and followed him' (Mark i. 16–20).

[1] A. M. Hunter, *Introducing N.T. Theology*, p. 18.

At this cross roads of decision, men did not divide themselves into 'the good' and 'the bad', the good following Jesus, the bad taking the other road. Some of the best and most respectable of people shied at this challenge. A young man once asked Jesus the secret of the complete life. Jesus directed him to the Commandments, 'Do not kill, do not commit adultery, do not steal, do not bear false witness, do not defraud, honour your father and your mother.' In utter sincerity the young man replied, ' "Teacher, all these have I observed from my youth." And Jesus, looking upon him, loved him, and said to him: "You lack one thing; go, sell what you have and give to the poor, and you will have treasure in heaven; and come, follow me!" At that saying, his countenance fell, and he went away sorrowful; for he had great possessions' (Mark x. 20–22; cf. Matt. xix. 16 ff; Luke xviii. 18 ff.). This is but one illustration of the warning Jesus gave: 'No one can serve two masters; for either he will hate the one and love the other, or he will be devoted to the one and despise the other. You cannot serve God and mammon' (Matt. vi. 24; Luke xvi. 13). If you have other 'hidden treasure'— for that is what mammon originally meant—then you cannot be willing to stake all on finding the 'treasure' which is the Kingdom of God (cf. Matt. xiii. 44).

Repent. This had likewise been the cry of John the Baptist; but there was a difference. John summoned the people to repent in view of 'the axe already laid at the root of the tree'. Jesus summoned the people to repent in the light of the 'good tidings', the gospel. That passage in the Old Testament, which Jesus so dramatically in the synagogue at Nazareth claimed to be fulfilled, turned upon the announcement of 'good tidings' to afflicted people (Isa. lxi. 1–2). Its justification lies in a God who cares for and delivers His people.

The fifteenth chapter of Luke's Gospel contains three parables about 'lost things'—a lost sheep (verses 3–7), a lost coin (verses 8–10), a lost boy (verses 11–32). But it is not the fact of their being lost which is of central significance. In each case there is an eager, loving search, and a great rejoicing when the lost is found. The shepherd, leaving his other sheep in the fold, goes forth in search of the one which is lost until he finds it. 'And when he has found it, he lays it on his shoulders, rejoicing. And when he comes home, he calls together his friends and his neighbours, saying to them, "Rejoice with me, for I have found my sheep which was lost" ' (verses 5–6). The poor woman turns the house upside down till she finds the elusive coin. Then she summons her neighbours, 'Rejoice with me, for I have found the coin which I had lost' (verse 9). The lost boy, hesitantly and shamefacedly turns home, to ask for a job among his father's workmen. But the father 'while he was yet at a distance, saw him and had compassion, and ran and embraced him, and kissed him' (verse 20). There must be a family celebration, 'for this my son was dead and is alive again; he was lost and is found' (verse 24).

Such, Jesus declared, is God's attitude to His rebellious children. He not only declared it, he lived it. Among His closest friends, there was a quisling, collecting taxes for the Roman occupation authorities, and, no doubt, lining his own pocket handsomely into the bargain (Matt. ix. 9, cf. the Zacchaeus story, Luke xix. 1–10). One might have thought that a man claiming to have been sent by God would have been careful of the company he kept, yet Jesus was often found with the 'untouchables', the riff-raff of society. Mark describes a meal when 'many tax collectors and sinners were sitting with Jesus and his disciples; for there were many who followed him' (Mark ii. 15; cf. Matt. ix. 10; Luke v. 28). When the self-appointed guardians of public morality and upholders of true religion protested, they were firmly told: 'Those who are well have no need of a physician, but those who are sick; I came not to call the righteous, but sinners' (Mark ii. 17).[1]

Here Jesus parted company with the most influential religious group of His day, the Pharisees, and roused their implacable hostility. The Pharisees knew what constituted true religion. God had made known to His people His 'Torah'. It was the duty of the sincerely religious both to understand and to keep every provision of the 'Law'. Only thus could a man further God's purposes. Indeed, were the whole of Israel only to keep God's Law in its entirety for twenty-four hours, the kingdom of God would come. It followed that those who, for one reason or another, were lax in the observance of the 'Law' were the enemies of God, 'sinners' the Pharisees

[1] Cf. C. H. Dodd, *History and the Gospels*, pp. 90 ff.

termed them, though many were respectable, hard-working people. At its worst, the attitude of the Pharisee produced self-righteousness and hypocrisy, about which Jesus had many a biting word to say (cf. Matt. xxiii. 13–33). At its best, and it was a noble best, it was separated from the attitude of Jesus by an almost impassable gulf. The interview between Jesus and Nicodemus, an influential and earnest Pharisee, makes this plain. 'Rabbi,' says Nicodemus, 'we know that you are a teacher come from God; for no one can do these signs that you do, unless God is with him.' Jesus answered him, 'Truly, truly, I say to you, unless one is born anew, he cannot see the kingdom of God' (John iii. 2–3). Born again? That is impossible, thinks Nicodemus, only to hear Jesus say, 'Truly, truly, I say to you, unless one is born of water and the Spirit, he cannot enter the kingdom of God!' (verse 5). In spite of Jesus attempt to explain His meaning by way of an illustration, Nicodemus is left asking, 'How can this be?' (verse 9). He is genuinely puzzled. To Nicodemus the focus of religion is on what a man does; he keeps God's commandments, and thus furthers God's kingdom. To Jesus, religion, first and last, centres upon what God does, a new life which God offers to man, the fruit of God's Spirit at work. The initiative is God's. To the utter astonishment of the Pharisees, Jesus can say that a 'taxgatherer', the hireling of Israel's oppressors, may be nearer the kingdom than they are. Jesus 'told this parable to some who trusted in themselves that they were righteous and despised others. "Two men went up into the temple to pray, one a Pharisee and the other a tax collector. The Pharisee stood and prayed thus within himself: 'God, I thank thee that I am not like other men, extortioners, unjust, adulterers, or even like this tax collector. I fast twice a week, I give tithes of all that I get.' But the tax collector, standing far off, would not even lift up his eyes to heaven, saying, 'God, be merciful to me a sinner'. I tell you, this man went down to his house justified rather than the other; for every one who exalts himself will be humbled, but he who humbles himself will be exalted" ' (Luke xviii. 9–14; cf. Luke vii. 36–50).

Jesus came with 'good tidings'. God was in action. His Kingship was 'at hand'; and this King was a Father who 'makes his sun rise on the evil and on the good, and sends his rain on the just and on the

unjust' (Matt. v. 45)—a Father eagerly concerned for the well-being
of *all* his children; 'the Son of Man came to seek and to save the
lost' (Luke xix. 10)—to seek and to save, not to condemn (cf. John
iii. 17).

John the Baptist had his doubts. Surely this could not be the axe
of God's judgement laid at the root of the tree? From prison, where
his uncompromising tongue had landed him, he sends messengers
to Jesus, 'Are you he who is to come, or shall we look for another?'
(Luke vii. 20). Jesus, continuing his works of healing and caring for
needy people, answers: 'Go and tell John what you have seen and
heard: the blind receive sight, the lame walk, lepers are cleansed, and
the deaf hear, the dead are raised up, the poor have good news
preached to them. And blessed is he who takes no offense at me'
(Luke vii. 22; cf. Matt. xi. 2–6). The words are an echo of Isaiah lxi.
1–2 read in the synagogue in Nazareth. This is God's kingship at
work in the world; it is 'good tidings' for the afflicted. 'And blessed
is he who takes no offense.' But there were many who did take
offence, and many who misunderstood.

III

The Gathering Storm. The outcome of Jesus' proclamation of
the Kingdom of God is surprising. John the Baptist has his doubts;
the influential Pharisees are antagonistic; what of the people as a
whole? The Synoptic Gospels give prominence to the fact that Jesus
sent His immediate disciples, the 'twelve' (cf. Matt. x. 2; Luke vi. 13)
out on a mission. 'And he called to him the twelve, and began to
send them out two by two, and gave them authority over unclean
spirits. He charged them to take nothing for their journey except a
staff; no bread, no bag, no money in their belts; but to wear sandals
and not to put on two tunics. And he said to them: "Where you
enter a house, stay there until you leave the place. And if any place
will not receive you and they refuse to hear you, when you leave,
shake off the dust that is on your feet for a testimony against them!"
So they went out and preached that men should repent. And they
cast out many demons, and anointed with oil many that were sick

and healed them' (Mark vi. 7–13; cf. Matt. x. 1, 5, 7–11; Luke ix. 1–5). Their message is to be the same as that of Jesus, 'the kingdom of God' (Luke ix. 2), and the reality of God's present kingship is demonstrated in the power delegated to them by Jesus to cast out demons. The mission is a partial success. Luke, reporting a similar mission by seventy of Jesus' disciples reports the seventy returning joyfully. ' "Lord, even the demons are subject to us in your name!" And he said to them, "I saw Satan fall like lightning from heaven" ' (Luke x. 17). Evil is being routed. But it is only a partial success. Central to the message of the kingdom is the call to repent. Mark tells us that Jesus, preaching in the synagogue in His home district, provoked astonished incredulity. ' "Where did this man get all this? What is the wisdom given to him? What mighty works are wrought by his hands! Is not this the carpenter, the son of Mary and brother of James and Joses and Judas and Simon, and are not his sisters here with us?" And they took offense at him. And Jesus said to them, "A prophet is not without honor except in his own country, and among his own kin, and in his own house." And He could do no mighty work there, except that He laid his hands upon a few sick people and healed them. And he marvelled because of their unbelief' (Mark vi. 2–6; cf. Mark ix. 19).

God's kingship, to be fully effective, required a people's response. Jesus looked in vain. Of the cities of Galilee, scene of His early ministry, scene of the missionary activity of His disciples, He can only say: 'Woe to you Chorazin! woe to you Bethsaida! for if the mighty works done in you had been done in Tyre and Sidon, they would have repented long ago, sitting in sackcloth and ashes. But it shall be more tolerable in the judgement for Tyre and Sidon than for you. And you, Capernaum, will you be exalted to heaven? You shall be brought down to Hades' (Luke x. 13–15; Matt. xi. 21–24). Approaching Jerusalem for the last time, He exclaims: 'O Jerusalem, killing the prophets and stoning those who are sent to you! How often would I have gathered your children together, as a hen gathers her brood under her wings, and *you would not*' (Matt. xxiii. 37; Luke xiii. 34; cf. Luke xix. 41). Like sulky children, refusing to join in any games, such is Jesus' verdict on the people of His generation (cf. Luke vii. 31–32). Offended by the stern asceticism of John the Baptist, they objected to Jesus as 'a glutton and a drunkard, a friend of tax collectors and sinners' (Luke vii. 34).

Not that Jesus lacked popularity. He always had the ability to draw a crowd. An incident like the feeding of the five thousand could make him dangerously popular.[1] The innumerable 'mighty works', the eager expectations roused by talk of the Kingdom of God, the magnetism of His teaching—all this was acceptable. But to the challenge of the Kingdom, to the call to repent, the people remain deaf. 'It is not waning popularity which compels Jesus to regard the Galilean ministry as a failure, and which drives Him to seclusion. It is popularity itself, and above all its facile character. The people do not repent. . . .'[2]

There comes a time when Jesus, deliberately turning His back on the crowds, seeks a period of seclusion (cf. Mark vii. 24, 31), during which, doubtless, He was pondering the significance of what had happened so far. Not long afterwards comes one of the most illuminating moments in the ministry of Jesus. Near Caesarea Philippi, not far from the source of the River Jordan, Jesus asks His disciples: ' "Who do men say that I am?" and they told him, "John the Baptist; and others say, Elijah; and others one of the prophets" ' —a great prophet, yes, but notice no suggestion that He is the Coming Ruler. Jesus did not measure up to popular expectation in this rôle. 'But you,' says Jesus, turning to the men who had responded to the challenge of the kingdom to share in God's work, 'who do you say that I am?' Peter, the most forthright among them, speaks for all when he says, 'You are the Christ' (Mark viii. 27–29), i.e. the Messiah, the Coming Ruler (cf. Matt. xvi. 13ff.; Luke ix. 18–21). The disciples know enough of Jesus by this time to realize that He *must* be the Coming Ruler, however much He differed from what was popularly expected. But even they did not, as yet, realize just how different this Coming Ruler was. 'Keep it a secret,' is Jesus' reply to this momentous confession; the risk of popular misunderstanding remained. Then 'he began to teach them that the *Son of Man must suffer* many things and be rejected . . .' (Mark viii. 31).

---

[1] Cf. p. 194.
[2] V. Taylor, *The Life and Ministry of Jesus*, p. 114; cf. T. W. Manson, *The Servant Messiah*, p. 71.

It is as if the disciples had been rudely awakened from a moment of religious wonder by a slap in the face. Peter will have none of it. He is still sufficiently at one with popular expectations to think of the Coming Ruler in terms of triumph and victory. He protests at this nonsensical talk of suffering and rejection, only to be stunned into silence by Jesus' vehement retort: 'Get behind me, Satan! For you are not on the side of God but of men' (Mark viii, 33). From now on, with ever increasing urgency, Jesus speaks to His disciples of coming suffering, rejection and even death, in close association with the enigmatic title 'Son of Man' (cf. Mark ix. 12; x. 33).[1] It is small wonder that after one such saying, Mark says that the disciples 'did not understand the saying, and they were afraid to ask him' (Mark ix. 32).

Why this talk of coming suffering, humiliation and death, and why the 'Son of Man'? Jesus, of course, has already made powerful enemies. Plans were early afoot to liquidate Him (cf. Mark iii. 6). But this in itself did not make what follows inevitable. Jesus could have avoided His enemies; instead Luke reports that 'he set his face to go to Jerusalem' (Luke ix. 51). The disciples had good reason to be afraid. With equal deliberation, Jesus stages His entry into Jerusalem, riding on the back of an ass' foal to the acclaim of His followers. The words of Zechariah spring to mind:

> 'Rejoice greatly, O daughter of Zion!
> Shout aloud, O daughter of Jerusalem!
> Lo *your king comes to you*;
> triumphant and victorious is he,
> humble and riding on an ass,
> on a colt, the foal of an ass.
> I will cut off the chariot from Ephraim
> and the war horse from Jerusalem;
> and the battle bow shall be cut off,
> and he shall command peace to the nations;
> his dominion shall be from sea to sea,
> and from the River to the ends of the earth.'
>
> (Zech. ix. 9–10)

[1] Was it now that He told the disciples the story of His baptism and temptations?

The claim to be the Coming Ruler is there, scarcely veiled, for anyone who has eyes to see it (Mark xi. 1–10; Luke xix. 29–38; Matt. xxi. 1–9; John xii. 12–15, the last two passages specifically quoting from Zechariah). When the disciples hail Jesus in the words of one of the Pilgrim Psalms (Ps. cxviii. 26): 'Blessed be the King who comes in the name of the LORD', 'some of the Pharisees in the multitude said to him, "Teacher, rebuke your disciples." He answered, "I tell you, if these were silent, the very stones would cry out" ' (Luke xix. 39–40).

The die is cast. Unless Jesus concealed some supernatural trump-card up His sleeve, *and were prepared to play it*, there could be only one outcome. A week of mounting tension, graphically described in the Gospels (Mark xi–xv; Matt. xxi–xxvii; Luke xix. 28–xxiii; John xii–xix) culminates on a Roman cross outside the city walls at 9 o'clock on Friday morning. Could it have been avoided? Yes, if Jesus had been prepared to pay the price of renouncing all that He had hitherto said and done. After speaking of His own coming suffering, Jesus warned His followers: 'If any man would come after me, let him deny himself and take up his cross and follow me. For whoever would save his life will lose it; and whoever loses his life for my sake and the gospel's will save it' (Mark viii. 34–35). Jesus could have side-stepped the cross. 'He could,' as has been said,[1] 'have saved his own life, but it would have meant the loss of all that he had lived for.' He came, proclaiming in word and deed the kingship of God, the kingship of a Father whose loving care reached out to all His children. That passionate concern for the despised and the outcast Jesus would never renounce, though it made Him implacable enemies. The challenge to repentance He could never renounce, even when it met with stony indifference. Luke records that on the last journey to Jerusalem Jesus 'sent messengers ahead of him who went and entered a village of the Samaritans[2] to make ready for him; but the people would not receive him because his face was set toward Jerusalem. And when his disciples James and John saw it, they said, "Lord do you want us to bid fire come down from heaven

[1] D. M. Baillie, *God was in Christ*, p. 182.
[2] There was as little love lost between Jew and Samaritan as there is between Jew and Arab at the present day, cf. John iv.; Luke x. 33.

and consume them?" But he turned and rebuked them' (Luke ix. 51-54).

If not 'consuming fire' then what? Some of our manuscripts add a very interesting rider to this incident: '. . . and he [i.e. Jesus] said, "You do not know what manner of spirit you are of; for the Son of man came not to destroy men's lives but to save them" ' (Luke ix. 55). But how do you 'save' in the face of indifference and enmity? How, but by continuing along the same caring, challenging path, prepared to go on loving, if need be to the bitter end.

Jesus 'set his face to go to Jerusalem', aware that the end would be bitter, but equally aware that only thus could He fully identify himself with God's searching love for men. This was His Father's will, and He knew the will of the heavenly Father as no one else ever did. All our sources agree that Jesus claimed a *unique* relationship to God. Jesus greets Peter's confession at Caesarea Philippi with the words,

'Blessed are you, Simon Bar-Jona! For flesh and blood has not revealed this to you, but *my* Father who is in heaven' (Matt. xvi. 17).

Or consider this statement: 'All things have been delivered to me by my Father; and no one knows who the Son is except the Father, or who the Father is except the Son and any one to whom the Son chooses to reveal him' (Luke x. 22; Matt. xi. 27)—a hard saying indeed, for any who would see in Jesus nothing more than a well-intentioned Galilean preacher.[1] On the evening of His arrest, we find Jesus praying in a place called Gethsemane: 'Abba, Father, all things are possible to thee; remove this cup from me; yet not what I will but what thou wilt' (Mark xiv. 36). How frequently the Aramaic word 'Abba' must have been on the lips of Jesus. Even when the Gospels were written in Greek, the Aramaic word remains, with an explanatory translation 'father'. Yet 'father' hardly does justice to this word. 'Abba' is more truly and startlingly translated 'Da-da'. It is the word of a little child, so familiar, so intimate a word that, as far as we can discover, no Jew ever dared use it in prayer. Yet Jesus used it. There was that degree of intimacy between Jesus and His heavenly Father. Out of that intimacy was born the conviction that suffering, humiliation and death were His Father's

---

[1] Cf. J. W. Bowman, *The Intention of Jesus*, pp. 174 ff.

will. 'Abba . . . what thou wilt.' He found confirmation of this in long meditation upon the Servant of the Lord in Isaiah xl. ff. If our interpretation of the Baptism and Temptation be correct, the figure of the Servant was with Jesus from the outset of His ministry, that Servant who, according to Isaiah liii, drinks a cup of bitter anguish for the sins of others. Only Luke xxii. 37 actually quotes from Isaiah liii, 'For I tell you that this scripture must be fulfilled in me'. 'And he was reckoned with transgressors;[1] for what is written about me has its fulfilment' (cf. Mark xiv. 49). There are, however, many echoes. Mark x. 45 talks about 'a ransom for *many*'; Mark xiv. 24, 'my blood . . . poured out for *many*'; we may compare Isaiah liii. 11 which describes the Servant as justifying *many* and bearing the sins of *many*. This was His Father's will, that He follow in the footsteps of the Servant of the LORD.

IV

This is the victory. Jesus, however, saw what awaited Him in Jerusalem, not as the tragic ending to a promising career, but as the fulfilment of His mission, the pathway to triumph. We talk of the 'Suffering Servant', but it is important to remember that the Suffering Servant is the Triumphant Servant. Broken, done to death, yet

'he shall see his offspring, he shall prolong his days;
the will of the LORD shall prosper in his hand;
he shall see the fruit of the travail of his soul and be satisfied.'
(Is. liii. 10–11.)

'The Son of man must suffer many things, and be rejected by the chief priests and the scribes, and be killed, and after three days *rise again*' (Mark viii. 31).

'The Son of man will be delivered into the hands of men, and they will kill him; and when he is killed, after three days he will rise' (Mark ix. 31, cf. x. 33).

'Truly I say to you, there are some standing here who will not

[1] Isa. liii. 12.

taste death before they see the kingdom of God come with power'
(Mark ix. 1; cf. Luke xxii. 28–30; Matt. xix. 28, 30).

So Jesus taught, and even if, as most scholars believe, some of
the references [e.g. to rising *in three days*] may have been made
more pointed in the light of what happened, there is no doubt that
Jesus associated suffering and death with ultimate victory.

At His interrogation before the Jewish authorities, Jesus is re-
ported as replying to the question, 'Are you the Christ?' with the
words, 'I am; and you will see the Son of man sitting at the right
hand of Power, and coming with the clouds of heaven' (Mark xiv.
62; cf. Matt. xxvi. 64; Luke xxii. 69). The words are an undoubted
reference to a passage in the Book of Daniel. In typical visionary
language we hear of four beasts who are to lord it for a period over
the earth. After the description of the destruction of the last and
most ruthless of these beasts,[1] the vision continues,

> 'I saw in the night visions,
> and behold, with the clouds of heaven
> there came one like a son of man,
> and he came to the Ancient of Days[2]
> and was presented before him.
> And to him was given dominion and glory and kingdom,
> that all peoples, nations and languages
> should serve him;
> his dominion is an everlasting dominion,
> which shall not pass away,
> and his kingdom one
> that shall not be destroyed.'
>
> (Dan. vii. 13–14)

There is evidence that this 'one like a son of man' was the object of
considerable speculation, and indeed, in certain circles, was equated
with the Coming Ruler. If, as seems most likely, it was from this
passage that Jesus took the enigmatic title 'Son of man', we must

---

[1] The reference is to the persecuting regime of Antiochus Epiphanes in the '60s
of the second century B.C.
[2] i.e. God.

note that it is of the very essence of this 'Son of man' that He appears in triumph to establish an everlasting kingdom. The originality of Jesus here, as in the case of the Coming Ruler, consists in His associating suffering and humiliation with the 'Son of man', but suffering and humiliation nonetheless, as the way to establish that everlasting kingdom. Deserted by His friends, surrounded by accusers, certain that death awaits Him, Jesus can speak with quiet confidence of the coming triumph of the 'Son of Man'.

A victory—but what *kind* of victory did Jesus associate with His suffering and death? Here we have less evidence, though what we have is suggestive. As Jesus and His disciples journey to Jerusalem, two of His disciples, James and John, approach Jesus with a request for positions of special privilege in His kingdom when it comes. You wish to be truly great? Then listen: 'Whoever would be first among you must be the slave of all. For the Son of man also came not to be served, but to serve, and to give his life as a ransom for many' (Mark x. 44–45). 'His life a ransom for many?' The Old Testament Law, in certain cases, provided for the payment of an agreed sum as a substitute for a life which has been forfeited (e.g. Exod. xxi. 30; xxx. 12). Furthermore, it laid upon the next of kin, 'the *go'el*, the duty of redeeming a kinsman for debt-slavery by paying his debt.[1] The great *go'el* was the LORD, who had delivered His people out of slavery in Egypt. Is not Jesus seeing Himself here as the new *go'el* of His people, the price to be paid, His own life? A strange phrase in a strange story may seem to confirm this. The incident at Caesarea Philippi is followed closely in the Gospels by the story of the Transfiguration. Luke's version is as follows:

Now about eight days (Mark and Matthew say six days) after these sayings he took with him Peter and John and James, and went up on the mountain to pray. And as he was praying, the appearance of his countenance was altered, and his raiment became dazzling white. And behold two men talked with him, Moses and Elijah, who appeared in glory, and spoke of his departure, which he was to accomplish at Jerusalem' (Luke ix. 28–31; cf. Mark ix. 2–4; Matt. xvii. 1–3). We cannot help but ask all manner of critical questions about this story; we are probably wise to admit that we can answer

[1] Cf. p. 83.

very few of them. One curious phrase in Luke's account claims our attention. Jesus, he says, spoke with Moses and Elijah, 'of his *departure* which he was to accomplish in Jerusalem'. The word 'departure' is literally in Greek, 'exodus'. Did Jesus think of what He was going to accomplish in Jerusalem in terms of a new Exodus, a new mighty deliverance wrought by God for His people?

A few hours before His arrest, Jesus, after careful preparation, shared a meal with His disciples in an upper room. It was to be the last of many fellowship meals. It was held as the Jewish people were preparing to celebrate Passover which, commemorating the Exodus, yearly renewed faith that as God had acted, so would He act again. Mark reports, 'As they were eating, he took bread and blessed, and broke it, and gave it to them, and said, "Take; this is my body." And he took a cup, and when he had given thanks, he gave it to them, and they all drank of it. And he said to them, "This is my blood of the covenant, which is poured out for many. Truly I say to you, I shall not drink again of the fruit of the vine until that day when I drink it new in the kingdom of God" ' (Mark xiv. 22–25; cf. Matt. xxvi. 26–29; Luke xxii. 19–20; 1 Cor. xi. 23 ff.).

Details in the different accounts vary, but all agree that Jesus, taking the cup, spoke about His blood as 'the blood of the covenant shed for many' (cf. Luke: 'this is the *new* covenant in my blood'). Who can doubt that Jesus had in mind that new covenant spoken of by Jeremiah[1] which would usher in a new and fruitful relationship between God and His people? As the covenant at Sinai had its roots in the wonder of God's deliverance of His people, so this new covenant has its roots in a new and even greater act of deliverance wrought by God through Jesus, in a ministry which finds its fitting climax on the Cross.

Such was the faith in which Jesus faced death. Never did it shine more brightly than in the hour of His death. What greater demonstration of patient love than the words of Jesus, uttered as the nails were hammered into the living flesh of His hands and feet, 'Father forgive them; for they know not what they do' (Luke xxiii. 34). What greater proof of the cost of such love than the haunting cry of agony, 'Eloi eloi, lama sabachthani, My God, my God, why hast

[1] Cf. pp. 150 ff.

thou forsaken me?' (Mark xv. 34). No purely physical pain drew that cry from Jesus. Was the full horror of man's defiance of the kingship of God overwhelming Him? We shall never know. We have no right to minimize what we do not fully understand, yet it is surely no accident that these words of dereliction are the opening words of Psalm xxii, which, beginning in darkness, ends with a confident assertion of God's triumphant sovereignty:

> 'All the ends of the earth shall remember
> and turn to the LORD;
> and all the families of the nations
> shall worship before him.
> For dominion belongs to the LORD,
> and he rules over the nations'
>
> (Ps. xxii. 27–28).

Was the Cross, indeed, the coronation of one who would rule over the nations? Or was it unrelieved tragedy, selfless love crushed by the opportunism, cowardice and self-centredness of men?

. . . . .

Unless the portrait of Jesus which we have sketched from the Gospels is wholly unreliable, there can be no denying that it bears a striking resemblance to the witness of the earliest missionaries. We find here no simple Galilean peasant destined mysteriously to don the garb of divinity in the mind of His followers. Declaring a decisive word, possessing power from God, seeing in Himself the fulfilment of all God's dealings with His people, the Coming Ruler, the 'Servant' Ruler going to the Cross in the confidence that thus God's kingship will triumph—*this* is Jesus of Nazareth.

Is it the portrait of a dangerously deluded religious maniac, or is it possible that, in sober truth, we *must* say that in this Jesus God was in action reconciling the world? If this were merely an academic question raised by research into the life of a man who lived over nineteen hundred years ago, we might well hesitate to commit ourselves to an answer; but the evidence is not yet complete.

10

The New People of God

The New Testament continues the story of the people of God, a new people of God, the 'ecclesia', the Church. The Church can be traced back into the ministry of Jesus in his deliberate choice of twelve men, symbolic of the twelve tribes of Israel. This is the nucleus of a new Israel. This community emphasis is also evident in some of the ways Jesus describes himself—the good shepherd with his flock, the vine with its branches, the 'Son of Man' which in Daniel is a title for the faithful remnant of God's people.

To look at the Church in the light of the New Testament witnesses is to see it as:

1. The Community of the Resurrection. *We cannot eliminate the Resurrection of Jesus from the New Testament even if there are many questions about the Risen Jesus we are unable to answer. The Church is built upon the Resurrection, bears the marks of the Resurrection, witnesses to the Resurrection, and shares a Resurrection life.*

2. The Fellowship of the Spirit. *Acts claims that Joel's prophecy about the outpouring of God's spirit has been fulfilled. The Holy Spirit is the exalted, triumphant Lord, active still among and through his people. To enter the Church means 'to receive the Spirit', to be called to life 'in the Spirit'. Every Christian shares in 'the gifts of the Spirit', the greatest of which is Christlike love. Christian 'virtues' are 'the fruit of the Spirit'. In worship and in prayer, the Christian is aided by the Spirit. For the Christian, Jesus is no fading memory, but a present, active Lord.*

3. The Body of Christ. *Paul's favourite description of the Church stresses that here is a new community*

　　　(a) cutting across all racial and social barriers, to unite men

*in sharing a common life. This 'oneness' is vividly represented in the
fellowship meal, the Lord's supper.*

    *(b) indissolubly linked to its Lord and Master, and intended to
express his 'fulness', being in the world to continue his 'ministry of
reconciliation'.*

THE Old Testament was the story of Israel, the people of God.
To the early missionaries, the murder of Jesus was the final
tragic act in this story of a stubborn, rebellious people. Stephen, the
first Christian martyr, flings in the face of the Jewish council this
accusation: 'As your fathers did, so do you. Which of the prophets
did not your fathers persecute? And they killed those who an-
nounced beforehand the coming of the Righteous One, whom you
have now betrayed and murdered' (Acts vii. 51–52). Is this the end
of God's attempt to establish in the world a community which will
reflect His purposes? Does the story of the Bible from this point onwards cease to be the story of a people, and become instead the story
of the salvation of the individual human soul? No, God's purposes
remain the same; they are merely diverted into a different channel.
Here is Peter, writing to scattered Christian communities in Asia
Minor. The Jewish nation has rejected God.

    'But you are a chosen race, a royal priesthood, a holy nation,
God's own people, that you may declare the wonderful deeds of
him who called you out of darkness into his marvellous light. Once
you were no people, but now you are God's people' (1 Pet. ii. 9–10).

    There is a reference here to Exodus xix. 5–6,[1] a passage des-
cribing Israel as the people of God. All this now applies to you,
says Peter. We Christians are the people of God (cf. Gal. iii. 29;
vi. 16; Phil. iii. 3; Rom. ix. 6).

    That there is in the world a new people of God is asserted in
that familiar word translated in our English Bibles as 'church' or
'churches' (e.g. Acts v. 11; vii. 38; 2 Cor. xi. 8; xii. 13; 1 Cor. i. 2;
Col. iv. 16; Rom xvi. 1, etc.). The word 'church' has a bewildering
variety of meanings for us. We talk about 'the Church of Rome',
'the Anglican Church', 'the Church of Scotland' and so forth,
meaning a particular branch of the Christian community distin-

   [1] Cf. p. 123.

guished from other branches by certain beliefs and practices. We talk about 'going to church' and what we mean, very often, is a particular building. We sometimes demand impatiently, 'Why does the Church not do something?' without being at all sure what we mean by 'the Church'. To the New Testament, however, the Church is neither a denomination nor a building; and where we are vague it is definite.

Ecclesia—this is the Greek New Testament word translated 'Church'.[1] It was a familiar enough word to a Greek. Strictly speaking, it meant the assembly of the people in a city state, summoned by the public herald to discuss matters of public interest. In course of time, it came to mean any public gathering, even the mob at Ephesus described so graphically in Acts xix. Does then 'ecclesia' simply mean in the New Testament, a gathering of Christians, a kind of religious club? Very rarely do we find any phrase remotely like an 'ecclesia of Christians' (cf. 1 Cor. xiv. 33—'the churches of the saints). When the ecclesia is described it is usually in one of two ways; either and more frequently, it is 'the ecclesia *of God*', e.g. 'To the church of God which is in Corinth' (1 Cor. i. 2; cf. x. 32; xi. 22; Gal i. 13; 1 Thess. ii. 14; 2 Thess. i. 4), or it is 'the ecclesia *of Christ*', e.g. 'All the churches of Christ greet you' (Rom. xvi. 16; cf. Gal. i. 22). These are but two different ways of saying the same thing. The 'ecclesia' is God's, called into being by what He has done in Jesus (cf. 1 Thess. ii. 14, 'the churches of God in Jesus Christ'). The background to this is not Greek city life, but the Old Testament, or rather the Septuagint, the Greek translation of the Old Testament, made for Greek-speaking Jewish communities. In the Septuagint, 'ecclesia' always translates the Hebrew word '*qahal*'[2] which tends increasingly to mean 'the people of God'. It describes, for example, the people gathered at Mount Sinai to share in the covenant. It is used of later gatherings at which the faith of the people is renewed. The 'ecclesia', the church is the people of God. True, the New Testament can talk about 'churches', but that does not mean that it believed in the existence of more than one people

[1] Cf. K. L. Schmidt, 'The Church' *Kittel's Bible Key Words*. Translation by J. R. Coates.
[2] Or words from the same root.

of God. Nor is it justification for our different denominations. We hear of the church at Cenchreae (Rom. xvi. 1), the church at Corinth (1 Cor. i. 2; 2 Cor. i. 1), the church of the Thessalonians (1 Thess. i. 1; 2 Thess. i. 1), but these churches are nothing other than outcroppings at different points on the map of the one people of God.

What made the early Christians think of themselves as the new people of God? Was it through reading the Old Testament story of God's people, and concluding, 'this is where we come in', or is there a deeper reason? We must retrace our steps to the ministry of Jesus. In the light of God's present kingship, Jesus summoned people to repent. He did more. He chose certain men, twelve men, to share in His work.

'And he [i.e. Jesus] went up into the hills and called to him those whom he desired; and they came to him. And he appointed twelve to be with him, and to be sent out to preach and have authority to cast out demons: Simon whom he surnamed Peter; James the son of Zebedee and John the brother of James, whom he surnamed Boanerges, that is sons of thunder; Andrew and Philip, and Bartholomew, and Matthew, and Thomas, and James the son of Alphaeus, and Thaddaeus, and Simon the Cananaean, and Judas Iscariot who betrayed him' (Mark iii. 13–19; cf. Matt. x. 1–4; Luke vi. 12–19).

No act of Jesus was done with greater deliberation. Luke says that, before He chose the 'twelve' He spent the whole night in prayer (Luke vi. 12). Why twelve? Twelve tribes together formed Israel, the people of God. The choice of twelve men is a symbolic action, pointing to the nucleus of a reconstituted people of God. The number 'twelve' was certainly regarded as of significance at an early date, since care is taken to choose one man to fill the vacancy caused in the ranks of the twelve by the defection of Judas Iscariot (cf. Acts i. 15–26).

Both Luke and Matthew call the twelve 'apostles'; Luke, indeed, claiming that Jesus gave them the name (Luke vi. 13). Behind this Greek word 'apostle' there lies an original Aramaic word, meaning 'one commissioned to act on behalf of, or in the name of another'. The twelve are sent out by Jesus to act in His name; they proclaim the kingdom is at hand; they exercise Jesus' power over disease and demons. By what they do they extend what Jesus is doing. Were not the people of God in the Old Testament summoned to reflect in their life what they had seen of God in action? Jesus has called into being a new people of God. John's Gospel makes the same point. 'I am the good shepherd,' says Jesus (John x. 11), the shepherd who lays down his life for the flock. The shepherd and his flock is a well-known Old Testament picture of God and His people.[1] Jesus is the 'true vine', His disciples the branches of that vine (John xv. 1 ff.). The vine and the vineyard are familiar descriptions of Israel, the people of God (cf. Ezek. xix. 10; Isa. v. 1–7). What is Jesus here claiming but that He is the foundation stone upon which is to be built a new people of God?

We noticed how Jesus favoured the title 'Son of man'. There is something about the Son of man in Daniel which we have yet to note. The Son of man who is to receive everlasting dominion and an indestructible kingdom is not a solitary figure. We are soon told that

'the kingdom and the dominion
and the greatness of the kingdoms under the whole heaven
shall be given to the *people of the saints of the Most High*;
their kingdom shall be an everlasting kingdom,
and all dominions shall serve and obey them.'
(Dan. vii. 27, cf. verses 18, 22)

The Son of man is a representative figure, the head of the community of God's faithful people. Was this, for Jesus, part of the attractiveness of the title? Certainly, from the choosing of the twelve till the words about a 'new covenant in his blood'[2] there is a marked community emphasis in Jesus' outlook.

Jesus died, but His followers, taught to regard themselves as the new people of God, lived on to perpetuate the memory of their master. Is this a fair description of the Church in the New Testament? If we think this is what happened, we should begin re-writing

[1] Cf. pp. 81ff.
[2] Cf. p. 213.

the New Testament, or rather, we should begin to write the New
Testament, because there would have been no Church, no New
Testament, and in all probability, none of us, except perhaps a few
professional historians, would ever have heard of Jesus of Nazareth.

I

The Community of the Resurrection. At his trial and crucifixion,
Jesus stood alone, deserted by His friends. The same Peter who
hailed Jesus as the Coming Ruler, when challenged as to whether
he is one of the followers of the arrested Jesus, curses and swears,
'I do not know this man of whom you speak' (Mark xiv. 71).
After the crucifixion, the disciples huddle behind bolted doors 'for
fear of the Jews (John xx. 19). Would the next footstep, the next
knock, signal their arrest? A beautiful dream had come to an end.
The kingship of God; where was it when Jesus died, hounded to
death by His fellow countrymen, crucified by the Romans? The
power of love; was it not only too plain that envy, hatred and
bigotry had the last word? They had jeered at Him, 'Aha, you who
would destroy the temple[1] and build it in three days, save yourself
and come down from the cross.' So also the chief priests mocked
Him to one another, with the scribes, saying, 'He saved others; he
cannot save himself. Let the Christ, the King of Israel, come down
now from the cross, that we may see and believe' (Mark xv. 29–32).
But He did not save Himself; the 'King' did not come down from the
cross. He died slowly and in agony. Late on Friday, a friend was
given permission to bury Him in a rock tomb, sealed with a stone
(Mark xv. 42 ff.). Jesus had not sown in the minds of His disciples
immortal ideas. He had made claims, every one of which was now
exploded.

It is Sunday morning. A few women go to the tomb to anoint
the body. As they go, 'they were saying to one another, "Who will
roll away the stone for us from the door of the tomb?" and looking
up, they saw that the stone was rolled back; for it was very large.
And entering the tomb, they saw a young man, sitting on the right

[1] Cf. John ii. 19; Mark xiii. 2.

side, dressed in a white robe; and they were amazed. And he said to them, "Do not be amazed; you seek Jesus of Nazareth who was crucified. He has risen, he is not here; see the place where they laid him. But go, tell his disciples and Peter that he is going before you to Galilee; there you will see him as he told you" ' (Mark xvi. 3–7; cf. Luke xxiv. 1–9; Matt. xxviii. 1–8; John xx. 1–2).

Later that Sunday, two of Jesus' friends walking home the seven miles from Jerusalem to Emmaus are joined by a stranger. They tell him of the tragic death of Jesus. They recount the amazing story of the women folk. But they are not convinced. The women had not seen Jesus. The stranger has surprising comments to make. 'So they drew near to the village to which they were going. He appeared to be going further, but they constrained him, saying, "Stay with us, for it is toward evening and the day is now far spent." So he went in to stay with them. When he was at table with them, he took bread and blessed, and broke it, and gave it to them. And their eyes were opened, and they recognized him; and he vanished out of their sight' (Luke xxiv. 28–31). Hurriedly they return to Jerusalem, to hear from others, 'The Lord is risen indeed and has appeared to Simon' (Luke xxiv. 34).

John's Gospel has its own stories. Mary meets a man in the garden. Mistaking Him for a gardener she asks Him whether He has disposed of Jesus' body, only to discover, as a familiar voice speaks her name, that the man is none other than Jesus (John xx. 1 ff.). Thomas, one of the twelve, is unimpressed by ghost stories. He wants proof. 'Unless I see in his hands the print of the nails, and place my finger in the mark of the nails, and place my hand in his side, I will not believe' (John xx. 25). A week later, Jesus says to Thomas, 'Put your finger here and see my hands; and put out your hand and place it in my side; do not be faithless but believing' (verse 27). The disciples are out fishing one night on the Sea of Tiberias. In the dim half light of morning a man hails them from the shore, ' "Children have you any fish?" They answered him "No". He said to them, "Cast the net on the right side of the boat, and you will find some." So they cast it, and now they were not able to haul it in for the quantity of fish. That disciple whom Jesus loved said to Peter, "It is the Lord" ' (John xxi. 5–7; cf. 9 ff.).

A matchless simplicity and reticence marks the telling of these stories. The 'risen Jesus' is familiar, yet different, sometimes unrecognized, then known in a characteristic word or deed. The marks of the crucifixion are on His body, yet He appears suddenly, passing through closed doors. Inevitably, we are thrown into a turmoil of questions, some of which we cannot answer. This much, however, is certain. These stories are not fabrications. A forger would have been more careful. We cannot fit all the Gospel stories easily into a harmonious picture, and when different Gospels recount the same story, there are marked divergences in detail (cf. Mark xvi. 5 with Luke xxiv. 4). Furthermore, in 1 Cor. xv. 4 ff. Paul quotes a tradition which mentions appearances not to be found in the Gospels. Were the disciples then in the grip of a powerful hallucination, the projection of their own inmost desires? What then of the empty tomb? No Burke and Hare act was performed on the body, since the scene in the tomb is orderly, a fact noted in John xx. 6. Did the disciples, then, make off with the body, and invent the story that Jesus had risen? It is surely a psychological monstrosity for a group of broken men to invent a story they knew to be false, a story which changed them from cowards into witnesses, from traitors into martyrs.

Had we only the resurrection stories, we might amuse ourselves by spinning theories to account for them. But we must account for the *fact of the Church*, and certain curious features in the life of that Church. If Jesus was not raised in triumph over death, then the missionary witnesses to Him are, one and all, liars. Paul says as much in a letter to the Corinthians. 'If Christ has not been raised, then our preaching is in vain, and your faith is in vain. We are even found to be misrepresenting God, because we testified of God that he raised Christ whom he did not raise' (1 Cor. xv. 14–15). From the beginning, the claim was, 'This Jesus God raised up, and of that we all are witnesses' (Acts ii. 32); witnesses or liars.

When men, accepting their witness as true, were constrained to join them in the new people of God, admission was by way of baptism. Baptism marked the breaking point in life. The old self-centred life was finished. There had begun the new God-centred life which was linked to the death and resurrection of Jesus. 'Do

you not know that all of us who have been baptized into Christ
Jesus were baptized into his death? We were buried therefore with
him, by baptism into death, so that, as Christ was raised from the
dead, by the glory of the Father, we too might walk in newness
of life' (Rom. vi. 3–4). 'You were buried with him in baptism, in
which you were also raised with him through faith in the working of
God, who raised him from the dead' (Col. ii. 12). As the convert
went down into the water, this marked the burial of the old life.
He came up out of the water, to share a new resurrection life. The
resurrection of Jesus was never solely a past event; it was a present
experience to be repeated in the life of every Christian. Henceforth
the Christian was called to live as raised with Christ.

'If then you have been raised with Christ, seek the things that
are above, where Christ is, seated at the right hand of God. Set
your minds on things that are above, not on things that are on
earth. For you have died, and your life is hid with Christ in God'
(Col. iii. 1–3).

For the Christian, life began with the resurrection; his entire life
thereafter was resurrection-centred[1] and at the end, the resurrection
gave him a defiant attitude to death.[2] This was the Christian experience, but was it not also the history of that community to which he
now belonged? Jesus, by choosing twelve disciples, was gathering
the nucleus of a new people of God. If the cross had been the end
for Jesus, would it now have seen the end of this people of God,
buried with Him in His death? But this people sprang into new,
vigorous life, raised from death by His resurrection. Upon the
foundation stone of the resurrection of Jesus, the shattered ruins
of the new people of God were rebuilt. The Church is the Community of the Resurrection, called into being by the Resurrection,
witnessing to the Resurrection, sharing the Resurrection life.

---

[1] His holy day was no longer Saturday, the Jewish Sabbath, but Sunday, the first
day of the week, the day on which Jesus was raised from the dead, the Lord's day.
[2] Cf. chapter 11. pp. 238ff.

The Fellowship of the Spirit. Acts i records an interview between the disciples and their risen Lord. Confident now that He has the answer to all their questions, they eagerly gather round Him to ask, 'Lord, will you at this time restore the kingdom to Israel?' (Acts i. 6). The reply is surprising: 'It is not for you to know times or seasons which the Father has fixed by his own authority. But you shall receive power when the Holy Spirit has come upon you; and you shall be my witnesses in Jerusalem and in all Judea and Samaria and to the end of the earth' (Acts i. 7–8).

You shall receive power *when the Holy Ghost has come upon you* (cf. the promise in Mark i. 8; John xv. 26). It is perhaps symptomatic of how much we are out of touch with the outlook of the Bible that, for many of us, the Holy Spirit is a Ghost, and even when 'Holy', a ghost not only remains a bit of a mystery, but is something of a 'rare bird'. Yet to the New Testament church, the Holy Spirit, far from being an intellectual puzzle, was the daily dynamic of life.

Acts i describes a promise; Acts ii relates its fulfilment.

'When the day of Pentecost[1] had come, they were all together in one place. And suddenly a sound came from heaven like the rush of a mighty wind, and it filled all the house where they were sitting. And there appeared to them tongues as of fire, distributed and resting on each one of them. And they were all filled with the Holy Spirit and began to speak in other tongues, as the Spirit gave them utterance' (Acts ii. 1–4).

'Amazing' was the comment of some of those who witnessed the after-effects of this experience; 'drunk' said others.

'But Peter, standing with the eleven, lifted up his voice and addressed them, "Men of Judea and all who dwell in Jerusalem, let this be known to you, and give ear to my words. For these men are not drunk, as you suppose, since it is only the third hour of the day [i.e. 9 a.m.]; but this is what was spoken by the prophet Joel,

[1] A Jewish harvest festival fifty days after Passover.

'And in the last days, it shall be, God declares,
that I will pour out my Spirit upon all flesh.'

(Acts ii. 14–17)

The New Age had dawned. God's Spirit had now come upon ordinary folk. The Book of Acts introduces us to a host of notable characters, Stephen, Philip, Peter, James, and above all Paul, yet the leading character in the entire narrative is the Holy Spirit. Stephen, at his martyrdom, is described as 'full of the Holy Spirit' (Acts vii. 55). Philip is prompted to his memorable meeting with the Ethiopian by 'the Spirit' (Acts viii. 29). Peter has some deeply ingrained prejudices overcome by 'the Spirit' (cf. Acts x. 19; xi. 12). The Holy Spirit is instrumental in having Paul and Barnabas set apart for overseas mission work (Acts xiii. 2). Paul is later 'forbidden by the Holy Spirit to speak the word in Asia' (Acts xvi. 6). This is not pious, metaphorical language. If the resurrection of Jesus is the foundation stone upon which the shattered ruins of the people of God are rebuilt, the Holy Spirit is the master-builder.

In his introduction to the Book of Acts, the author informs us that in a previous volume [i.e. Luke's Gospel] he deals 'with all that Jesus *began* to do and teach'. Acts is the story of what Jesus continued to do. For the Holy Spirit—'the Spirit', 'the Spirit of Christ', 'the Spirit of God', the New Testament uses them all—is none other than God in action, the God who was in Jesus, in action still. 'No apostle,' it has been said, 'ever *remembered* Jesus.'[1] Jesus was not an ever-receding memory. He was the risen, triumphant Lord who poured out His Spirit upon His people. He was in action, now and for ever.

When a man responded to the Gospel he 'received the Spirit' (Gal. iii. 2), that is to say, he entered a community in which the Spirit of God was actively at work and came under the direction of this Spirit. The entire Christian life is life 'in the Spirit', as opposed to the old self-centred life 'in the flesh' as Paul describes it.

'You are not in the flesh, you are in the Spirit, if the Spirit of God really dwells in you. Any one who does not have the Spirit

---

[1] Cf. A. M. Hunter, op. cit. p. 75.

P

of Christ does not belong to him. But if Christ is in you, although your bodies are dead because of sin, your spirits are alive because of righteousness. If the Spirit of him who raised Jesus from the dead dwells in you, he who raised Christ Jesus from the dead will give life to your mortal bodies also through His Spirit which dwells in you' (Rom. viii. 9–11). The old self-centred rebellious life spelt death, the new life 'through His Spirit' is the resurrection life.

Every Christian receives 'from the Spirit' certain gifts to use 'for the common good' (1 Cor. xii. 7).

'To one is given through the Spirit the utterance of wisdom, and to another the utterance of knowledge according to the same Spirit, to another faith by the same Spirit, to another gifts of healing by the one Spirit, to another the working of miracles, to another prophecy, to another the ability to distinguish between spirits, to another various kinds of tongues. All these are inspired by one and the same Spirit, who apportions to each one individually as he wills' (1 Cor. xii. 8–11). There has always been a tendency, especially in the heady days of revivalism, to stress the abnormal as evidence of the working of the Spirit. Christians at Corinth were much enamoured of 'speaking with tongues', weird, unearthly utterances, unintelligible to others yet evident signs of a man gripped by the Spirit. Paul did not deny that there was such a gift, but he was not greatly impressed.

'I thank God that I speak in tongues more than you all; nevertheless, in church I would rather speak five words with my mind, in order to instruct others, than ten thousand words in a tongue' (1 Cor. xiv. 18–19). There was a far more important 'Harvest of the Spirit', vital to the continuing life and witness of the new people of God.

When we think of daily conduct, of what is desirable and what is not desirable, we talk of 'virtue' and 'vice'. These words are foreign to the New Testament, pagan words which by-pass the Holy Spirit. The New Testament thinks of the contrast between the self-centred life apart from God, and the God-centred life controlled by the Spirit. The outcome of the self-centred life—the 'works of the flesh' to use Paul's phrase—is plain 'immorality, impurity, licentiousness, idolatry, sorcery, enmity, strife, jealousy, anger, selfishness, dissension, party spirit, envy, drunkenness, carousing, and the like' (Gal. v. 19–21). These are not 'the sins of the flesh' in our modern understanding of that phrase. Though such sins are included (e.g. immorality, drunkenness), what we would term 'spiritual' sins, jealousy, anger, selfishness, envy, are well to the fore. Such is the consequence of our self-centred living, taking different forms in different lives. In contrast, Christians are bidden to 'walk by the Spirit' (Gal. v. 16), to be under the directing control of that ever-active Spirit of Christ. Of such a life, the outcome, the 'harvest of the Spirit' is 'love, joy, peace, patience, kindness, goodness, faith-fulness, gentleness, self-control' (Gal. v. 22). That Christian love of which Paul speaks so memorably in 1 Corinthians xiii is the greatest 'gift of the Spirit'.

Turn for a moment from conduct to prayer and worship. What are we doing in prayer and worship; thinking our way through to some remote God; reaching upwards in the hope that we may find Someone? This was not the experience of the first Christians. They kneel in prayer; the Spirit of Christ is with them prompting them to say, as Jesus had said, ' "Abba! Father!" it is the Spirit himself bearing witness with our spirit that we are children of God' (Rom. viii. 15–16; cf. Gal. iv. 6). They do not know what to pray for? '. . . the Spirit helps us in our weakness; for we do not know how to pray as we ought, but the Spirit himself intercedes for us with sighs too deep for words' (Rom. viii. 26). Meeting together for worship and prayer 'they were all filled with the Holy Spirit' (Acts iv. 31; cf. ix. 13; xiii. 2). The God they knew in Jesus was gripping them. He was present.

There is a saying of a Jewish Rabbi to the effect that '. . . if two sit together and the words of the Law (are spoken) between them the *Shekinah* [i.e. the manifest Presence of God] rests between them.'[1] Matthew's Gospel attributes to Jesus the words '. . . where two or three are gathered in my name there am I in the midst' (Matt. xviii. 20). If Jesus knew the Rabbi's saying, then He is claiming that for His disciples He is and henceforth shall be the very Presence of God. Certainly the early Christians testify that the Spirit of Christ was ever with them. The new people of God was no society

[1] Cf. J. W. Bowman, *The Intention of Jesus*, p. 182.

solemnly inaugurated to preserve the memory of Jesus and His resurrection. It is the *fellowship of the Spirit*, created by the out-poured Spirit of its risen, triumphant Lord, utterly dependent in life, witness and worship upon the ever-active Spirit of Christ.

III

The Body of Christ. A well-known Asian Christian likes to say that the census of the world is always one short. The missing one? . . . Jesus. He does not mean that Jesus is in the world vaguely and invisibly. No, Jesus is here concretely, visibly *in the Church*, the Church which is the *body of Christ*. Round this phrase, 'the body of Christ', there gather many of the most important things which the New Testament has to say about the new people of God.

A

'. . . Just as the body is one and has many members, and all the members of the body, though many, are one body, so is it with Christ. For by one Spirit we were all baptised into one body . . .' (1 Cor. xii. 12–13). We are all baptised into *one body*, the body of Christ; therefore this is a community which cuts across all the barriers, national, political and social, which divide men in this world. We divide our world into Communist and non-Communist. The Jew divided his world into Jew and non-Jew [i.e. Gentile]. The two were separated by an iron curtain, erected by the Jewish claim to have exclusive possession of God's Law. But in this community, the body of Christ, the iron curtain must disappear. It had been dynamited by Christ.

'For he is our peace, who has made us both one and has broken down the dividing wall of hostility . . . that he might create in him-self one new man in place of the two, so making peace, and might reconcile us both to God in one body through the cross, thereby bringing the hostility to an end' (Eph. ii. 14–16). Peace has broken out. The warring camps are now at one with God and with each other in the one body. Non-Jews, formerly regarded as religiously 'outside the pale', are now well and truly inside. You non-Jews, says the author of Ephesians, are 'no longer strangers and sojourners, but you are fellow citizens with the saints and members of the household of God, built upon the foundation of the apostles and prophets, Christ Jesus himself being the chief corner-stone' (Eph. ii. 19–20). The metaphors change with bewildering rapidity—'in one body', 'fellow citizens', 'belonging to God's family', 'a building' —but the meaning remains the same. In this community, the body of Christ, the deep-seated racial religious barrier which divided Jew and Gentile, has no longer any meaning. 'There is neither Jew nor Greek . . . for you are all one in Christ Jesus' (Gal. iii. 28; cf. Rom. x. 12; Col. iii. 11).

As with the racial religious barrier, so with the social. The Graeco-Roman world was a world of 'freemen' and slaves. The lot of the slave varied from the hell of sweated labour in the mines to positions of trusted responsibility in a family. But the distinction between slave and free was unambiguous. The penalty for a runaway slave was crucifixion. Paul met such a runaway slave, Onesimus by name. He persuaded him to do an unheard-of thing, to return of his own free will to the master from whom he had absconded, relying on nothing more than a covering note from Paul to his master Philemon, and the all-important fact that master and slave were now both Christians. In the covering note Paul requests Philemon to receive Onesimus 'no longer as a slave, but more than a slave, as a beloved brother, especially to me but how much more to you, both in the flesh and in the Lord. So if you consider me your partner, receive him as you would receive me. If he has wronged you at all or owes you anything, charge that to my account' (verses 16–18). The very fact that Philemon preserved the letter is proof that he acceded to Paul's request.

'. . . there is neither slave nor free . . . for you are all one in Christ Jesus' (Gal. iii. 28).

B

To belong to the new people of God meant not only a total disregard of such racial and social barriers, but a common sharing of life's resources and experiences. No dull uniformity or totalitarian regimentation, designed to crush individual distinctions, was involved. The body is a complex organism with many different members, eyes, ears, hands, feet, each with different functions (cf. 1 Cor. xii. 14–24). So in the body of Christ, some are apostles, some prophets, some teachers, some have gifts of healing, some administrative talents, some 'speak with tongues' (Cf. 1 Cor. xii. 28–30). But there is no room here for superiority or inferiority complexes. All are bound to one another,

'That there may be no discord in the body, but that the members may have the same care for one another. If one member suffers, all suffer together; if one member is honoured, all rejoice together' (1 Cor. xii. 25–26). It is a picture of true family life on a large scale, laughter and tears, successes and failures being shared. There was nothing 'airy-fairy' about this sharing.

'Now the company of those who believed were of one heart and soul, and no one said that any of the things which he possessed was his own, but they had everything in common. . . . There was not a needy person among them, for as many as were possessors of land or houses sold them and brought the proceeds of what was sold and laid it at the apostles' feet; and distribution was made to each as any had need' (Acts iv. 32, 34–35). This has been called 'primitive communism', 'impossible idealism', a passing folly till the Church learned better. It is none of these things. It is a serious attempt to give practical expression to the fact of a belonging together in the one body of Christ.

In this particular form it did not last for long. It remains, nonetheless, more realistic than we who, criticizing from a distance, give so little evidence of our total oneness in the body of Christ.

Nowhere was this oneness more vividly portrayed than when the members, together in the body of Christ, met to share their family meal. 'For I received from the Lord what I also delivered to you, that the Lord Jesus on the night when he was betrayed took bread, and when he had given thanks, he broke it and said, "This is my body which is for you. Do this in remembrance of me". In the same way also, the cup, after supper, saying, "This cup is the new covenant in my blood. Do this as often as you drink it, in remembrance of me". For as often as you eat this bread and drink the cup you proclaim the Lord's death until he comes' (1 Cor. xi. 23–26). Earlier in this letter Paul has an interesting comment to make upon the significance of sharing in this, the LORD's table.

'The cup of blessing which we bless, is it not a participation in the blood of Christ? The bread which we break, is it not a participation in the body of Christ? Because there is one loaf, we who are many are one body, for we all partake of the same loaf' (1 Cor. x. 16–17).

Sharing a meal was always a highly significant action in the East. It was the pledge and symbol of brotherhood. It was part of the darkness of Judas Iscariot's dastardly deed that he rose from sharing a meal with Jesus to betray Him. As in response to their LORD's command, Christians shared the wine and loaf, they were demonstrating their oneness with the LORD and *with one another* in the body of Christ; the many sharing the one loaf and the one body.[1]

The bread—'my body'; the new covenant in 'my blood'; this do in remembrance of me—the emphasis throughout is strongly upon the close relationship which exists between the new people of God and their LORD. That is why the church is described not simply as a body, but the *body of Christ*. 'He is the head of the body, the church' (Col. i. 18).

Nowhere in the New Testament is greater stress laid upon what God accomplishes in Jesus than in the letter to the Ephesians; and nowhere do we find a more exalted picture of the church. 'God,' claims the author, 'has put all things under his [i.e. Jesus'] feet and has made him the head over all things for the church *which is his body, the fullness of him who fills all in all*' (Eph. i. 23).

In Christ, says Colossians i. 19, 'all the fullness of God was pleased to dwell'. Paul is here speaking to people influenced by a

[1] Cf. our word 'companion', literally 'one who eats bread with you'.

current of thought which would have ascribed to Jesus *one* place in the divine scheme of things alongside other heavenly beings and powers. No, claims the writer, Christ has *the* place, 'all the fullness of God' is in Him. If you would know God, look to Jesus, and, continues, Ephesians, if you would know Jesus, look to the Church, for there is His 'fullness'. It is there He is to be found, it is there He is actively at work. You cannot separate Jesus and the church which is His body.

A passage in Ephesians v. 21 ff., concerning that most intimate of all human relationships, husband and wife, serves further to underline this truth. Feminists may object, but, asserts this writer, 'as the church is subject to Christ, so let wives also be subject to their husbands' (verse 24). It is not slavery, but a glad and willing submission which is intended. The word to wives is followed by a word to husbands. 'Husbands, love your wives, as Christ loved the church and gave himself up for her' (verse 25). Husband and wife being one, 'Even so, husbands should love their wives as their own bodies. He who loves his wife loves himself. For no man ever hates his own flesh, but nourishes and cherishes it, as Christ does the church, because we are members of his body. "For this reason a man shall leave his father and mother, and be joined to his wife, and the two shall become one." This is a great mystery and I take it to mean Christ and the church' (Eph. v. 28–31).

The Church is the one body of Christ, indissolubly linked to Christ, Who, nourishing and cherishing it, is ever actively at work in it through the Spirit. 'There is one body and one Spirit, just as you were called to the one hope that belongs to your call, one LORD, one faith, one baptism, one God and Father of us all, who is above all, and through all and in all' (Eph. iv. 4–6).

To be 'in Christ', one of Paul's favourite expressions,[1] describes a vital religious experience, but it is not the mystic's solitary pursuit of the Infinite. To be 'in Christ' means to be 'in the body of Christ', to belong to the new people of God and thus to 'have power to comprehend with all the saints what is the breadth and length and height and depth and to know the love of Christ which surpasses knowledge, that you may be filled with all the fullness of God'

[1] This, or a similar phrase, occurs over 160 times in Paul's letters.

(Eph. iii. 18–19). But it can only be *'with all the saints'*. This knowledge is not open to the religious isolationist.

The people of God does not, however, exist for its own sake. As a man expresses his personality and achieves his aims in life through his body, so the church as the body of Christ exists to continue and to express in the world the work of Christ. The ministry of Jesus was confined almost wholly to His own country and fellow Jews; but there is no evidence that He shared their attitude of exclusiveness. The hero of one of His best-known parables is a hated Samaritan (Luke x. 25–37). He rewards the persistent faith of a foreign woman (Mark vii. 24–30). He cures the slave of a Roman centurion and highly commends his faith: 'I tell you, not even in Israel have I found such faith' (Luke vii. 9). Matthew caps his version of this story with the words, 'I tell you, many will come from east and west and sit at table with Abraham, Isaac and Jacob in the kingdom of heaven, while the sons of the kingdom [i.e. Jews] will be thrown into outer darkness: there men will weep and gnash their teeth' (Matt. viii. 11). Above all Jesus thought of Himself as the Servant of the LORD, destined, let it never be forgotten, to be 'a light to the nations' (Isa. xlii. 4, 6–7; xlix. 6). The church led by His Spirit, though not without initial misgivings (cf. Acts x and xv), found herself committed to a world-wide mission to all men, Gentile as well as Jew. And the object of this mission?

'God through Christ reconciled us to himself *and gave us the ministry of reconciliation*' (2 Cor. v. 18). This is the continuing task of the Church as the body of Christ, to continue in the world His work of reconciliation and to demonstrate its reality in her own life. What is the Church of the New Testament but the nucleus of that new humanity of God's intending, the new people of God wherein men led by the Spirit of Christ are at one with God and with one another?

11

In the End, God

The decisive act in God's dealings with men lies in the past, has present reality, but awaits a future consummation. The symbols in New Testament visions are not literal fact, but ultimate certainties.

1. The Abolition of Death. *The Old Testament had for long enough little positive to say about life hereafter. Some of the Psalms (e.g. Ps. 73) point to a depth of communion with God defying death. This links up with the emphasis in John's Gospel about 'eternal life'.*

Faith in God's righteousness in the persecutions of the second century B.C. *led to belief in the Resurrection of the dead (Daniel). The New Testament witness, far from sharing Greek views about the immortality of the soul, regards death as an enemy, defeated by the Resurrection of Jesus, and finally to be banished. The Resurrection of Jesus is the 'first fruit' of the Resurrection of all believers.*

Instead of speculations about the conditions of personal survival, we find the Resurrection hope set within the context of renewal for the whole world.

2. The Coming of Christ. *The early Christians expected a speedy return of their Lord. The Old Testament 'Day of the* LORD' *becomes 'the day of our Lord Jesus Christ'. Paul discouraged speculation as to the date; a later generation produced its sceptics. But the 'Coming of Christ' emphasises that God's purposes for the world await a future fulness, with Christ at its centre.*

This 'Coming' means—as every 'coming' of God has meant—judgement upon all failing to respond to God's invitation to share in His concern. Yet the New Testament believes in the reconciliation of 'all things' to God.

3. The New Heaven and the New Earth. *A renewed world, with pain, suffering and death banished, with men and nations living*

together in harmony—such is the climax of the New Testament hope.
At its centre stands the people of God gathered round their Father,
seeing Him 'face to face'. Though we strain language to try to describe
the indescribable, the certainty upon which this hope is grounded may
be seen in Rom. viii. 28–31.

THE decisive act in the story of God's dealings with His world
has taken place. There is no going back on that.

'For the Son of God, Jesus Christ, whom we preached among
you,' writes Paul to the Corinthians, '. . . was not Yes and No; with
him it is always Yes. For all the promises of God find their Yes in
him' (2 Cor. i. 19–20). God's kingship is fact. Jesus' confident words
to His accusers were to be vindicated. Dying He conquered death.
God raised Him to triumph.

'We see Jesus, who for a little while was made lower than the
angels, crowned with glory and honor because of the suffering of
death. . . .' (Heb. ii. 9).

The story of the Ascension (Luke xxiv. 50–53; Acts i. 9–12)
which ends the appearances of the risen Lord to His disciples
symbolizes Jesus exalted to the place of supreme authority at God's
right hand. The New Age has dawned. Death conquered, the Spirit
poured out upon His followers by the exalted Lord (Acts ii. 33),
the existence in the world of the new people of God—these are its
evident signs. It has dawned, yes, but the full brightness of noon-
tide is still to come. Christians live somewhat uneasily between
what is and what is yet to be. They share the new resurrection life,
but a greater wonder is in store.

'For you have died, and your life is hid with Christ in God.
When Christ who is our life appears, then you also will appear with
him in glory' (Col. iii. 3–4). *You have died* [i.e. to the old sinful
life]; *there* is the glorious fact of the present: you *will appear*; *there*
is the future hope.

The faith of the New Testament does not encourage wishful
thinking or mental blindness. The Epistle to the Hebrews thinks of
Jesus as Representative Man. The portrait of man in Ps. viii. 4–6,
crowned with glory and honour, the lord of creation, has come to
life in Jesus to whom even death is subject. Yet there is a flaw.

'As it is, we do not yet see everything in subjection to him' (Heb. ii. 8). Why, even within the new people of God old tensions and frustrations keep cropping up. Within the church at Corinth there was party bickering (1 Cor. i. 11–12; xi. 18), flagrant immorality (1 Cor. v.) and personal animosity (1 Cor. ix; 2 Cor. x.). In his letter to the Philippians, a letter radiating joy and thankfulness, Paul urgently pleads for unity within the church (ii. 1 ff.), warns against heretical teaching (iii. 1 ff.) and openly rebukes two quarrelsome women (iv. 2). Little wonder that another writer can say, 'My little children, I am writing this to you so that you may not sin; *but if anyone does sin*, we have an advocate with the Father, Jesus Christ the righteous' (1 John ii. 1).

The old self-assertiveness kept rearing its ugly head; the Holy Spirit was not in full control. Moreover death 'the last enemy' (1 Cor. xv. 26) had still to be faced by all. Defeated it may have been by Jesus, but His followers still died, died sometimes as martyrs in a persecuting world. Inevitably the cry goes up, 'O Sovereign Lord, holy and true, how long before thou wilt judge and avenge our blood on those who dwell upon the earth' (Rev. vi. 10). The Lordship of Christ was fact, unquestionable fact in the experience of men (cf. Phil. iv. 13), but sin and suffering remained to infect the whole created world. True to the outlook of the Old Testament which binds together man and the rest of creation for weal and woe,[1] Paul can say 'we know that the whole of creation has been groaning in travail together until now' (Rom. viii. 22); and like Christians the whole creation is waiting with an eager expectancy (Rom. viii. 19).

We must not conclude that it was sheer frustration which gave rise to 'pipe' dreams of a brighter future. As with the Old Testament, what *had* happened is decisive for what is yet to come. The opening verses of Romans v. will show us how inextricably past, present and future are woven together in the New Testament.

'Therefore, since we are justified by faith, we have peace with God through our Lord Jesus Christ. Through him we have obtained access to this grace in which we stand, and we rejoice in our

[1] Cf. pp. 153 ff.

hope of sharing the glory of God. More than that, we rejoice in our sufferings, knowing that suffering produces endurance, and endurance produces character, and character produces hope, and hope does not disappoint us because God's love has been poured into our hearts through the Holy Spirit which has been given to us' (Rom. v. 1–5).

We begin with the past, with what God *has* done in Jesus; that is the basis of our present at-one-ment with God. Because of our present experience, 'the grace in which we stand', we look to the future, confident of 'sharing in the glory of God'. Past, present, future, then the passage returns to the present. Christian hope is no deluding mirage, because the hope is already partly realized, through the presence of the Holy Spirit.

In Ephesians, Christians are described as 'Sealed with the promised Holy Spirit, which is the guarantee of our inheritance until we acquire possession of it, to the praise of his glory' (Eph. i. 13–14; cf. 2 Cor. i. 22; v. 5). 'The *guarantee* of your inheritance', the word really means the 'down payment' or 'first instalment', the pledge of future full payment. The working of the Holy Spirit is the foretaste of what is to come. Present experience, rooted in a past event, pointed forward to the final unveiling of God's glorious purposes. The New Testament writers 'believed in a final triumph of Christ, because they believed in a victory already won by him. They expected cosmic confirmation of Christ's victory, because they held inexpugnably to his present Lordship'.[1]

To what was expected in that final cosmic victory, we must turn; but first a word of warning. To speak of things beyond this present world of sense and time, we cannot employ the same kind of language as we would use in describing an accident or a football match. In visualizing what lies 'beyond our ken', we are driven to picture language, poetic visions, symbols. It is as futile to press the literal truth of such pictures as it is to regard the 'myths' of the opening chapters of Genesis as bald statements of fact. Many indeed of the pictures used by the New Testament, though given a distinctive slant, are traditional, drawn from the Old Testament, and in particular from a type of literature known as 'Apocalyptic' [i.e.

[1] A. M. Hunter, op. cit., p. 85.

it claims to 'draw back the curtain' veiling the future.][1] Such literature has had a fatal fascination for people who have seen in it an open invitation to speculation about the future, a kind of cosmic crossword puzzle, which, provided you can read the clues correctly, gives the solution to all that is destined to happen. But it is neither dates nor details, but ultimate certainties which such pictures provide. What are these ultimate certainties?

I

The Abolition of Death. For those who believe that the chief purpose of religion is to give men a certain hope of life beyond the grave, the Bible is a disappointing book. For long enough the Old Testament had nothing positive to say about life hereafter. Down under was a vague shadowy abode of the departed, Sheol, a place of no real life where a man was cut off from God (cf. Isa. xxxviii. 16–19; Ps. lxxxviii. 10–12). But even Sheol came to be within the jurisdiction of the LORD (cf. Amos ix. 2; Ps. cxxxix. 7–8). Neither this vague underworld, however, nor psychic phenomena (cf. 1 Sam. 28) provide the Old Testament with a faith in life beyond.

In certain of the Psalms there are indications of a depth of communion with God which would rob even death of all its meaning:

'Whom have I in heaven but thee?
And there is nothing on earth that I desire besides thee.
My flesh and my heart may fail,
but God is the strength of my heart and my portion for ever.
For lo, those who are far from thee shall perish;
thou dost put an end to those who are false to thee.
But for me it is good to be near God;
I have made the LORD God my refuge,
that I may tell of all thy works.'

(Ps. lxxiii. 25–28)

[1] Daniel is the one true example of an Apocalyptic book in the O.T. (but cf. Isa. xxiv.–xxvii.), though such books abounded in later Judaism. Revelation is the one complete N.T. example though many passages of apocalyptic flavour are to be found, e.g. Mark xiii.; 1 Thess. iv. 13; 2 Thess. ii. 6 ff; 2 Pet. iii.

We are on the path here which leads to John's Gospel, where 'eternal life' has its beginnings here and now in that intimate communion with God made possible for men through Jesus. 'This is eternal life, that they know thee, the only true God, and Jesus Christ whom thou hast sent' (John xvii. 3). To Martha, mourning the death of a brother, Jesus says, 'he who believes in me, though he die, yet shall he live, and whoever lives and believes in me shall never die' (xi. 25–26; cf. iii. 15; iv. 14; vi. 54). Notice that such eternal life is God's gift to men in Jesus, a by-product of communion with Him.

The Bible's chief triumph song over death, however, is set in a different, if related, key. We must go back to the sixties of the second century B.C., dark days of persecution for the faithful in Israel. The Book of Daniel seeks to strengthen the resistance of the freedom fighters by assuring them of the imminent triumph of God's sovereignty. For a moment, the tyrant may flourish, but judgement is about to be given for God's faithful people. They shall enter into their rightful kingdom here on earth.

> 'The kingdom and the dominion
> and the greatness of the kingdoms under the whole heaven
> shall be given to the people of the saints of the Most High;
> their kingdom shall be an everlasting kingdom,
> and all dominions shall serve and obey them.'
>
> (Dan. vii. 27)

But what of the faithful who die before the coming of this kingdom? Are they not to share in its triumph? What of the persecutors who die before that day? Do they escape just punishment? Surely this would fly in the face of the righteousness of God. There is only one solution. On the day of God's triumph when His people are delivered, 'many of those who sleep in the dust of the earth shall awake, some to everlasting life and some to shame and everlasting contempt' (Dan. xii. 2). Similarly, in Isaiah xxvi. 19 (Isa. xxiv–xxvii may come from the same, or a similar situation to that of Daniel), we hear, 'Thy dead shall live, their bodies shall rise.'

Resurrection, this is the key word in what the Bible has to say of

life heraefter. An age of persecution saw it as the inevitable corol-
lary of the righteousness of God. Turn to the New Testament and
we find that it is the supreme demonstration of this righteousness,
the raising of Jesus from the dead, which is central to its hope.

Nowhere does our ordinary Christian thinking tend to be more
out of touch with the Bible. If in life we are followers of Jesus, in
death many of us switch our allegiance to Plato and the Greek
philosophers.[1] 'John Brown's body lies a-mouldering in the grave
. . . but his soul goes marching on.' Is this, in popular terms, the
Christian hope? There are two assumptions here, one about the
kind of people we are, the other about death, both of which are
foreign to the New Testament. We think of ourselves as people with
a double nature. We have a body which quite definitely perishes at
death; but we also have a 'soul', which, after all, is the real us. Far
from perishing at death it goes 'marching on', by very nature immortal. Its destination is the only uncertain factor. To the truly
religious man, death is consequently a friend in disguise. The body
is rather a drag on the soul. (Plato called it the 'prison' of the soul.)
Death is a happy release, the natural fulfilment of a life which has
been concerned to escape from the entanglements of the body to the
things of the 'spirit'.

Now listen to the New Testament. Death a friend? No, man's
inescapable enemy, the 'last enemy' who must be destroyed. (1 Cor.
xv. 26; cf. Rev. xx. 14.) It is an intruder into God's world, the dire
result of man's self-centred rebellion against his creator. According
to the 'myth' of Genesis iii, 'Everyman's' expulsion from the garden
involved the erection of an impassable barrier between him and the
tree of life 'lest he put forth his hand and take of the tree of life,
and eat, and live for ever' (Gen. iii. 22).

'Therefore,' comments Paul, 'as sin came into the world by one
man, and *death through sin*, so death spread to all men because all
men sinned' (Rom. v. 12; cf. 1 Cor. xv. 22). Everyman's story is our
story. In rebellion against the Creator of life, we reap death, 'the
wages of sin is death' (Rom. vi. 23).

Man an uneasy alliance of body and soul, the one perishable, the
other immortal? The New Testament is too firmly rooted in the

[1] Cf. O. Cullmann, *The Resurrection of the Dead and the Immortality of the Soul.*

Old Testament outlook so to regard man. God created man as a unity.[1] True, he has an 'inner' and an 'outer' self, but both coming from God are utterly dependent on God for continued existence. Both may be under the dominant spell of evil, both may be set free by God's spirit. There is no false devaluation of the body in the interests of the soul, nor is there any full life which does not find expression in a body.

With this in mind, let us look at death and what lies beyond through the eyes of Paul. He is writing to a Greek community which, trained to think of the 'immortality of the soul' found difficulty in understanding the 'resurrection' hope. 'You do not believe in the resurrection of the dead?' says Paul, 'then what about Jesus?' 'If Christ has not been raised, then our preaching is in vain and your faith is in vain. We are even found to be misrepresenting God, because we testified of God that he raised Christ, whom he did not raise, if it is true that the dead are not raised. For if the dead are not raised, then Christ has not been raised' (1 Cor. xv. 14–16). But the resurrection of Jesus is not an isolated bolt out of the blue. Just as Adam is Everyman, so Christ is Representative Man (in verse 45 he describes Christ as the 'last Adam'). He conquered death and everyman may share His victory.

'For as by a man came death, by a man [i.e. Jesus] has come also the resurrection from the dead' (verse 21).

The Risen Christ is but 'the first fruits of those who have fallen asleep' (verse 20). The full harvest is still to come. 'For as in Adam all die, so also in Christ shall all be made alive. But each in his own order: Christ the first fruits, then at his coming, those who belong to Christ. Then comes the end when he delivers the kingdom to God the Father after destroying every rule and every authority and power. For he must reign until he has put all his enemies under his feet. The last enemy to be destroyed is death' (verses 22–26).

Paul does not think of this 'resurrection' as happening to the individual believer immediately after death. He associates it with 'the coming of Christ' which heralds the End. It is but part of a greater cosmic event in which death, along with other enemies of

[1] Cf. p. 31.

O

God, will be finally destroyed, to make way for 'new heavens and a new earth'. Until then—if 'until' has any meaning outside the world we know—the dead are 'asleep' (1 Thess. iv. 13; cf. Rev. xiv. 13), without any prejudice to the share they are to have in the wonder life which is to break in upon this world. Elsewhere, the 'sleep' is described as being 'with the Lord' (Phil. i. 23), or being 'at home' (2 Cor. v. 8). Though Paul obviously regards this state as desirable, the New Testament is noticeably and wisely reticent about speculation as to the condition of the individual immediately after death. It is part of our preoccupation with self that we tend to think of death solely as a personal problem, and life hereafter as in-dividual bliss or the opposite. The New Testament sets its hope in the context of a larger hope for the whole of creation.

'But some one will ask, "How are the dead raised? With what kind of body do they come?"' (1 Cor. xv. 35)—a fair enough question. The resurrection 'body' will naturally differ from the body of flesh and blood we know. There is no suggestion that the body which rots in the grave will somehow or other 'unrot'. Use your eyes, says Paul. Even in this world there is rich variety of bodies of different kinds and texture, men, animals, birds, fish, planets (cf. verses 36–41). (Does it need to be emphasized that this is the layman's point of view, not the professional scientist's?) If so, then why should God not give us another kind of body, fit for that wonder life to come, 'a spiritual body' (verse 44) Paul describes it, as distinct from the body of flesh and blood we now possess. He is thinking, perhaps, of the resurrection body of the Risen Jesus (cf. verses 47 ff.). In Philippians he describes Christians as waiting for the coming of Jesus 'who will change our lowly body to *be like his glorious body* by the power which enables him to subject all things to himself' (Phil. iii. 21).

What are we to make of all this? In the first place this faith has nothing to do with the kind of people we are, i.e. people with immortal souls which necessarily survive death. This hope is firmly rooted in God, in what He has done for us in Christ, and in the ultimate triumph of all His purposes in Christ. Life hereafter is a new creative act of God, the God we know in Jesus, as much *His* doing as the creation of life in this world. At this point as at all others, the

Christian says 'All my hope on God is founded'. Secondly, this future life is no 'ghost' existence with innumerable spirits flitting around. The resurrection involves the whole personality, real people, far more real indeed than we are now, since the defects in our lives will be a thing of the past. This is what is safeguarded by talking of the resurrection of the *body*.

II

Caught up in a world of tension and crises, we must often have wondered, 'Is there any purpose behind it all? Yes, there is, claims the New Testament; and we know what that purpose is. It is now an open secret.[1] God 'has made known to us in all wisdom and insight the mystery of his will, according to his purpose which he set forth in Christ as a plan for the fullness of time, to unite all things in him, things in heaven and things on earth' (Eph. i. 9–10). This is God's purpose made known in Christ, to gather up the broken fragments of a world gone wrong, and fit them all together again in Christ. As Jesus stands at the very heart of the New Testament witness to God, so He stands at the centre of its ultimate hope for the world.

A

The Coming of Christ. Because Jesus is Lord, so the New Testament looks forward to His 'coming' in triumph to establish His universal lordship.

Philippi was a Roman colony. Its citizens were intensely conscious of belonging to a greater commonwealth, the commonwealth of Rome. But Christians at Philippi—or elsewhere—have even greater citizen rights, 'our commonwealth is in heaven and *from it we await a saviour, the Lord Jesus Christ*' (Phil. iii. 20). Elsewhere Christians are bidden steadfastly to continue in the faith 'so that when he appears we may have confidence and not shrink

---

[1] This is the meaning of 'mystery' in the N.T.—something once hidden but now known.

Q*

from him in shame at his coming' (1 John ii. 28). His *coming*[1]—in secular literature the word is used to describe the official state entry of a ruler into a city or province. Jesus had come once into His world, unrecognized, finally rejected by men; the Church awaits His triumphant state entry into a world His by right. Such a state entry was always a significant day, a 'holy day' in the life of a community: hence another way of speaking of His 'coming' is 'the day of the Lord' (2 Thess. ii. 3), or 'the day of our Lord Jesus Christ' (1 Cor. i. 8; cf. Phil. i. 10). The Old Testament 'Day of the LORD'[2] becomes significantly 'the day of our Lord Jesus Christ'.

There is no doubt that many in the early Church believed that 'Day' and 'His Coming' to be imminent, so much so that in a fervour of religious excitement, certain Christians at Thessalonica downed tools, on the pretext that further work was a waste of time (2 Thess. ii. 1 ff.; iii. 6 ff.). Calendar pinpointing, an occupational disease of religious cranks, was firmly discouraged by Paul (2 Thess. ii. 1 ff.). The only certainty is that it will come when least expected. 'But as to the times and the seasons, brethren, you have no need to have anything written to you. For you yourselves know well that the day of the Lord will come like a thief in the night. When people say 'There is peace and security', then sudden destruction will come upon them as travail comes upon a woman with child, and there will be no escape' (1 Thess. v. 1–3; cf. 2 Pet. iii. 10; Luke xii. 39–40; Matt. xxiv. 43–44). Meanwhile, the Christian's orders are so to live that he will always be ready no matter when his master comes. No longer in the dark, he is to be 'sober, and put on the breastplate of faith and love, and for a helmet the hope of salvation' (1 Thess. v. 8; cf. Eph. vi. 10 ff.). The thought of His 'coming' should be a spur, not to idleness or curiosity, but to resolute and consistent Christian living. 'Therefore, beloved, since you wait for these, be zealous to be found by him without spot of blemish, and at peace' (2 Pet. iii. 14).

A later generation of Christians, grown accustomed to the world continuing its familiar course, produced its sceptics, who asked, 'Where is the promise of his coming? For ever since the fathers fell

[1] Cf. 1 Cor. xvi. 22; xv. 23; James v. 7; 2 Pet. iii. 4; 1 Thess. iii. 13; 2 Thess ii. 1; Acts i. 11.
[2] Cf. pp. 135ff.

asleep, all things have continued as they were from the beginning of creation' (2 Pet. iii. 3). There have been sceptics ever since. We must indeed beware of treating as literal fact the pictorial language of passages such as 1 Thessalonians iv. 16–17:

'For the Lord himself will descend from heaven with a cry of command, with the archangel's call and the sound of the trumpet of God. And the dead in Christ will rise first; then we who are alive, who are left shall be caught up together with them in the clouds to meet the LORD in the air.'

But we are untrue to the witness of the New Testament if we do not confess that God's purposes for the world await a future final consummation, and at the heart of this consummation stands Christ. As to the when, a wise agnosticism will echo the words of Jesus himself, 'But of that day and hour no one knows, not even the angels of heaven, nor the Son, but the Father only' (Matt. xxiv. 36).

B

Judgement. God's activity in this world, says the Bible, always involves judgement. Pharaoh hardens his heart (Exod. vii. 13) and meets with catastrophe. The people of God refuse to give to God that moral obedience required of them, and there is an inevitable 'day' of judgement (cf. Amos). Jesus appears among men, and there is a parting of the ways. 'Do not think that I have come to bring peace on earth; I have not come to bring peace but a sword' (Matt. x. 34; cf. Luke xii. 51). Jesus can say that He came, 'not to judge the world but to save the world' (John xii. 47); nevertheless, by their response to, or their rejection of the 'good tidings' He brings, men are judged (cf. John iii. 36).

As it has been throughout, so it will be on the day of God's final act. This is 'that day when ... God judges the secrets of men by Christ Jesus' (Rom ii. 16). Do not pass judgement, writes Paul to the Corinthians, 'before the time, before the Lord comes, who will bring to light the things now hidden in darkness and will disclose the purposes of the heart. Then every man will receive his commendation from God' (1 Cor. iv. 5). Then comes the final divine reckoning, 'when the Lord Jesus is revealed from heaven with his mighty angels in flaming fire, inflicting vengeance upon those who do not know God and upon those who do not obey the gospel of our Lord Jesus. They shall suffer the punishment of eternal destruction and exclusion from the presence of the Lord and from the glory of his might, when he comes on that day to be glorified in his saints, and to be marvelled at in all who have believed because our testimony to you was believed' (2 Thess. i. 7–10; cf. Rev. xxii. 15).

Lest we think that the outcome of this judgement depends upon our being able to produce the correct religious password, or to subscribe to an orthodox creed, we would do well to recall the great parable of judgement upon the nations in Matthew xxv. 31 ff. There will be surprises. All are not sheep who think themselves sheep, and all are not goats whom others regard as goats!

'The King will say to those at his right hand: "Come, O blessed of my Father, inherit the kingdom prepared for you from the foundation of the world; for I was hungry and you gave me food, I was thirsty and you gave me drink, I was a stranger and you welcomed me, I was naked and you clothed me, I was sick and you visited me, I was in prison and you came to me.' Then the righteous will answer him, "Lord, when did we see the hungry and feed thee, or thirsty and give thee drink? And when did we see thee a stranger and welcome thee or naked and clothe thee? And when did we see thee sick or in prison and visit thee?" And the King will answer them, "Truly I say to you, as you did it to one of the least of these my brethren, you did it to me." Then he will say, to those at his left hand: "Depart from me, you cursed, into the eternal fire prepared for the devil and his angels; for I was hungry and you gave me no food, I was thirsty and you gave me no drink, I was a stranger and you did not welcome me, naked and you did not clothe me, sick and in prison and you did not visit me." Then they also will answer, "Lord, when did we see thee hungry or thirsty or a stranger or naked or sick or in prison, and did not minister to thee?" Then he will answer, them, "Truly, I say to you, as you did it not to one of the least of these, you did it not to me." And they will go away into eternal punishment, but the righteous into eternal life'

(Matt. xxv. 34-46; cf. vii. 21). A true response to the 'good tidings' of God's concern for us must express itself in sharing that concern.

But is eternal punishment God's last word for some? We dare not minimize the element of judgement in the New Testament (cf. Rev. xx. 11-15), but neither must we transfer dramatic pictures into sober statements of everlasting torment and agony. There are at least hints in the New Testament of another vision. In 1 Tim. ii. Christians are urged to pray for 'all men' especially those in positions of high responsibility, because 'This is good, and it is acceptable in the sight of God our Savior, who desires (rather "wills") all men to be saved and to come to the knowledge of the truth' (1 Tim. ii. 3-4). Later in this letter God is described as 'the Saviour of *all men*, especially of those who believe' (1 Tim. iv. 10; cf. Rom. xi. 32). There is little reason to believe that the last phrase is meant to be exclusive. If it be true that in Him 'all the fullness of God was pleased to dwell, and through him to reconcile to himself *all things*, whether on earth or in heaven, making peace by the blood of his cross' (Col. i. 19-20), may it not be that even through and beyond judgement, there is hope for all?

C

The New Heaven and the New Earth. The coming of Christ and judgement are both preludes to something which staggers the imagination in its sweep and brilliance.

'Then I saw a new heaven and a new earth; for the first heaven and the first earth had passed away, and the sea was no more. And I saw the holy city, new Jerusalem, coming down out of heaven from God, prepared as a bride adorned for her husband; and I heard a great voice from the throne saying, "Behold, the dwelling of God is with men. He will dwell with them and they shall be his people, and God himself shall be with them; he will wipe away every tear from their eyes, and death shall be no more, neither shall there be mourning nor crying nor pain any more, for the former things have passed away" ' (Rev. xxi. 1-4; cf. 2 Pet. iii. 13).

The universe as God meant it to be, rid of all the ravages caused by man in revolt—this, no less, is the New Testament hope. That is why there is to be no more sea. In the mythology of the Near East, the 'Sea' is the enemy of the God of order. A yachting addict would no doubt have had a different vision! Of greater significance, the whole of life, as we know it, is radically transformed. The agony of human history is at an end. The tragedy of the Garden of Eden is undone. The vigilant divine security guard around the 'tree of life' is withdrawn. In the renewed world, the author of Revelation depicts a city through whose streets there flows 'the river of the water of life' (Rev. xxii. 1), 'also, on either side of the river, *the tree of life*, with its twelve kinds of fruit, yielding its fruit each month; and the leaves of the tree were for the healing of the nations (xxii. 2). Here is the fulfilment of that old prophetic hope that 'Nation shall not lift up sword against nation, neither shall they learn the art of war any more' (Mic. iv. 3; Isa. ii. 4). The tears, the mourning, the anguish, the pain, even death itself are things of the past, 'then shall come to pass the saying that is written:

> "Death is swallowed up in victory."
> "O death where is thy victory?
> O death where is thy sting?" '
> (1 Cor. xv. 54–55, quoting Isa. xxv. 8 and Hos. xiii. 14.)

At the heart of this renewed universe we find not the religious hermit, rapt in solitary ecstasy, but the community of God's people, their long pilgrimage ended. 'We shall always be with the LORD' (1 Thess. iv. 17).

Moses, according to the Book of Exodus, once addressed to God a plea which has echoed across the centuries,

'I pray thee, show me thy glory' (Exod. xxxiii. 18).

It was a request to tear apart the veil which hides God from human sight. Moses is assured that he will have ample cause to know God's goodness, 'But,' God said, ' "you cannot see my face; for man shall not see me and live" ' (verse 20). In the presence of the consuming splendour of a holy God, rebellious warped man would shrivel up. (The story naively continues that as a special concession Moses was allowed to see God's back!) The New Testament takes up this story. As the storm clouds gather, Jesus tries to reassure His frightened disciples. One of them, Philip, is not wholly satisfied with what He has told them.

'Philip said to him, "Lord, show us the Father and we shall be satisfied.' Jesus said to him, "Have I been with you so long, and yet you do not know me, Philip? He who has seen me has seen the Father; how can you say, 'Show us the Father?' Do you not believe that I am in the Father and the Father in me?" ' (John xiv. 8–10).

'He who has seen me has seen the Father'—yet even here, the full glory of God has to be veiled in a human life. In the heavenly city of Revelation, however, we find the people of God gathered round the throne of God and of the Lamb.[1]

'They shall see his face and his name shall be on their foreheads. And night shall be no more; they need no light of lamp or sun, for the Lord God will be their light, and they shall reign for ever and ever' (Rev. xxii. 4–5).

The final barriers are down. Man's revolt is at an end. God's wandering children have been gathered again into their Father's home with joy and gladness to see their Father face to face.

Inevitably, as the New Testament is well aware, we are straining language, adding picture to picture in an effort to describe something which in the last analysis is indescribable in terms of our present life. 'For now we see in a mirror dimly, but then face to face. Now I know in part; then I shall understand fully, even as I have been fully understood' (1 Cor. xiii. 12).

But the pictures are no mere flight into fantasy. They are an attempt to give expression to a great certainty, rooted in Jesus Christ, and verifiable in daily Christian experience.

'For I am sure,' says Paul, 'that neither death, nor life, nor angels, nor principalities, nor things present, nor things to come, nor powers, nor height, nor depth, nor anything else in all creation, will be able to separate us from the love of God in Christ Jesus our Lord' (Rom. viii. 38–39). If to 'us' we add 'the whole of God's creation' and affirm that that love from which nothing can ever

[1] I.e. Jesus.

separate us, must in the end triumph, is not this the hope of the New Testament?

.   .   .   .   .

We live in troubled uncertain times. Man, possessing the power of self-destruction, trembles on the brink of a fearsome abyss. Whether he will hurl himself into the abyss or not, no one knows. But what the Bible does affirm is that the last word can never be spoken by the hydrogen bomb, or any 'improvement' upon it which man may invent. For, as in the beginning, so shall it be in the End—*God*, the God who has made Himself known to us in the story of His people, and decisively, in the man Christ Jesus.

Epilogue

There was a television commentary on one of Donald Campbell's successful attempts on the world water-speed record. It fell into two parts, the first of which was a film taken by cameras set on the boat and at various vantage points, a film of Donald Campbell in action. The film ended, viewers were taken to the studio, there to see Donald Campbell face to face. Is this not an illustration of what we find in the Bible?

In the Old Testament we have a series of shots of God in action in the life of a nation, shots taken from all different angles through the lens of poets, historians, story tellers, hymn writers. In the New Testament, the claim is made that in Jesus of Nazareth, we are face to face with this God.

We have but to strip the story of the Bible to its bare essentials to realize that from beginning to end it is a 'challenge story'. The Bible speaks; it would be truer to say it *witnesses* to God and His dealings with men. There is nothing tentative about what the Bible has to say in this respect. It does not with disarming modesty profess to offer one among many possible interpretations of life. We do it a grave disservice if we think it speaks the last word on matters historical or scientific; we do it an even greater disservice if we do not realize that it does claim to speak a decisive word from God. It witnesses to a God who, far from being an idle spectator of life, is ever in action, His word of judgement inevitably written in the crisis headlines of a rebellious world. Yet even in judgement there comes His word of renewing steadfast love, a word which can never be fully understood by the arm-chair student of religion. God's dealings with men involve the creation of a people who will hear His demands and serve His purposes. That people is in our midst. With all its imperfections—and those who know it best are most aware of its imperfections—the Church remains the people of God created by Him, the fellowship wherein His Spirit binds men together in an adventure into newness of life. The Bible speaks, and the challenge it leaves with us is not merely, 'Do you believe what this book has to say?' but 'will you in response to God's initiative, commit yourself to His people?'

The story of the Bible, the story of God and His people, is a continuing story in which we are all involved. So shall it be until 'The kingdom of the world has become the kingdom of our Lord and of his Christ, and he shall reign for ever and ever' (Rev. xi. 15).

Index of Biblical Passages